MORE NINETEENTH CENTURY STUDIES

More Nineteenth Century Studies

A GROUP OF HONEST DOUBTERS

By

BASIL WILLEY

HONORARY FELLOW OF PEMBROKE COLLEGE AND
KING EDWARD VII PROFESSOR EMERITUS OF ENGLISH LITERATURE
IN THE UNIVERSITY OF CAMBRIDGE

Columbia University Press

NEW YORK

Published in Great Britain (1956) by
Chatto & Windus Ltd.
London

*

First Published in United States of America 1956
Second Impression 1969
Third Impression 1977

Printed in the United States of America

Preface

IN the Preface to *Nineteenth Century Studies* (1949) I said that I hoped to write a sequel which might 'fill in some of the gaps and bring the story down to the end of the century'. The present volume is only a partial fulfilment of that hope. Its central theme is 'the loss of faith', or (as it might often be called) the re-interpretation of current orthodoxy in the light of nineteenth century canons of historical and scientific criticism. I have not attempted to be exhaustive, nor have I harped incessantly on the central topic. Instead, I have tried, in six fairly detailed chapters, and using a method partly biographical and partly critical, to illustrate some phases of Victorian liberal thought from a group including historians, theologians and men of letters.

I hope to have presented these writers as more than a mere set of 'worm-eaten' period pieces. If faith today has recovered tone and confidence, it owes this largely to the work of these pioneers who compelled it to abandon many impossible positions. Even now this debt is not always properly acknowledged, and some of the 'liberal' or 'agnostic' criticisms are conveniently forgotten rather than properly faced. It may be that the liberal tradition—not in its older form, but chastened by twentieth century experience—is due for a revival.

My acknowledgments are due, and are gratefully given, to the Principal and Fellows of Lady Margaret Hall, Oxford, and Miss Margaret Deneke, for permission to include (in Chapter II) parts of my Deneke Lecture (1952) on Tennyson; to the Oxford University Press and Dr R. Hale-White for permission to quote from the works of William Hale White and Mrs Dorothy V. White; to Messrs Macmillan and Sir Charles Tennyson for permission to quote from the works of Viscount Morley and from Sir Charles Tennyson's *Alfred Tennyson*; and to the Stanford University Press for permission to quote from Wilfred Stone's *Religion and Art of Mark Rutherford* (1954). I should like to record here also (as

5

PREFACE

I have done in the text and footnotes of Chapter V) my gratitude to Mr Stone for his book, which is not only the best yet written about Mark Rutherford but is also a first-rate contribution to the spiritual history of the period.

B. W.

PEMBROKE COLLEGE, CAMBRIDGE

1956

Contents

CONTENTS

8

CONTENTS

To
Z. M. W.

CHAPTER I

FRANCIS W. NEWMAN

(1805-1897)

1. *Phases of Faith*

IN the history of nineteenth century English thought there is no story more striking, or more full of moral significance, than that of the divergent courses of the brothers Newman. It is as if two rivers, taking their rise in the same dividing range, should yet be deflected by some minute original irregularity of level, so that one pours its waters into the Mediterranean, the other into the German Ocean. The *Morning Leader* newspaper, shortly after the death of Francis (1897), called John 'a spiritual Tory' and Francis 'a spiritual radical'. Long before this—even five years before his own conversion to Rome—John took his younger brother as an omen of the dangers of Protestantism: 'Whether or not Anglicanism leads to Rome,' he wrote to his sister Jemima, 'so far is clear as day, that Protestantism leads to infidelity.' The career of Francis, indeed, seemed to him the clearest and most painful illustration of one of his own deepest beliefs, that there is no logical standing-point between Romanism and Atheism. One of my main objects in what follows will be to suggest that this antithesis represents a dangerous half-truth. The foundations of nineteenth century Protestantism were indeed insecure, and out of this insecurity there was bound to emerge, and did emerge, a drift on the one hand towards Rome and on the other towards unbelief. The brothers John and Francis Newman had a great deal in common; far more than might at first sight be supposed. They had not only drunk the same milk of evangelical doctrine in their childhood, but they both had subtle and dissolvent intellects, and the instinctive scepticism which questions received assumptions. But scepticism, as history has repeatedly shown, may be the basis of orthodoxy as well as of heresy; according to the proportion it bears to

MORE NINETEENTH CENTURY STUDIES

other elements in a man's make-up it may lead him either towards dogma or denial. The all-corroding intellect, if allied with a mystical temper and a deep reverence for tradition, may itself suggest—as it did to John Henry Newman —the need for certainties beyond the reach of mere intellect, given and attested by supernatural authority. John's scepticism carried him as far as the exposure of the Anglican dilemma; the Church of England, Romish in its liturgy, Protestant in its articles, Erastian in its government, and committed to an untenable bibliolatry, could not without a drastic overhaul stand up to the nineteenth century. His scepticism went no further; or rather, it induced him to take the one step further, amid the encircling gloom, which led towards the kindly light of Rome. If the Church of England was wrong, Rome must have been right all along. In Francis Newman this corrosive mind was unchecked by any respect for the powers that be, and accordingly it carried him far beyond the rejection of his own youthful evangelicalism to a radical critique of the whole structure of dogmatic Christianity. The spiritual history of Francis was in no way exceptional, as John's was; what happened to him happened to so many in the nineteenth century that his life-story may be said to conform to the standard pattern. Yet to say this would be to overlook the most interesting point: Francis was Newman enough never to end up in the agnosticism of a Leslie Stephen, a Huxley or a John Morley. After peeling off layer after layer of the doctrinal husk, he was left—not with nothing, but with a solid core of certainty: a certainty not buttressed by Church or dogma, but by reasons of the heart and spirit. In the rejuvenated Church of today he might have found a place as a modernist of the mystical type; in his own time he could only exist outside its pale.

The Newman household at Ealing in the early days seems to have been harmonious enough. The prevailing influence, that of intense evangelical piety, came mainly from the mother, but it was strongly reinforced by Walter Mayers, a master at the Rev. George Nicholas's school to which both John and Francis went. Mr Newman, the father, a banker and man of the world, admired Franklin and Jefferson and

12

had 'learned his morality more from Shakespeare than from the Bible'.[1] He was therefore, from the standpoint of the 'twice-born' Francis, not a Christian, and it is interesting to find that the son, who claimed in later life to be 'anti-everything', showed his first intransigence in resisting the paternal authority—resisting it, however, in the interests not of emancipation but of greater strictness. On September 30, 1821, when the lad was sixteen, J. H. Newman wrote in his diary: 'After dinner today I was suddenly called downstairs to give an opinion whether I thought it a sin to write a letter on a Sunday. I found dear F[rank] had refused to copy one. A scene ensued more painful than any I have experienced.'[2] In his youth, as his mother lamented later, 'Frank was adamant', but he afterwards changed his mind about his father, growing to admire him as 'an unpretending, firm-minded Englishman, who . . . rejected base doctrine from whatever quarter'. Later experience taught him to rate honest humanity higher than fanatical saintliness, and he saw his father and brother as types of that antithesis. At the time of the scandal over Queen Caroline and George IV, John, whose 'zeal for authority, as in itself *sacred*, was the main tendency perverting his common-sense', supported the Ministry and the King against the Queen, because they were 'the Government'. '"Go on!"' said Newman senior: '"Persevere! Always stand up for men in power, and in time you will get promotion."'[3]

I have been quoting some phrases from a work of Francis Newman's old age, the *Contributions Chiefly to the Early History of the Late Cardinal Newman, with Comments* (1891), written shortly after the Cardinal's death. It is a book which even the sincerest admirers of Francis find difficult to forgive, for it breathes a spirit of bitterness, jealousy and wilful incomprehension hard to reconcile with the writer's known character. To many it seemed like an act of treachery, or at least brotherly disloyalty, against the memory of a great saint whom the whole world, Protestant, Catholic and infidel

1 F. W. N., *Early History of the Late Cardinal Newman* (2nd ed., 1891), pp. 6-7.
2 Quoted by Maisie Ward, *Young Mr Newman* (1948), p. 60.
3 F. W. N., *loc. cit.*, pp. 9-11.

alike, had learnt to reverence. The book was, in fact, the discharge of a lifetime's accumulation of embittered feelings against a brother whose views he abhorred, whose treatment of himself he had resented, and of whose character he saw the least ideal aspects. Why did he write it? Not only to vent his spite, but because he cared for truth above all else, and sincerely feared that the Cardinal's true image would be falsified by obituary piety. The present generation, he said, sees him through a mist, but he belongs to English history and so should be rightly seen. 'The splendour of his funeral makes certain that his early life will be written; it must be expected that the more *mythical* the narrative the better it will sell.' In reading the book, therefore, we have to make allowances for this strain of feeling. Yet read it we must, for it contains valuable reminiscences and is indispensable to an understanding of the two brothers. Nor is it wanting in generous acknowledgment of all that John had done for him in youth:

> 'In my rising manhood I received inestimable benefits from this (my eldest) brother. I was able to repay his money, but that could not cancel my debt, for he supported me not out of his abundance, but when he knew not whence weekly and daily funds were to come. I have felt grateful up to his last day, and have tried to cherish for him a sort of *filial* sentiment.'[1]

Such deliberate gratitude, such calculated transference of filial feelings on to a very superior and somewhat coldly arrogant elder brother, was not likely to generate anything but painful repressions. But what ruined the relationship was the religious difference: 'the Church was to him everything, while the Church (as viewed by him from the day of his ordination) was to me, NOTHING. Hence we seemed never to have an interest nor a wish in common.' And so 'a most painful breach, through mere religious creed, broke in on me in my nineteenth year, and was *unhealable*'.

From boyhood up Francis saw his brother as cold, reserved, aloof, humourless, unsympathetic, holding inflexibly and fanatically his predetermined course. Like Cassius,

[1] *Op. cit.*, p. vi.

John never relaxed; he never played any games at Dr Nicholas's school, but founded instead a secret society with himself as Grand Master. In his temperament there was 'nothing boyish, popular or self-distrusting'. It is of course hard for brothers to agree when each represents to the other the very views he most detests and fears; to Francis, John was the embodiment of blind reaction, while to John, Francis was the personification of that poisonous liberalism against which his whole life was a crusade. Readers of the *Apologia* will not accept Francis's version of his brother; they will feel that the real man is revealed there, and in such a passage as this (from a letter John wrote soon after his mother's death in 1836):

> 'Of late years my mother has much misunderstood my religious views, and considered she differed from me; and she thought I was surrounded by admirers, and had everything my own way; and in consequence I, who am conscious to myself I never thought anything more precious than her sympathy and praise, had none of it ... I think God intends me to be lonely ... I think I am very cold and reserved to people, but I cannot ever realize to myself that anyone loves me.'[1]

At Oxford the brothers were at first much thrown together, John coaching Francis, and living with him in the same lodgings, for a year before the latter's matriculation (1822, at Worcester College). John was much impressed with the younger man's abilities, and reported that Francis was a better Greek scholar and a better mathematician than himself. The first open breach came two years later, when Francis, fitting up a new set of rooms on his own, discovered a picture of the Virgin Mary hanging on the wall there. He at once went to the print shop to have it removed, and learnt that his brother had ordered it. 'I am sure he thought me an ungrateful brother,' he comments. Francis had subscribed the Thirty-Nine Articles on admission, according to the rule of those days, but he soon began to have doctrinal qualms. In what sense were the sufferings of Christ applied to the sinner for salvation—and was his righteousness also

---

1 Quoted by Sieveking, *Memoir and Letters of F. W. Newman* (1909), p. 64.

imputed? How could Christ's body have ascended to heaven, when it is written that 'flesh and blood cannot inherit the Kingdom of God'? Were the Oriel heretics, who approved of Sunday cricket, perhaps right after all? Perhaps the Puritans and Evangelicals had been wrong in making the Old Testament a rule of life for Christians. And here, before I leave the subject of the fraternal relations, I must quote the most interesting of all Frank's references to his brother; it occurs in *his* 'Apologia', called *Phases of Faith* (1850), of which more later:

> 'One person there was at Oxford, who might have seemed my natural adviser: his name, character and religious peculiarities have been so made public property, that I need not shrink to name him: —I mean my elder brother, the Rev. John Henry Newman. As a warm-hearted and generous brother, who exercised towards me paternal cares, I esteemed him and felt a deep gratitude; as a man of various culture and peculiar genius, I admired and was proud of him; but my doctrinal religion impeded my loving him as much as he deserved, and even justified my feeling some distrust of him. He never showed any strong attraction towards those whom I regarded as spiritual persons: on the contrary I thought him stiff and cold towards them. Moreover, soon after his ordination, he had startled and distressed me by adopting the doctrine of Baptismal Regeneration; and in rapid succession worked out views which I regarded as full-blown "Popery". I speak of the year 1823-6: it is strange to think that twenty years more had to pass before he learnt the place to which his doctrines belonged.' [1]

The world is now acquainted with that agony of twenty years; to Francis, John's whole Tractarian phase seemed, both at the time and still more later, to be a period of treachery to the Church and deception of others and himself. It is notable that the rift was caused, not by Frank's heresies, but by his Protestantism and his consequent suspicion of John's romanising trends. His main grievance against John always was that at this time he was 'pushing on the Romish line in the garb of an Anglican'; once he had become an avowed Papist the charge of dishonesty lapsed automatically.

[1] *Phases of Faith*, pp. 10-11.

16

Francis himself had the stubborn and prosaic kind of honesty which makes the satirist; his gaze pierced through external trappings—as when, for example, he saw Bishop Howley, who confirmed him, as no more than 'a *made-up* man, and a mere pageant'. Disrespect for bishops, indeed, was one of the faults for which John reproved him at Oxford. But he soon left off trying to maintain spiritual intimacy with John; the latter's arguments, he complains, were too fine-drawn and subtle, 'often elaborately missing the moral points and the main points, to rest on some ecclesiastical fiction'. A man who could believe in Baptismal Regeneration could believe anything, and moreover could not possibly know by experience what regeneration really is. John, in Frank's opinion, could have been a great barrister; he only needed a concession from you, some first principle ('he could get no concessions out of me!'), and you were entangled as by a Socrates. Admittedly, first principles cannot be proved, but a disbelief in magic is nowadays a reasonable first principle, and this John could never see.

Francis Newman did brilliantly at Oxford, graduating B.A. with a double first (1826), and gaining a Balliol Fellowship. In order to take his degree he had to subscribe the Articles once again. He did so, but with deep misgiving, for he now had grave doubts on the lawfulness of Infant Baptism —whereas Article XXVII asserts it to be 'most agreeable with the institution of Christ'. It began to dawn upon him that he could never take Orders, as it had been assumed he would; in fact, he never even took his M.A., and in six years' time he resigned his Fellowship. In doing this he set a precedent for a succession of honest doubters in the later decades of the century. Subscription was a hopeless stumbling-block to such minds; 'all who subscribe', says Francis, 'labour under a common difficulty, in having to give an absolute assent to formulas that were made by a compromise and are not homogeneous in character'. The difficulties which first worried him, it is worth remarking, had nothing to do with science or the higher criticism; they were simply such as might and did then confront any rigorous Protestant mind in its independent scrutiny of the Bible—any mind, that is, for which Rome was an impossible alternative. The High Church and Roman doctrine of Baptismal Regeneration, for instance, seemed to him a superstitious perversion based upon 'carnal inability to understand a strong spiritual metaphor'. Episcopacy again, whatever its pretensions, stood self-condemned for him by the worldliness and supineness of the bishops themselves. He also began to note discrepancies and 'dislocations' in the Gospel narratives—points which are the very alphabet of modern criticism, but which were then most disturbing to one who still believed the Bible to have been 'dictated by the immediate action of the Holy Spirit'.

I propose now to notice some of the main stages of Newman's development as given in *Phases of Faith*. His difficulties may have ceased to terrify, and his conclusions—many of them—are now the unquestioned data of every beginner. Yet it remains an interesting and touching spectacle to watch a pioneer winning, inch by painful inch, the vantage-ground we now occupy. Moreover, in enjoying our present immunities, we may easily forget how they were gained, and how recently; and it is salutary to look back with gratitude on the costly struggles which purchased for us what now we take for granted. Newman's struggle commands our respect and sympathy all the more because it was, on the whole, worked out in solitude and estrangement. He lacked the intellectual supports enjoyed by later religious liberals. 'If at this period', he writes, 'a German divinity Professor had been lecturing at Oxford, or German books had been accessible to me, it might have saved me long peregrinations of body and mind.'[1]

The year (1827) after his Balliol Fellowship Newman went to Dublin as tutor in the household of Lord Congleton. He was at this time brimful of missionary zeal (as indeed he never ceased to be throughout his long life), and eager to do good by spreading the purest, most primitive kind of Christianity amongst unbelievers. Like John Wesley and others before and since, he longed to prove himself capable of giving up everything for Christ. He was then also, and

[1] *Phases*, p. 24.

for some years to come, in the throes of an unrequited passion for Maria Rosina Giberne. It was while in this state of over-wrought feeling that he fell in with a group of religious enthusiasts who fed the flames with appropriate fuel. Lord Congleton himself, a youth of Newman's own age, had just experienced conversion and was eager for action. And there was also Anthony Norris Groves, a dentist from Devonshire who consorted much with Congleton, and whose tract *Christian Devotedness*, advocating renunciation of all personal property and all money-making, Newman read with the greatest admiration. But the dominating influence was that of John Nelson Darby—the 'Irish Clergyman' of *Phases*, who is best known as the founder of the Plymouth Brethren. This extraordinary character, who as Newman says 'everywhere displayed a wonderful power of bending other minds to his own, and even stamping upon them the tones of his voice and all sorts of slavish imitation', was at this time living a life of apostolic austerity as a curate in the Wicklow mountains. Ascetic, bearded, crippled, taking no thought for food or raiment, vying in emaciation with a monk of La Trappe, he seemed to Newman the embodiment of the Christian character in its utmost purity. For a while this man, with his imperious demand, fully supported by his own practice, for unflinching consistency in living out the last consequences of Gospel Christianity, held Newman completely in thrall. He taught Newman to despise all his Oxford learning as mere dross; he expected the Second Coming and the speedy destruction of the earth by fire, and in view of this deprecated all worldly study or work for distant objects. 'The highest Christian must necessarily decline the pursuit of science, knowledge, art, history,—except so far as any of these things might be made useful tools for immediate spiritual results.'[1]

Having given up all thought of ordination, Newman now took up, under Darby's influence, the notion of preaching to the heathen—a task for which, according to New Testament precedent, neither Anglican nor any other kind of Orders seemed necessary. At this very time Congleton and Groves

[1] *Ibid.*, p. 34.

received a joint communication, of a mystical character, concerning the mind of God towards them: 'that we should come together not waiting on any pulpit or minister, but trusting that the Lord would edify us together by ministering as He pleased'.[1] This revelation, which was the basis of Plymouth Brethrenism, supplied an equally satisfactory basis for a missionary exploit, and so began the most fantastic episode in Newman's life, and one of the queerest in nineteenth century biography. Groves, accompanied by Mrs Groves, had gone to Baghdad with a view to taking by storm, and singlehanded, that central citadel of Islam. And in September 1830 Newman set forth—'with some Irish friends', as he says—to join them. It was a strangely assorted party, consisting of Congleton ('Mr Parnell'), Congleton's fiancée Nancy Cronin, his prospective brother-in-law Dr Edward Cronin, his prospective mother-in-law Mrs Cronin, Cronin's baby (an infant in arms recently left motherless), a certain Mr Hamilton and Francis Newman. They travelled anything but light, having many hundredweights of trunks, chests, hampers, bags, baskets, etc. They suffered untold hardships by land and by sea, hardships worthy of St Paul himself; they crossed wild and desert tracts on horse and camel, Cronin carrying the baby in his arms; they were attacked and stoned by hostile tribes; they experienced famine and fever. But all this was as nothing compared with the tragic deaths, in rapid succession, of all the women of the party: Mrs Groves dying of plague before the others arrived, and Congleton's bride (married to him in Aleppo) and her mother succumbing to exposure and over-exertion. Newman himself was twice at death's door, and Hamilton gave up the venture in mid-course.

Newman gives many picturesque details about this ill-fated expedition, but says nothing of the actual missionary work carried on in Baghdad by the faithful remnant. The little we do know suggests that Islam was unperturbed by their Lilliputian arrows. On Newman himself, however, the effects were deep and lasting. Other Victorian freethinkers had been exposed to the spiritual east winds of the century;

---

[1] Quoted Sieveking, *op. cit.*, p. 28.

none but Newman had confronted the East itself. Satirists, for the purpose of exposing Christianity, had long spoken through the lips of some imaginary oriental, perfectly wise and rational, to whom the anomalies of orthodoxy were patent. Newman alone knew at first-hand what it was to try to explain Christianity—let alone impart it—to the adherents of a rival religion equally sure of its own unique and exclusive credentials. Before setting out he had reflected on the theory of proselytism, and come to some wise and far-seeing conclusions. Academic divines might bicker about Christian evidences, but the only evidence likely to influence Muslims and Hindoos was the saintliness of Christians.

'While nations called Christian are known only to heathens as great conquerors, powerful avengers, sharp traders,—often lax in morals and apparently without religion,—the fine theories of a Christian teacher would be as vain to convert a Mohammedan or Hindoo to Christianity, as the soundness of Seneca's moral treatises to convert me to Roman paganism.'[1]

And so he had dreamed of a sort of collective religious colony, animated by love, primitive faith and disinterestedness, and exhibiting such tokens of Christian living as might move the natives in the end, and powerfully support the efforts of the actual preachers. The dream was harshly dispelled—and besides, Newman at once found himself entangled with doctrine. He had himself begun to wrestle with St John and the Athanasian Creed on the metaphysics of the Trinity; were these two authorities perfectly agreed on the status of the Son? He suspected that 'the Creed really teaches polytheism, but saves orthodoxy by forbidding anyone to call it by its true name'. Now, how would all this appear to an intelligent Mohammedan? One missionary incident, the only one Newman has recorded, is relevant and significant here. He had a religious conversation with a Mohammedan carpenter at Aleppo which left on him a lasting impression. Newman tried especially to disabuse him of the notion, current amongst his people, that our gospels are spurious narratives of late date. The man listened

[1] *Phases*, p. 44.

attentively, waited till he had done, and then delivered himself thus:

> "'I will tell you, Sir, how the case stands. God has given to you English a great many good gifts. You make fine ships, and sharp penknives, and good cloth and cottons; and you have rich nobles and brave soldiers; and you write and print many learned books . . . all this is of God. But there is one thing that God has withheld from you, and has revealed to us; and that is, the knowledge of the true religion, by which one may be saved."' [1]

It was long before the full meaning of that interchange disclosed itself, but the memory of it told in favour of his growing conviction that the germ of Christianity, and the possibility of spreading it, existed in the moral and spiritual sphere, not the metaphysical and the historical. This impression was strengthened by another interview he chanced to have at Aleppo, this time with an English infidel, a man of low tastes and lax morals, who insisted upon attacking the historical foundations of Christianity. Compelled to defend the faith on these grounds, Newman found himself wondering what the Mohammedan carpenter could have made of such complexities, or what religious meaning he could possibly attach to them. After-reflection once again suggested that not on that ground must the battle be fought; Christianity must win, if at all, by a contagiousness to which even a Mohammedan would not be immune.

After two years Newman returned to England. Ostensibly this was to gain new recruits for the East, but stronger and deeper currents were driving him home. He had tried unsuccessfully to induce Maria Rosina to join him and marry him in Baghdad; he must see and speak with her again. He must have known too, though he may not have admitted it to himself, that the eastern mission was foredoomed. At any rate he never went back there. He found enough at home to preoccupy and disturb him. The star-crossed brothers, John and Francis Newman, landed in England on the very same day in 1833, Francis from Baghdad, John from Sicily. At their first meeting Frank found John dignified, stiff and

[1] *Ibid.*, pp. 52-3.

distant. Soon, with the Tractarian movement about to begin, John 'separated himself entirely from my private friendship and acquaintance'. To Frank's consternation, he found that 'painful reports' had been spreading against him for unsoundness in faith, and that his former friends, including even the saintly Darby, were cold-shouldering him. In bitterness of heart he resolved never again to court friendship with any but banned heretics; he began, too, to look with a new understanding on people—such as his father had been—who were not 'twice-born'. 'It was pleasant to me to look on an ordinary face, and see it light up into a smile, and think with myself:—"*there* is one heart, that will judge of me by what I am, and not by a Procrustean dogma."' Doubtless this was how he felt when, rejected by Maria Rosina, chilled by his brother and repulsed by Darby, he met and wooed Maria Kennaway of Ottery St Mary. In her eyes, at least, he figured as the Christian hero who had given up brilliant chances at Oxford for the Gospel's sake. Comforted by the sympathy of one who saw nothing wolfish beneath his sheep's clothing, he married this charming girl (1836)—perhaps not reflecting, for his part, that as a Plymouth Sister she must of course be twice-born, and for the time not noticing or caring that she was and must ever be 'outside his mental door' (in his biographer's phrase). Nevertheless the marriage, though childless, was happy enough; they were devotedly attached, Francis making no impossible demands, and Mrs Newman, while distressed at her husband's steady drift towards infidelity, yet blending with her anxious love the hope that somehow, some day, he would return to the fold.

It was in 1834, two years before his marriage, that Newman was appointed Classical (and apparently also mathematical) Tutor at Bristol College. This institution, which had been founded in 1831, was housed in Park Row. It was run on liberal lines, giving religious instruction—on Anglican principles—only to those boys whose parents wished it. This alone was enough to arouse the suspicion and hostility of the Bishop and other clergymen, and in 1841 Bristol College expired in competition with its newly founded rival,

Bishop's College. Yet in its ten years of existence it had numbered amongst its pupils Edward Fry, George Gabriel Stokes and Walter Bagehot. At Bristol Newman was a worshipper at the Broadmead Baptist Chapel, where he underwent re-baptism; but he was not long associated with that or any other denomination. In 1840 he took the post of Classical Lecturer at the Unitarian 'Manchester New College', lately removed thither from York (later to be removed to London, and again later, as Manchester College, to Oxford). To complete the outline of his career it is convenient to add at once that in 1846 he became Professor of Latin at University College, London, and that he held this Chair until 1863.

We may now neglect chronology awhile in order to follow the later developments of his thought as revealed in his *Phases of Faith*. The next stage was the rejection of Calvinism, under which he specially refers to the doctrines of Reprobation, Atonement, the Fall and Total Depravity. Holding fast to his central insight that a man must not be judged by his ostensible creed, he remarks that human nature 'has a singular art of not realizing all the articles of a creed', and adds his discovery that 'to be able to define my own notions on such questions had exceedingly little to do with my spiritual state'.

Knowing as we do how acutely Newman analysed the religious weakness of Protestantism,[1] we shall not be surprised to find him, in his next phase, coming to grips with Bibliolatry. In the article I have just mentioned (in the footnote) he makes the same point as his brother, though his conclusion is the reverse: Protestantism is in a cleft stick— it has admitted 'private judgment' as against Rome, only to set up Scripture instead, and to deny the right of appeal against *that*. Apply the same judgment to Scripture, and the foundations crumble. From the vulnerability of the Bible, its inability to stand the test of modern criteria of evidence, John inferred the need for a divinely instituted and guided Church; Francis, the need for a faith grounded upon mystical and spiritual experience. Francis—it cannot be too

[1] See his article (1858) of that title: *Miscellanies*, vol. ii (1887).

strongly emphasized—did not drift into unbelief, though he became quite heterodox by all the standards of his time. Sufficient proof of this is his book *The Soul* (1849)—of which more anon—a work which, in my view, deserves a much higher rank in devotional literature than is usually assigned to it.

After a century of biblical scholarship, Newman's critique on the infallibility of Scripture has lost its edge, and we need not dwell long upon its details. It must be remembered, of course, that he had the tremendous initial handicap, from which we are now delivered, of having to extricate himself step by step from the doctrine of verbal inspiration. If we bear this always in mind when reading him, his account takes on a new vitality and pathos. To establish the principle that human error may occur in the scriptural books, it was enough to note such trivial discrepancies as Matthew's faulty arithmetic in counting the generations, or the two divergent accounts of the creation in Genesis. But, the principle once established, where could its application be checked? Must one crucify the understanding to such things? By the fourth decade of the century, too, the geological difficulties of the Mosaic cosmogony were 'exciting much attention'. 'It had become notorious to the public, that Geologists rejected the idea of a universal deluge as physically impossible.'[1] How could the whole human race have descended from Adam in six thousand years? And did not the fossils show that death had come into the world before sin? Perplexed by these and other problems, Newman sought guidance from the oracle of Liberalism, the great Dr Arnold of Rugby—leader and hero of the anti-Tractarian hosts. We do not know precisely when this interview took place, but Arnold died in 1842, and we may plausibly assign it to the period 1834-42. 'To my surprise,' says Newman—but not to ours, if we have read our Dr Arnold—

> 'Dr Arnold treated all these questions as matters of indifference to religion . . .'

calling Noah's deluge 'mythical' and Joseph's story 'a

[1] *Phases*, p. 122.

25

beautiful poem'. Newman was 'staggered at this'; 'I was unable', he goes on,

'to admit Dr Arnold's views; but to see a vigorous mind, deeply imbued with Christian devoutness, so convinced, both reassured me that I need not fear moral mischiefs from free enquiry, and indeed laid that enquiry upon me as a duty'.[1]

From that duty he did not flinch, and his further enquiries led on to still more drastic misgivings. There were deeds recorded in the Bible as commanded or approved by God which were repugnant to our moral sense: Jael's perfidious murder of Sisera; Abraham's intended slaughter of Isaac; Joshua's treatment of the Canaanites. In the New Testament there were miracles lacking in moral dignity: the therapeutic napkins taken from Paul's body; the curse on the barren fig-tree; the tribute-money found in the fish's mouth. There were, too, in the first three evangelists disquieting marks of credulity; they clearly shared the vulgar error of their time about demoniacal possession and the casting out of devils. Moreover, human frailty appeared in all four Gospels, and in the Acts, in the misapplication of Old Testament quotations.

Newman again consulted the Rugby oracle, and was glad this time to find that Arnold rested Christianity mainly on the Fourth Gospel. Newman had always preferred St John's 'mysterious Jesus' to the synoptic portrait, and he agreed with Arnold's estimate of John's narrative as vivid and simple, deeply spiritual, and comparatively undeformed by credulous legend. We may now take stock of his conclusions on the scriptural question. He tabulates them thus:

'1. The moral and intellectual powers of man must be acknowledged as having a right and duty to criticize the contents of the Scripture.

'2. When so exerted, they condemn portions of the Scripture as erroneous and immoral.

'3. The assumed infallibility of the entire Scripture is a proved falsity, not merely as to physiology, and other scientific matters,

[1] *Ibid.*, pp. 110-11.

26

but also as to morals: and it remains for further enquiry, how to discriminate the trustworthy from the untrustworthy within the limits of the Bible itself.'[1]

"You will become a Socinian!" somebody had told him at Oxford (just as Blanco White had said to his brother "Ah! Newman! if you follow that clue it will draw you into Catholic error"). Well, says Francis now, recalling that prophecy about himself, if following the truth leads that way, so be it. Had not Coleridge said ' "If any one begins by loving Christianity more than truth, he will proceed to love his Church more than Christianity, and will end by loving his own opinions better than either"?'[2] So clearly did his new insights now enable him to distinguish between creeds and true spirituality, that he not only reproached himself for his early misjudgments of the 'once-born', but even felt a change of heart towards his brother John:

> 'I had a brother, with whose name all England was resounding for praise or blame; from his sympathies, through pure hatred of Popery, I had long since turned away. What was this but to judge him by his creed? . . . my brother surely was struggling after truth, fighting for freedom to his own heart and mind, against church articles and stagnancy of thought. For this he deserved both sympathy and love: but I, alas! had not known and seen his excellence.'[3]

Accordingly he wrote John a letter of contrition and conciliation, and John responded, one is glad to find, with brotherly cordiality. Yet the doctrinal gulf still yawned between them: ' "It is a great joy to me",' John wrote to their sister Jemima (November 1840),

> '"that I have made it up with Frank . . . his tone is, I rejoice to say, as different as possible from what it was years ago. . . . [But] I think he has that great defect of imagination or mysticism . . . which will act always in keeping him from the Catholic system."'

[1] *Phases*, p. 115.
[2] So quoted by Newman, *ibid.*, p. 117.
[3] *Ibid.*, pp. 118-19.

A few months later he writes again, more gravely, that it is a question, not merely of defective imagination, but of 'most painful' doubts:

"'Whether the beginning of St John is written by the Apostle, whether it is inspired, and whether the doctrine is not taken from Philo. And he said in the course of his letter, God forbid he should ever doubt Our Lord's Resurrection. Indeed I do not see where he is to stop. It is like [Blanco] White. It is like the Genevans, the Germans, like Protestantism generally. Whether or not Anglicanism leads to Rome, so far is *clear as day* that Protestantism leads to infidelity.'"[1]

Frank's own comment is the natural complement to John's: 'it is to me a painfully unresolved mystery, how a mind can claim its freedom in order to establish bondage'. But 'the germ of Romanism', he adds, 'lies in the contradictions and bigotries of Protestantism itself'. For 'germ' read 'need' or 'proof', and the brothers speak with one voice.

From now on, his armoury reinforced with weapons of the latest German type (he had begun to read Michaelis, De Wette and Neander), Newman's attacks on bibliolatry became more and more confident. He pronounced, from evidence of literary style alone, that the Apocalypse could not be by the author of John's gospel and epistles, nor Hebrews by St Paul. The Song of Solomon, from the same standpoint, was revealed as no mystical allegory, but a plain love-song. He disentangled the Elohistic and Jehovistic narratives in the Pentateuch, characterizing those books as conglomerates of older materials mechanically joined. '"Of course, then,"' he makes an imaginary reader say, '"you gave up Christianity?"' '"Far from it,"' he retorts; '"I gave up all that was clearly untenable, and clung the firmer to all that still appeared sound."'[2] 'Those who believe that the apostles might err in human science, need not the less revere their moral and spiritual wisdom.'[3]

The question of miracles could not long remain in abey-

[1] Quoted by Maisie Ward, *Young Mr Newman*, pp. 359-60.
[2] *Phases*, p. 141.
[3] *Ibid.*, p. 121.

ance, and Newman now confronts it squarely. On what principles of evidence should miracles be tested? Ought we to receive moral truth in deference to an apparent miracle of sense? What sort of evidence convinced Paul or John?—clearly not the sort which we should now demand. Or, putting the matter the other way, ought we to accept sensible miracles *because* they recommend some moral truth? Jesus himself is said sometimes to have rebuked the demand for miracles, but sometimes to have expected faith on their account. What sort of miracle could or should alter my opinion on a moral question?—certainly not a voice from heaven commanding me to do wrong, as Abraham and Hosea were commanded—or Joshua, Samuel, Elijah and Josiah. At last Newman uncovered what he felt to be the underlying false assumption: that Reason and Conscience are *not* God's mode of revelation to man, and that only sights and sounds (or especially these) *are*. 'Miraculous phenomena will never prove the goodness and veracity of God, if we do not know these qualities in Him without miracle.'[1] Bishop Butler and his followers deduce rightly that 'a really overpowering miraculous proof would have destroyed the moral character of Faith: yet they do not see that the argument supersedes the authoritative force of miracles entirely'.

Having thus abandoned all 'faith at second-hand'—that is to say, faith depending upon the unconvincing testimony of others, Newman makes a final assault upon the whole concept of 'historical' Christianity, and issues a Declaration of Independence—independence of all such alleged foundations. If, he reflected, he had been spending seven years labouring in vain to solve the 'vast literary problem' of Scripture, it must be 'an extreme absurdity to imagine that the solving of it is imposed by God on the whole human race'. Since he cannot solve 'literary problems concerning distant history', these 'can form no part of my religion'. Has he therefore, he asks again, abandoned Christianity itself? It is a question still to be asked today by those who, enjoying the freedoms won for them by such as Newman, yet profess

¹ *Ibid.*, p. 157.

themselves Christians. In what sense do they deserve the title, if at all? Let us hear Newman's own reply. After eight years of anxious enquiry and struggle, he can say that his religion has not dwindled.

'I still felt the actual benefits and excellencies of this religion (oh how contrasted to Paganism!) too remarkable a phenomenon to be scorned for defect of proof . . . the Bible is pervaded by a sentiment, which is implied everywhere,—viz. the intimate sympathy of the Pure and Perfect God with the heart of each faithful worshipper.'[1]

And this it is that edifies still. He can say to any Evangelical:

'I know, that the spiritual fruits which [you value] have no connection whatever with the complicated and elaborate creed, which [your] school imagines to be the roots out of which they are fed.'[2]

But there are Christians, he goes on,

'Christians of another stamp, who love their creed *only* because they believe it to be true, but love truth, as such, and truthfulness, more than any creed: with these I claim fellowship. *Their love to God and man, their allegiance to righteousness and true holiness, will not be in suspense and liable to be overturned by new discoveries in geology and in ancient inscriptions, or by improved criticism of texts and of history, nor have they any imaginable interest in thwarting the advance of scholarship.* It is strange indeed to undervalue *that* Faith, which alone is purely moral and spiritual, alone rests on a basis that cannot be shaken, alone lifts the possessor above the conflicts of erudition, and makes it impossible for him to fear the increase of knowledge.'[3]

Protestant bigotry and bibliolatry are driving many each year to Rome; in others, they are producing an intense reaction against religion in any form. One class of critics attacks it harshly and crudely, not knowing in what deep and holy soil it is really rooted; others, knowing this, are afraid

[1] *Phases*, pp. 187-8.
[2] *Ibid.*, p. 201.
[3] *Ibid.*, p. 202 (italics in the middle sentence mine).

to speak out. One of the last paragraphs of the book opens with this sentence, which sums up much of the argument:

> 'Religion was created by the inward instincts of the soul: it had afterwards to be pruned and chastened by the sceptical understanding.'[1]

II. *The Soul*

Newman's other chief religious work, *The Soul, Its Sorrows and Aspirations: An Essay towards the Natural History of The Soul as the True Basis of Theology*, appeared in 1849, the year before *Phases of Faith*. I have chosen to speak of the later book first because it is the more negative and destructive, whereas in *The Soul* we can see how Newman rebuilt his faith on new and firmer foundations—or perhaps he would prefer us to say, found out by excavation on what basis it had really rested all along. *The Soul* is, of all Newman's writings that I have read, by far the most beautiful; in it there breathe a pure spirituality, and a noble aspiration, which make intelligible George Eliot's somewhat gushing and Carlylish description of him as 'our blessed St Francis' whose 'soul is a blessed *yea*'.[2] Though it lacks the personal, biographical interest of *Phases*, it greatly excels it in elevation of tone and charm of style. It deserves to be better known.

Newman means by 'the soul' the organ whereby spiritual truth is spiritually discerned. James Martineau complained that this was to restrict its meaning unduly, leaving Conscience, Reason, etc., out of account. But this is really irrelevant to Newman's main purpose, which is to vindicate the autonomy of religious experience. He dissociates this from all 'proofs' and 'evidences' which depend upon history, bibliolatry, metaphysics and logic—all of which are in his sense 'unspiritual' in that they do not derive their authority from spiritual experience as such. In this Newman is carrying on the tradition of Coleridge and Thomas Arnold; his 'soul' covers much of the meaning of Coleridge's 'Reason'.

---

[1] *Ibid.*, p. 232.
[2] Cross's *Life* (1885), vol. i, pp. 193-4 (in a letter to Sara Hennell, 1848).

Approaching religion from the personal, subjective side, his book becomes an account of the psychology of religious experience. In the Preface to the first edition he says:

> 'Those truths, and those only, are properly to be called Spiritual, the nature of which admits of their being directly discerned in the Soul, just as Moral truths in the Moral Sense: and *he* is a spiritual man, not who believes these at second-hand (which is a historical and dead faith), but who sees internally, and knows directly.'

And so he proceeds to trace the origins of faith from the situation in which the individual finds himself in relation to the Infinite.

If the soul is 'the organ of specific information to us' concerning its own subject-matter (viz. things spiritual), we must ask how it arrives at its ideas of supernatural reality, of infinity, of divine existence and power, of God. We begin with the emotions of awe and wonder which are typical of infancy and of the childhood of the human race; emotions linked with fear of parents, of the dark, of the unknown; fear, too, of magic, of idols, of the underworld; also emotions bound up with a sense of the sublime in mountain or sea. Next comes the feeling of admiration, distinguished from wonder by its greater tranquillity; it is a 'resting of the soul, on whatever form of beauty', which 'tends to impart cheerfulness . . . and mute thankfulness'. Newman uses Wordsworthian language on this theme, and appropriately, for he associates the feeling especially with love of natural beauty. Mere sensibility will not make a man religious, but if he possesses it he has a 'temperament on which true religion may be happily superinduced'. Mere morality, on the other hand, provides no incentive from within itself; it needs to be supplemented by some enthusiasm, whether of love, of poetry or of religion, to 'throw the heart out of Self'. Following upon this admiration comes the sense of order, constancy and law in Nature—and the sense of design, derived from noticing the adaptation of means to ends. We know we ourselves have Mind: 'whence have we picked it up?' It is not self-generated in us, so we may *prima facie* 'expect to find Mind in the Universe acting on some stupendous scale, and

32

of course imperfectly understood by us'.[1] In some such way
(I am greatly condensing the argument) we arrive at an idea
of a Boundless, Eternal, Unchangeable, Designing Mind—
and we call this God.

These are the hackneyed topics of theistic argument, but
what follows immediately after is in Newman's most original
vein. Religious knowledge, he insists, is essentially imperfect, approximate and 'popular', and from this it follows that
'no long deductions, following logical (that is to say verbal)
processes, can be trusted in Theology. . . . A system of
Theology, constructed like a treatise on Mechanics, by fine-
drawn reasonings from a few primitive axioms or experi-
mental laws, is likely to be nothing but a sham Science.'[2]
We know, therefore, that any language we may use about
the Divine Nature must be imprecise and inaccurate; it can
at most be metaphorical. Metaphorical, yes: but it is the best
we have got; thus

> 'to refuse to speak of God as loving and planning, as grieving and
> sympathizing, without the protest of a *quasi*, will not tend to
> clearer intellectual views, . . . but will muddy the springs of affec
> tion. Metaphorical language in this whole subject is that which
> the soul dictates, and therefore must surely express our nearest
> approximation to truth, if the soul be the eye by which alone
> we see God. *Jealously to resist metaphor, does not testify to depth of
> insight.*'[3]

I ascribe originality to this last aphorism of Newman's,
because resistance to metaphor—the replacement of image
by abstraction—had for long been considered the secret of
theological progress.

The transition—always difficult—from "Sense of Order
and Design" to "Sense of Goodness and Wisdom" is effected
by Newman from-within-outwards, in accordance with his
whole plan. We find in the human spirit certain possibilities
or germs of perfection; but these must be only a faint shadow
of the divine perfection. It is the exact reverse of Feuerbach's

[1] *The Soul* (1905 ed.), p. 88.
[2] *Ibid.*, pp. 89-90.
[3] *Ibid.*, p. 94 (my italics).

argument: that 'God' is simply a name for the highest human ideal. Newman, presupposing God, and finding a limited goodness and wisdom in man, infers that the Creator of man must be perfectly good and wise. Generations of schoolmen had argued likewise, but even to this hackneyed theme Newman adds an original variation—I mean his warning that we must not expect to find God's wisdom and goodness exemplified in ways which might be satisfying to our limited moral views. In particular, it is not in Nature that we must seek God's moral will; in the whole realm of Nature, as far as we know, 'moral considerations are uniformly overborne by mechanical ones'.[1] Gravitation will not cease if you, however holy, step over a precipice. This line of reflection, used by J. S. Mill as an argument for the limited power of whatever God might be, indicates for Newman simply that God's wisdom and goodness are disclosed, not to the scientific intellect, but to the devout heart. The course of *history*, unlike that of Nature, may illustrate the wisdom and moral government of God, but here too we must guard against appealing too crudely to any particular historical events, or to alleged 'providences', 'mercies', etc., as 'proofs' of God's superintendence. Our sense of divine wisdom is mainly a matter of '*a priori* discernment'; the human soul itself, imperfect as it is, remains our best 'type' of the divine. It is when the soul comes into play—as in the posture of reverence—the soul and not the understanding, that religion begins. The greatest step forward occurs when the religious sentiment is linked with the moral sentiment, and God is seen to be concerned with the heart and the conscience. Idolatry, the oldest of all perversions of natural religious sentiment, is with us still in the form of Church-worship and Bible-worship; and here, in a section on 'English Idolatry', the more controversial Newman of *Phases* peeps out. 'Bibliolatry' is the typical British form of idolatry.

> 'No book-revelation', he says, 'can (without sapping its own pedestal) authoritatively dictate laws of human Virtue, or alter our *a priori* view of the Divine Character.'

[1] *Ibid.*, p. 92.

34

'What God reveals to us, he reveals *within*, through the medium of our moral and spiritual senses.'

'Three centuries of Protestantism demonstrate, that the supremacy of the letter will never give an end of bitter controversy, nor any of that enlarged wisdom and recognition of goodness, in which we are so scandalously deficient.'[1]

In the "Sense of Sin", Newman goes on to show, we have a particular aspect of man's feeling of personal relation to God—the consciousness of having offended the Most High and Holy. He both censures and praises the evangelical approach to sin. He condemns the Calvinistic doctrine of Total Depravity; the conception of Original Sin should be replaced by that of the 'necessary imperfection of every created existence'. The great difficulty for every sinner—that is to say, the central spiritual problem for every man—is how to get out of 'evil feelings and *into* holier thoughts and aspirations'. If 'total depravity' is indeed our state of being, what incentive is there to strive—by repentance, and prayer, and spiritual exercises—towards communion with God, to hunger and thirst after righteousness, to pursue an ever-receding vision of perfection? The doctrine of total depravity, by discounting effort, may even become an excuse for ignoble acceptance of removable evil. Self-righteousness is indeed to be abhorred, but true spiritual advancement will not produce it; a holy soul, though far above a remorseful sinner's, will weep with loathing (though not with despair) over its own shortcomings. What Newman does approve in evangelicism is its approach to the unconverted sinner: 'Come to Christ just as you are! do not try to be good *first*!' This is correct spiritual psychology: if you 'come' in this way, it proves the birth in you of higher longings which may in time grow permanent. Sudden conversion is a verified fact; it needs, however, to be followed up by good habits.

Chapter III, on the "Sense of Personal Relation to God", contains Newman's most striking plea for the autonomy and validity of spiritual experience, and also shows him in his

---

[1] *Ibid.*, pp. 115-23.

loftiest mood. He has to refute the 'scientific' objections that all such 'experience' is illusory, that it is all subjective, that the soul itself does everything and God nothing. Newman, like Matthew Arnold twenty years later, brushes metaphysics aside; his concern, he says, is with 'popular' facts. But such facts demand scientific recognition; they may not be amenable to investigation, but they cannot be abolished by a shrug.

'The men of science [must] treat with tender thoughtfulness the facts alleged by the unscientific men who have felt them; and shall cease to shower on them vague phrases of contempt, as mysticism, fanaticism, etc.'[1]

Granted that we can no more apprehend the mind of God than a dog his master's; granted that our spiritual vocabulary is vague and metaphorical; yet it will not be by 'refusing to become experimentally acquainted with the facts' that we shall get clearer conceptions or an improved terminology. One of these alleged 'facts' is the efficacy of prayer, to which all spiritual persons bear testimony. '"Yes,"' replies the scientist, '"that is the heart acting on itself."' But he might dispose in the same way of the evidence of sense: *perhaps* there is no outer world, and our internal sensations *are* the universe? Syllogistic proof of an outer world will never be gained, nor syllogistic proofs that God exists or listens to prayer. If by 'sense' we make contact with this undemonstrable world, so by a specific sense—the Soul—do we come into contact with God. 'Let us not deal more slightingly with its testimony, than with that of the Touch or the Taste.'[2] The instinct for God is perhaps the most powerful in man: let us follow it without fear of the critics. We ourselves shall get holiness, peace, and joy; and perhaps we may bequeath a few 'facts' for future men of science. 'If we drink the heavenly nectar ourselves, others may analyse our juices when we are dead.' Speaking in praise of a 'womanly' or childlike state of the soul, Newman breaks into mystical chant recalling Traherne or George Fox or John Smith:

[1] *Ibid.*, p. 181.
[2] *Ibid.*, p. 183.

'Thus the whole world is fresh to us with sweetness before untasted. All things are ours, whether affliction or pleasure, health or pain. Old things are passed away; behold! all things are become new: and the soul wonders, and admires, and gives thanks, and exults like the child on a summer's day;—and understands that she *is* as a new-born child: she has undergone a New Birth! It is not birth after the flesh, but a birth of the Spirit, birth into a heavenly union, birth into the family of God. Why need she scruple to say, that she is "partaker of the divine nature", if God loves her and dwells in her bosom?

'Reader, accept these mystical metaphors as such. Behold in them the soul labouring to express her feelings; but freeze them not into logical terms, or they will become *the letter that killeth*.'[1]

'To despise wide-spread facts is *not* philosophic', and when such 'facts' prove to be bound up with goodness and happiness it is better to learn them by personal experience before theorizing about them. Paul was not boasting, but stating the simple truth, when he said that the spiritual cannot be judged by the unspiritual.

A few of Newman's comments on the doctrine of a future life (Chapter V) are worth briefly noting. All attempts, from Plato's to those of today, to prove the immortality of the soul by logical demonstration, inevitably fail because they are addressed not to the soul but to the pure intellect. If the soul could be proved immortal by such means, this would become a truth of science and not a religious doctrine. A pure soul, conscious of union with God, hopes that such beatitude may be lasting; he 'believes' it by faith, whereas the grounds of belief proposed to the mere understanding have nothing to do with faith at all. The resurrection of Christ, even if we could believe it, would have no demonstrative relevance to this question, since it was by definition an 'exceptive phenomenon'. Newman is the first writer I know who has pointed out what has long seemed a confusion in the Pauline teaching on this matter. How can the resurrection of Christ be an argument for the resurrection of ordinary, non-divine, sinful men? Unless His resurrection was *unique*, it can have no

[1] *Ibid.*, p. 195.

doctrinal significance. Newman himself did not believe it, but that does not affect the point here discussed.

Finally a word about Chapter IV, "On Spiritual Progress", and Chapter VI (the last), entitled "Prospects of Christianity". These two chapters alone, I think—and especially the second—would justify us in giving Newman a high place amongst the religious writers of the nineteenth century. No one saw more clearly into the causes of the widening gulf between the theology and the science of the day; no one declared more roundly that insofar as theologians were without genuine conviction, and insofar as scientists spoke of what they knew to be truth, it was the theologians who must yield. Merely to destroy superstition will not produce religion, yet 'the destruction is necessary, if religion is to flourish'.

> 'Our misery has been, that the men of thought have no religious enthusiasm, and the enthusiastically religious shrink from continuous searching thought; and this must go on until our Theology is shifted away from its present basis.'

The 'mere understanding' or 'scientific intelligence', suspect when it trespasses into the spiritual zone, has supreme authority within its own sphere, and it must no more be sacrificed to the soul than the soul to it.

> '. . . wherever there is true Faith, there is an unhesitating conviction that there cannot possibly be any real collision between these two parts of human nature. It is now no common guilt, when a man uses his spiritual influence to frown down any honest intellectual endeavour.'[1]

(I do not know whether T. H. Huxley had read Newman, but he made the very same point in 1860 when rebutting Bishop Wilberforce's attacks on Darwin.)

Finally, looking to the future prospects of Christianity, Newman enquires how it may best be propagated, not only over 'the remoter parts of the world', but nearer home: in Europe, where amongst the educated little formal belief survives, or in our own towns, where 'horrid heathenism'

[1] *Ibid.*, p. 247.

largely prevails. Speaking from his own missionary experience, he pronounces the difficulties to be very great. What hinders Christian missionaries in dealing with 'acute Hindoos or Mohammedans', and what hinders them amongst our pagans at home, is 'the unmanageable character of what are called Christian Evidences'. The modern missionary is committed, as the Apostles were not, to belief in an 'infallible Book', and this exposes him to attacks from 'every bold and sharp-witted man'. Christian doctrine, too, often aims at, without attaining, logical exactness; it is, moreover, burdened with the metaphysics of the first century A.D., whence manifold perplexities. The intellectual formulations of Paul and John were fallible, though their spiritual perceptions were sound and holy.

The modern evangelist, setting out to attack sin, should be girt with the sword of the Spirit; nothing else is of first importance. Instead, what do we find?—

'A study-table spread over with books in various languages; a learned man dealing with historical and literary questions; referring to Tacitus and Pliny; engaged in establishing that Josephus is a credible and not a credulous writer; enquiring whether the Greek of the Apocalypse and of the Fourth Gospel can have come from the same hand; searching through Justin Martyr and Irenaeus, in order to find out whether the Gospels are a growth by accretion and modification, or were originally struck off as we now read them . . . and other important but very difficult studies . . . all remote from the sphere in which the Soul operates.'[1]

All this belongs to the sphere of the 'critical understanding'; it has nothing to do with *religion*. Theology, instead of being the 'science of God', based like any other science on its own specific and verifiable data, has become an affair of biblical interpretation and historical criticism. 'Christianity has been turned into a LITERATURE, and therefore her teachers necessarily become a literary Profession.'

In the climate of the nineteenth century something other than all this is needed. Those who have no *hereditary* faith, or who have deliberately rejected Christianity on account of

1 *Ibid.*, pp. 319-20.

the hypocrisy and worldliness of alleged Christians, will not
be converted by such means.

> 'It is absolutely impossible to recover the tens of thousands who
> have learned to scorn Christian faith, by arguments of erudition
> and criticism. Unless the appeal can be made directly to the Con-
> science and the Soul, faith in Christianity once lost by the vulgar
> is lost for ever.'[1]

The large towns of England will be overspread with 'black
infidelity'; the cultivated will become poetical Pantheists,
with an intellectual belief in a plastic Spirit or Life in the
Universe, but no more 'moral affection towards God' than
Atheists. In the Christianity of today there is indeed enduring 'iron'—'the pure morals and spiritual doctrine, of which
the Conscience and Soul take cognizance'; but there is also
'miry clay'—the 'historical element, of which the Soul can
take no cognizance at all'. Anticipating most strikingly the
argument of *Literature and Dogma* and *God and the Bible*
(Matthew Arnold, who had read Newman, ought, one feels,
to have recognized a forerunner and a kindred spirit, instead
of affecting to despise him),[2] Newman urges that

> 'the real problem for those who wish to save cultivated Europe from
> Pantheism, Selfishness, and Sensuality (such as flooded and ruined
> ancient Greece), is,—to extract and preserve the heavenly spirit of
> Christianity, while neglecting its earthly husk'.[3]

It will be asked, what then (for Newman) was 'heavenly
spirit', and what 'earthly husk'? How much was left to him
after so much drastic paring? I will conclude this section by
quoting his own words—they occur near the end of his book:

> '. . . do you believe in Sanctification of the Spirit by Peace and
> Communion with God? in the New Birth of the Soul by believing
> in God? in the Free Grace of Him, who loved us before we loved
> Him? in Justification of the Sinner, in the midst of his sins, by
> simple Faith in God? in the permanent Union of the believing Soul
> with God? what know you of the love of God shed abroad in the

---

[1] *Ibid.*, p. 324.
[2] Cf. *Letters of M. Arnold to A. H. Clough*, ed. Lowry (1932), p. 115.
[3] *The Soul*, pp. 332-3.

heart by the Spirit, and of the Hope thence arising? or of man's insight into the heart of God, when he has received somewhat of that Spirit which searcheth even the deep things of God? of a Faith that overcomes the World? of a Spirit that guides by a higher rule than Law? *Such sentiments and experiences (not propositions) are the true heart of Christianity*:[1] and if the reader hold them not, he may haply have the shell of Christian truth, but he has not the kernel. If he rightly knows them, he will not say, "They are all worth nothing, without a belief in Historical and Metaphysical paradoxes."'[2]

III. Translating Homer

To many general readers of today, and many literary students, Francis Newman is perhaps only known—along with Sir Charles Adderley, Mr Roebuck, Miss Cobbe, the Bishops of Winchester and Gloucester, and the Rev. W. Cattle—as a fly preserved in the Arnoldian amber. He is one of Arnold's symbols of the eccentricity and wrongheadedness of the British Philistine class; of their lack of poise; of their ignorance of M. Sainte-Beuve. Arnold and Newman were both liberals, and their respective attempts to extract and preserve the 'spirit' of Christianity at the expense of the 'husk' might well, one would have thought, have given them a sense of common purpose. Yet whenever they come within sight of each other there is a skirmish. Arnold, after reading *The Soul* (? *Phases of Faith*), calls Newman 'an hass'; Newman, after reading *Literature and Dogma*, reproves Arnold both for flouting and bantering two bishops on the score of their belief in a Personal God ('as if in all Christendom and Jewdom only two bishops held this creed'), and also for having 'the infatuation to correct the translation of the celebrated verse in John iv to "God is an influence"'.[3] A clear case of imperfect sympathies; and in Newman's articles of 1872 and 1873 (about Arnold's religious writing) his resentment against the debonair smatterer who from the Oxford Chair of Poetry had ridiculed his Homer still glows hotly.

[1] My italics.   [2] *Ibid.*, pp. 334-5.
[3] *Miscellanies* (1887), vol. ii, pp. 311-12.

It is not part of my present purpose to discuss the theory of Homeric translation, nor even to adjudicate between the rival views of Arnold and Newman; all I have space or competence to attempt is to illustrate the nature of their antagonism. For Arnold, Homer was the embodiment of many of those qualities which made Hellenism so 'salutary' for Victorian England; above all, he was 'noble'; he had the grand manner. Homer's other qualities: his rapidity, his plainness and directness of substance and style, must be so rendered as not to sacrifice his essential 'nobility'. Cowper had failed because he was too Miltonic, too intricate and laboured in movement; Chapman had failed because he was too curiously conceited; Pope because he was too artificial and literary; and now Newman, though his syntax and evolution of thought are faithful to Homer, fails in 'nobility'. His version is, in fact, 'eminently ignoble'. To this there can be only one reply, the reply that Newman made: Homer is *not* noble, or not uniformly so; he is often 'quaint', 'garrulous', prosaic and low. The aim of any translator must be, it is said, to reproduce upon the ears of his own countrymen as much as possible of the effect produced by the original upon the ears of its contemporaries. To do this, however, always turns out far more difficult than at first appears; for example, if 'naturalness' is an essential character of the original, then naturalness must be sought in the translation, and this can seldom be attained by strict faithfulness to the original in movement and syntax. The problem is complicated enough even when there is no dispute about the qualities to be reproduced; some may hold that 'faithfulness' means copying the original at all costs, without much care for what will sound natural in one's own language; others, that the effect of the original, if it had been there attained by methods most un-English, must be sought in translation by methods native and proper to the English language—that is, by an analogous rather than a strict rendering. But Arnold and Newman were not agreed about the essential qualities of Homer himself; to Newman, Homer was not the personification of Hellenism and the grand manner, but an old bard and ballad-monger, often odd, archaic and remote. By what criterion, or by what tribunal, can such a dispute be adjudicated? Shall appeal be made to the alleged effect of Homer upon, for example, Sophocles and his contemporaries? Arnold, holding it impossible to know what this was, appealed to the best scholarship of his own time, and urged that a translation must reproduce the effect of Homer upon the Provost of Eton, Professor Thompson and Professor Jowett. He airily assumed, perhaps with justice but certainly without proof, that their views must necessarily correspond with his own. It was this assumption—that he had the 'living scholar' on his side—that especially annoyed Newman: 'What if I were bluntly to reply: "Well! I am the living scholar"?' Let Mr Arnold confess his own ignorance, Newman goes on—'let him confess for himself that he does not know, and *not for me, who know perfectly well*, whether Homer seemed quaint or antiquated to Sophocles. Of course he did, as every beginner must know.'[1] If he had translated Homer in the style of the following (not that he recommends it):

> 'Dat mon, quhlch hauldeth Kyngis-af
>   Londis yn féo, niver
> (I tell 'e) feereth aught; sith hee
>   Doth hauld hys londis yver.'

—he would have been using 'a style *far less* widely separated from modern English than Homer from Thucydides'. For Newman, moreover, Homer was not merely antiquated 'relatively to' the age of Pericles, but absolutely, as 'the poet of a barbarian age'. This is his justification for using a form of ballad measure in his translation, and for besprinkling his vocabulary with those odd archaic or dialect words which aroused the Arnoldian scorn: *bragly*, for 'proudly fine'; *bulkin*, 'a calf'; *plump*, 'a mass', and the like. 'Where, indeed, Mr Newman got his diction, with whom he can have lived, what can be his test of antiquity and rarity for words, are questions which I ask myself with bewilderment.' The tones were those of the voice which later exclaimed over Shelley's

---

[1] In M. Arnold, *Essays Literary and Critical* (Everyman), p. 296. Newman's *Reply* (1861) is printed here (my italics).

social circle 'What a set!', and Newman was touched on the raw: 'he wonders *with whom Mr Newman can have lived, . . .* I suppose I am often guilty of keeping low company'. Not at all, said Arnold in his rejoinder; Mr Newman is 'one of the few learned men we have', and as for his companions, we know that he 'lived with the fellows of Balliol'. Yet 'his having lived with the fellows of Balliol does not explain Mr Newman's glossary to me'.[1]

A candid reader of this controversy will feel, I think, that Newman cuts no contemptible figure even when matched with Arnold. His translation may be unreadable, but—to judge from the samples Arnold gave of his own work—so would Arnold's have been. Newman had at least the moral advantage of having gone through the toil of translation. ('In the midst of numerous urgent calls of duty and taste, I devoted every possible quarter of an hour for two years and a half to translate the Iliad, toiling unremittingly in my vacations and in my walks, and going to large expenses of money, in order to put the book before the unlearned; and this, though I am not a Professor of Poetry nor even of Greek.'[2]) He makes the right criticisms of Arnold's own specimen-hexameters, and of the English hexameter in general. Of the former he simply records (what others besides himself can echo) that for a while he 'seriously wondered whether [Arnold] meant his first specimen for metre at all'; 'my "metrical exploits"', he adds, 'amaze Mr Arnold; but my courage is timidity compared to his'. And of the English hexameter in general he remarks, rightly as I think, that to the English ear it always sounds like 'odd and disagreeable prose', and cannot therefore be the right medium where 'naturalness' is the effect aimed at—however closely its movement may resemble that of Homer's own verse. 'If the metre can inspire anything,' says Newman, 'it is to frolic and gambol with Mr Clough.'

Arnold's controversial methods are well known: the affected humility and ignorance, coupled with a bland identification of himself with critical headquarters, and of his opponent with the lunatic fringe or the intellectual under-

[1] *Ibid.*, pp. 234, 302, 339.　　　　[2] *Ibid.*, p. 313.

world. These methods are seen in action here, as with suavity and sweetness he tries to force Newman into the rôle of a tiresome and crotchety pedant. But it does not quite come off; Newman, in virtue not only of his learning but of a certain gritty good sense, partly escapes Arnold's silken toils. He not only hits back effectively at Arnold's own impossible hexameters, but he succeeds in convincing us that Arnold's 'Homer'—so noble and civilized, and so comprehensible to Professor Thompson, Professor Jowett and Dr Hawtrey—is possibly a mirage of the schools, and that the real Homer was something so very much more rough-hewn and uncouth that, were he to reappear, 'Mr Arnold would start from him just as a bishop of Rome from a fisherman apostle'. Newman also exposes the danger besetting all translators of ancient literature into modern English—that of 'melting up the old coin and stamping it with a modern image', of 'obliterating everything characteristic', and cutting out whatever cannot be made 'stately'. Arnold, on the other hand, is in a stronger position when he suggests that Newman's very learning has got in his way, that he has been too much preoccupied with scholarly niceties, and that the real problem is 'not one of scholarship, but of a poetical translation of Homer'.[1] Newman, with all his great merits, was not a poet; he was not *ondoyant et divers*; his spirit was not sufficiently 'free, flexible and elastic'. And if this is the 'last word' on the subject, then Arnold has it.

iv. Newman the Man: Later Years

Space forbids me to enlarge upon Newman's friendships —with Clough, with Martineau and many others—or to speak at length about the numerous activities and literary productions of his later years. I must be content with a rough sketch of his personality and interests.

I have already tried to extricate him from the ignoble army of Arnold's martyrs, and I will go on to suggest that Miss Maisie Ward does him less than justice when she says that 'to some extent he seems to have filled the place of

[1] *Ibid.*, p. 350 (from *Last Words*).

faith with a number of fads'.[1] There is truth in this, but not
the whole truth; he never 'filled the place of faith' with
anything else, and his 'fads' were the natural preoccupations
of an ardent Victorian 'progressive'. 'He seemed', as Miss
Ward rather naïvely admits, 'more aware than [his brother]
John of the horrors of modern poverty.' He was indeed, and
if we enquire what were these so-called 'fads' we find that
they were interests and concerns which he shared with some
of the finest spirits of the age. If he was a faddist, so was
Kingsley for caring about drains and housing, Mill for
caring about the emancipation of women, Maurice and Ludlow for wishing to Christianize our social order, Morris and
Ruskin for trying to restore joy and pride in fine craftsman-
ship. Newman had, what it is not usual to censure in other
eminent Victorians, a highly developed social conscience—
the last phase, no doubt, in the evolution of an escaped
evangelical. Man is not totally depraved: his condition is
indefinitely improvable. But improvable only by taking
thought and action, and meanwhile he lives in avoidable
degradation; lose no time, therefore! What were, then, these
interests of Newman's? Women's Suffrage ranked high
amongst them. He was in the habit of classifying the others,
under four main headings, as the Four Barbarisms of Civilization: War, the Penal System, the Degradation of Man
(by drink), and Cruelty to Animals (blood-sports and vivisection). It may have seemed eccentric in his time, but
hardly seems so now, to examine in all seriousness the
possibility of eliminating war by an armed peace-federation
of the united nations. The defects of the penal system can
hardly be contemplated, even in their present mitigated
state, with total complacency. Opinions may differ about
'temperance-reform', blood-sports and vivisection, but they
are still topics upon which it is not contemptible to hold
strong views. But Newman did not, as the true crank is apt
to do, confine his thought and energy to any one or more of
these causes. He pleaded for such far-seeing measures as
administrative decentralization, with the establishment of
provincial chambers for local legislation; for land reform, to

[1] *Young Mr Newman*, p. 166.

bring in small holdings and a property-owning peasantry; for Indian self-government. A comment of his on the Indian question will illustrate the quality of his thinking on public questions:

'Nothing but an abundance of black faces in the highest judicature, and intelligent Indians of good station in the high police, could administer India uprightly. . . . Every year that we delay, evils become more inveterate and hatred accumulates. To train India into governing herself, until English advice is superfluous, would be to both countries a lasting benefit, to us a lasting glory.'[1]

On the drink question I will merely allude to an incident of the year 1867, which brings out strongly the contrasted attitudes of Francis and John Henry Newman. On October 22nd in that year, Newman found himself on the same platform as Archbishop (afterwards Cardinal) Manning, at a meeting in the Manchester Free Trade Hall. Manning had come to co-operate with Protestants 'against the enormous excess of the trade in Intoxicating Drink'. Manning's speech, and his courage in defying sectarian criticism, filled Newman with enthusiasm and joy, and he wrote at once to his brother, believing that at last they had found a common interest. John's reply was:

'"As to what you tell me of Archbishop Manning, I have heard that some also of our Irish bishops think that too many drink-shops are licensed. As for me, I do not know whether we have too many or too few."'

'This seemed to curdle my heart like a lump of ice,' says Francis.[2]

Newman, largely because of his brush with Matthew Arnold, has been so much misrepresented and ridiculed that the true proportions of his character and work are blurred. Even so penetrating a critic as Lionel Trilling—although, in his admirable book on Arnold, he is naturally concerned to present Newman as Arnold saw him, leaves it too much to be inferred that Newman was, as Arnold thought, the mere embodiment of British crankiness and provinciality.

---

1 Quoted in Sieveking, *op. cit.*, p. 321.
2 *Early History of Cardinal Newman*, pp. 109-10.

Throughout his very amusing passage on Newman, Mr Trilling is content, by a clever selection of anecdotes, to raise a series of laughs at Newman's expense. Unimplicated and irresponsible, Mr Trilling even scores one telling point by a piece of sheer perversity. Newman, he tells us, was 'a partisan of Hungarian independence and believed that Hungary would benefit considerably from the introduction of the Bactrian camel'.[1] What is the foundation of this statement? When Newman was a Professor at University College, London, he used sometimes to invite students to breakfast at his house. He was ill at ease on such occasions, and his hospitable intentions were not sufficient to break the ice. At one such breakfast, held, as our informant Sir Alfred Wills says, 'in singularly gloomy and bitter weather in the winter or very early spring of 1849', the social frigidity was matched by the temperature, and conversation must have been a hollow mockery. There was no fire, and 'I have not often been colder'. Only one non-student was there, a certain Herr Vukovich, who had been Hungarian Minister of Justice under Kossuth. Picture the scene: a group of embarrassed boys, blue with cold, and with nothing much to say to each other and less still to say to this strange and rather sinister exotic. In comes Newman, hoping by brisk action to save the situation: '"Gentlemen," says he, "this is Herr Vukovich, lately Minister of Justice in Hungary."' He turns to Vukovich, and goes on, with mounting desperation, '"I shall not introduce these gentlemen to you by name, as it would be of no interest to you; and besides, you would forget their names at once."' This little piece of vivacity flutters to the ground like a wounded bird; there is a pause of incomprehension, a tightening of the breast. Something must be done at all costs, and Newman plunges blindly: '"I have never been able to understand, Herr Vukovich, how it is that you have never introduced the Bactrian camel into Hungary...."'[2] Any don who has ever been in Newman's predicament, even after dinner and in reasonable warmth, will interpret the Bactrian camel correctly (no doubt Mr

[1] L. Trilling, *Matthew Arnold* (1939), p. 170.
[2] Sieveking, *op. cit.*, pp. 107-8.

Trilling is such a don, but he was guying Newman and such nuances went for nothing). Mr Trilling also manages to convey by his tone—and here he is not alone, for Miss Ward and Matthew Arnold do the like—that there was something ridiculous about Newman's phenomenal linguistic range, which included (besides Hebrew, Latin, Greek, Sanscrit, Spanish, German, French, Italian and Danish) Berber, Libyan, Arabic, Abyssinian, Gothic, Chaldean, Syriac and Numidian. But his intrepid pioneering was surely admirable, and the specialists of today will not despise their amateur forerunner.

Eccentricities there certainly were in Newman (would that there were more in our own contemporaries!), but they were of the kind which, when seen in their true proportions, soften the beholder's heart. Many of them arose from his excessive seriousness, his concentration upon his own thoughts, and his total disregard for the impression he was making on others. He was, to put it in other words, lacking in sense of humour. The photograph of him in middle age, by Davies of Weston-Super-Mare, shows him (as might have been foretold) both strikingly like and yet unlike his brother the Cardinal. He has the same broad brow, the great curved yet finely chiselled nose, the large, tight mouth with jutting underlip. The expression is stately and sad. But the total effect is utterly changed, mainly by a square-cut goatee beard (he was otherwise clean-shaven) which, together with the uncompromising gaze, and the hint of intransigence about the mouth and lines, gives him a curiously Yankee appearance—an effect still more pronounced in the bronze bust (by Mrs Bainsmith), which reminds one simultaneously of Uncle Sam, Thoreau and Abraham Lincoln. We have several accounts of him as Professor at University College, written by people who had attended his lectures. It is evident that they admired him as an intellectual giant, without being unaware (as he was himself) of his oddities. He was, says Sir Alfred Wills,

'of middle stature, very well made, with a face that always reminded me of the type of the North American Indian. . . . His complexion was dark, his hair very black with no tendency to curl, and he wore it long, and his nose was aquiline. He had a "carrying" voice; his eyes were blue, bright, very expressive, and his smile, not very often seen, peculiarly sweet and engaging.'[1]

In winter, we are told, 'he would wear three coats, the top one green with age, and over the coats a rug with a hole for his head. Beneath these appeared trousers edged with several inches of leather, and above all an immense dirty white hat.'[2] Newman's hats, which were a byword, provide an anecdote which exactly illustrates this side of him. Emerging once from the railway station at Penrith, he was beset by a crowd of little boys who followed him along shouting "Who's your hatter?"—a catch-phrase of the time. Afterwards,

> 'The Professor described to Dr Nicholson what an extraordinary interest the boys had shown. "They repeatedly asked me", he said, "to tell them who was my hatter, and really, Nicholson, at the time I could not remember the man's name."'[3]

Always the experimenter, always eager to awaken interest in his pupils, he translated *Hiawatha* and *Robinson Crusoe* into Latin; he introduced the continental pronunciation of Latin; he made his students speak Greek. His first lectures were the wonder of all who listened, so full were they of every variety of knowledge: antiquarian, philological, historical and literary.

'I am anti-everything', he once said, and amongst the causes he espoused we find (in addition to teetotalism, non-smoking, anti-vivisection and anti-vaccination) vegetarianism, which he took up (in 1867) chiefly because he had a horror of slaughter-houses. He permitted himself, and others, milk and eggs as well as vegetables; the term 'vegetarian', therefore, was not strictly applicable, so he proposed as an alternative 'anti-creophagist'. ' "The Professor considered", an informant tells us, "that our molar teeth clearly indicated grain, roots and nuts as our food, and the incisors

---

[1] Sieveking, *op. cit.*, p. 106.
[2] Maisie Ward, *op. cit.*, p. 166.
[3] Sieveking, *op. cit.*, p. 120.

as clearly suggested fruit, but at that time [a Manchester conference of the Vegetarian Society in the 'seventies] he was in some doubt about the canine teeth.'''[1]

It is in matters like these that we feel the lack in Newman of that 'free, flexible and elastic' spirit which Arnold missed in his Homer. That humourless veracity, that crude honesty unenriched by subtlety or instinctive tact, which led him so often into absurdity, appears with an effect of grotesque pathos in the epitaph he inscribed upon his wife's grave at Weston-Super-Mare:

> '*With no superiority of intellect,* yet by the force of love, by sweet pity, by tender compassion . . . by a constant sense of God's presence, by devout exercises, private and social, she achieved much of Christian saintliness and much of human happiness. She has left a large void in her husband's heart.'[2]

Newman, ill-starred in several ways, has been especially unfortunate in his biographer (I. G. Sieveking). The book could not have been worse if it had been written by his wife; it would perhaps have been better, since although she had 'no superiority of intellect' she had love for her husband, whereas it is difficult to see what impelled Miss Sieveking to write her book, except the fact that Newman was once in love with her aunt. She has no understanding of his ideas or sympathy with them; Mr Newman to her was a very clever man (really cleverer than John if the truth were known), who had some queer ideas—but after all women *may* get the vote some day, who knows? and drink *is* a dreadful temptation to the working classes. Her incomprehension of his religious views almost reaches sublimity: a terrible free-thinker, oh yes—and for forty-five years, too. But what are forty-five years in the sight of Him to whom a thousand ages are but an evening gone? After all, Newman returned to the Christian faith at the end. What lies behind this last statement? James Martineau reported that Newman had said he wished it to be known that he died in the Christian Faith; and Newman, at the age of ninety-two, wrote to Anna

---

[1] Sieveking, *op. cit.*, p. 118.
[2] *Ibid.*, p. 51 (my italics).

Swanwick that he wished 'once again definitely to take the name of Christian'. Miss Sieveking raises a hallelujah over what she takes to be an eleventh-hour repentance. But if we read a little more of the evidence she herself supplies, we find that it was nothing of the sort. Newman meant by 'Christianity' what, by the stages we have followed, he had long come to regard as the spirit within the husk: 'my now sufficient definition of a Christian', he writes, is 'one who in heart and steadily is a disciple of Jesus in upholding the prayer called the Lord's Prayer as the highest and purest in any known national religion . . . this supplants all creeds.'[1] A few years earlier he had written to Mrs Kingsley:

> 'I suppose I must say "Alas!" that the older I become [85] the more painfully my creed outgrows the limits of that which the mass of my nation, and those whose co-operation I most covet, account *sacred* . . . yet I uphold the *sacred moralities* of Jew and Christian . . . with all my heart. Two mottos, or say *three*, suffice me:—
>
> The Lord reigneth.
> The righteous Lord loveth righteousness.
> The Lord requireth Justice, Mercy, and Sobriety of thought, not ceremony or creed.'[2]

With two more sentences from letters written in old age— sentences which show him ardent, philanthropic and inquisitive to the last—we may fitly bid him farewell:

> 'More than ever I see that our best work for God is to work for God's creatures . . .' (1889).[3]

> 'The longer I live, the more hopeful and more interesting I find the whole world' (1891).[4]

---

[1] *Ibid.*, p. 215.   [2] *Ibid.*, p. 381.
[3] *Ibid.*, p. 384.   [4] *Ibid.*, p. 385.

CHAPTER II

TENNYSON

(1809-1892)

1. Somersby

IN a well-known passage of *Science and the Modern World* A. N. Whitehead selected, as the representative long poems of their respective times, *Paradise Lost*, the *Essay on Man*, *The Excursion* and *In Memoriam*. Although I should have substituted *The Prelude* for *The Excursion*, the choice was otherwise good. In this chapter I propose to consider Tennyson from this point of view, as a representative nineteenth century sage caught between religion and science, faith and doubt; facing the newest discoveries of the century, at once excited and disturbed by them but ending virtually in a 'Lord, I believe; help thou my unbelief'. I shall dwell mainly upon *In Memoriam*, but I also want to emphasize Tennyson's achievement as a 'poet of science', and to connect with this the extraordinary accuracy of his observation of Nature.

Tennyson's life spanned the greater part of the nineteenth century, and his years of poetic activity coincided fairly closely with those of Queen Victoria's reign. Throughout most of the Victorian Age, and more especially during its latter half, he lived, moved and had his being close to its spiritual centre, expressing in his verse all its inmost conflicts, its unexpressed assumptions, its half-certainties, its hopes and its daydreams. Turn over the pages of any of the biographies, and you will find them sprinkled with all the famous and significant names, from the Queen herself downwards; Church and State, science, history, theology, philosophy, the arts, education—all are represented by some close personal link. Through Gladstone, for example, he was in touch with politics; through Carlyle with the 'Germano-Coleridgean' stream; through Stanley, Jowett, Ward and Maurice with theology; through Fitzgerald, Patmore, Palgrave, the Brownings (and hosts of others) with contemporary letters; through Ruskin and Watts with the arts; through Kingsley and Maurice with 'Broad Church' and Christian Socialism; and his membership of the Metaphysical Society gave him access, through such men as Huxley, Tyndall, Frederic Harrison, John Morley and Leslie Stephen, to the worlds of science, speculation and agnosticism. This is not to say that Tennyson was ever a man of society; he was by temperament solitary, brooding, sensitive and shy, and in his earlier years his existence was largely obscure and nomadic. But his personal attachments were exceptionally strong, and many of them connected him with people of distinction. In these ways he came to epitomize his age more fully than any other single figure. Moreover, from the time of his full recognition as England's leading poet—that is, from the appearance of *In Memoriam* and his succession to the Laureateship (1850)—he was never left alone. Not only his poetic fame, but his romantic melancholy, his bardic quality, his noble appearance and his very eccentricities—his sombrero and cloak, his formidable and abrupt manner, his lonely walks by day and night—all exerted a strong fascination, and he was pursued to his rural retreats by troops of visitors, ranging from the deserving to the importunate, as well as by his own welcome and valued friends.

English society in those days had a cohesion, a solidarity, which it has since lost. Still essentially aristocratic, it moved in regular orbits, following the seasons in unvarying curves from London to the country houses, and revolving round certain fixed luminaries. At the London dinner or reception, or at the country house-party anywhere from Cornwall to Caithness, you met the same people, or the same kind of people. Statesmen, bishops, landowners, physicians, lawyers, administrators, freethinkers, scientists, novelists, poets and painters—all were there, all mixed on an equal footing; and though there could be sharp differences of belief, all spoke the same language. All had had the same sort of upbringing, came from the same kind of schools, and inherited the same values and presuppositions. Beneath all the surface divergencies there was a wonderful unanimity; the arguments, like cricket matches or Parliamentary debates, were friendly contests between gentlemen who shared a common tradition and took the same things for granted. True, one of the most admirable things about this social heaven was that great gifts, without birth or wealth, could procure you entrance to it. Thus Carlyle, for example, was drawn into its orbit. Tennyson, of course, was of the squirearchy, a son of the rectory, and belonged to it by right of birth as well as of genius. Within it there was a real interchange of ideas, a real circulation of results; the latest volume of verse, the latest scientific theory, was not just something out of the void: it was the work of that charming, that very peculiar, or that rather terrifying Mr So-and-So whom you had met last year at Lady Ashburton's or the Duchess of Argyll's.

Tennyson, the sixth child of a family of twelve, was nurtured in the bosom of the Anglican Church and his mind was stamped with religious impressions from the beginning. His father was the Rev. Dr George Tennyson, Rector of Somersby and Bag Enderby; and his mother, Elizabeth *née* Fytche, was the daughter of a clergyman and niece of a bishop. Elizabeth Tennyson was much more earnestly religious than the Reverend Doctor, and her intense evangelical piety was probably by far the strongest of the early influences. Alfred worshipped her as the ideal mother, as these lines from *The Princess* show:

> 'Not learned, save in gracious household ways,
> Not perfect, nay, but full of tender wants,
> No Angel, but a dearer being, all dipt
> In Angel instincts, breathing Paradise,
> Interpreter between the Gods and men . . .
>   Happy he
> With such a mother! faith in womankind
> Beats with his blood, and trust in all things high
> Comes easy to him.'

This mother survived until 1865, when her son had reached the height of his fame, and the quality of her watchful love may be seen in the letter she wrote to him (1859) on the publication of the first four *Idylls of the King*, expressing her joy on finding that they breathed the spirit of Christianity.[1] When she died, six years later, Tennyson told the parson who conducted the funeral that 'she was the beautifullest thing God Almighty ever did make'. A man does not grow up under such influence, and live unrebelliously with it till the age of fifty, without being decisively affected. Tennyson early lost his simple faith, but the believing temper, the propensity to trust the larger hope, believing where we cannot prove, was implanted in him from infancy and never left him.

But the milk of Paradise, thus early infused into his system, encountered there a darker humour, an atrabilious strain derived, it is to be feared, from his clerical father. Allied to heaven on his mother's side, he was, on the father's, linked with the world, the flesh and the devil. Not that the Doctor was a wicked man; far from it, he was an earnest and hard-working country parson. But he was a frustrated and embittered being, the black sheep of his family, and acquainted with moods of depression from which, in later years, he sought escape in drink. Forced into Holy Orders by a tyrannical father, he did his best to be worthy of the office, but it was against the grain and, as we are told, he 'took a great deal of snuff in the pulpit'. The portrait we have of him as a young man shows him as rather coarsely handsome: the strong, irregular lines suggesting indolence and self-indulgence accompanied by a smouldering Byronic or Satanic energy. Though he was the eldest son of his family and the natural heir to a large property, he had early been disinherited by his father in favour of his younger brother Charles, and this produced in him a lifelong Esau-complex which ate into his vitals and poisoned his whole existence. The sense of being unjustly dispossessed, cheated of his birthright and condemned to poverty and uncongenial struggle, was a constant torment to him and haunted the Somersby household like a spectre. It must be reckoned an important formative influence upon Alfred, second only to his mother's; it works itself out not only in his character and career, but also in his poetry, where it appears as a recurring

[1] See Sir Charles Tennyson, *Alfred Tennyson* (1950), pp. 318-19.

pattern. Had there been only one voice within him, whether of heaven or of the world, he might never have been heard of. But there were two, and from their contradictions his poetry sprang. If Tennyson had become a parson, or if he had been the son of a ruling squire, he would probably have written no poetry, or none worth remembering.

The worldly success-story of the Tennysons is to be read in the life of the usurping uncle Charles, who went into politics, became a Member of Parliament and a Privy Councillor, changed his name to d'Eyncourt, and succeeded to the Manor of Bayons. What Charles did with Bayons is worth noting, for it is a vivid expression of the decadent romanticism of the nineteenth century new-rich: of their desire, at whatever cost in money and in flamboyant unreality, to create for themselves a bogus Valhalla. As soon as he came into the property he began to rebuild the old house, first adding a mediaeval hall, and then by degrees transforming the whole place into a faked-Gothic castle. 'Cottages were pulled down', writes Tennyson's grandson and biographer,

'and roads sunk and diverted, to form a fine rolling park, which was populated with deer and horned sheep. A moat was made along the western front and the lake below stocked with curious aquatic birds. Stained glass, tapestry, armour and old pictures were purchased for the interior. . . . Special portraits were commissioned of Edward III and other royal personages who figured in the new pedigree. As for the general plan, Charles had endeavoured to give the impression of an ancient manor house, which had gradually evolved out of a feudal castle. Accordingly, the architecture was of many different mediaeval periods, the ruined keep on the rocky eminence behind the house being Anglo-Saxon or Early Norman; the eastern towers, the curtain, the large central flag-tower and two of the gates of a period ending about the accession of Edward III, the great hall and its oak fittings in the style of Richard II and the more decorated portion towards the west representing for the most part the period between Henry V and Henry VII.'[1]

This digression has a purpose: we shall understand the

[1] *Ibid.*, p. 159.

nineteenth century all the better if we can see Charles's Folly as a symbol—as a counterpart in domestic architecture of a trend which found expression also in the novels of Scott, in the Oxford Movement, in Pugin and the pre-Raphaelites, in Ruskin, and in parts of Tennyson's own poetry. To build a pseudo-mediaeval castle after the Reform Bill, when modern democracy was being shaped, when Chartism and the hungry 'forties were just round the corner—how absurd, how anachronistic! Yet Charles d'Eyncourt was only doing what many would have loved to do if their means had allowed it. The game of pretending to live in the Middle Ages was played with all the more zest because the new industrialism was undermining the old order with such alarming speed. The oncoming world is raw and hideous: very well, let us pretend that the old order is unchanging, that the feudal hierarchy persists, that landed property, not industrial capital, still controls politics and society! A decaying order is never so fanatically upheld as when it is touched by the finger of death. And this pattern of life, this notion of success, of what it is worth while to do with money, a pattern so blatantly visible at Bayons, runs through the whole fabric of upper- and middle-class Victorian life and thought. It is important for the understanding of literature that such things should be remembered, because it was with such patterns in mind, or buried in subconsciousness, that part of the literature of the Victorian age was written. Tennyson's own pageantry was more insubstantial, but Camelot, the city of shadowy palaces, is his Bayons none the less.

One other early influence calls for mention, because of its own importance, and because of its relevance to one of my purposes in this chapter: the scenery of Lincolnshire. The Lincolnshire scene in Tennyson's boyhood was—as in part it is still—pastoral, agricultural and untouched by the Industrial Revolution. Centuries of peaceful habitation and cultivation had made it a patchwork of farmlands and parklands, sparsely populated yet besprinkled with innumerable quaint villages and studded with castles and manorial halls. Its every human symbol told of continuity with the feudal past and denied all connection with those sinister changes which, in neighbouring counties to the north and west, were devastating the land and shaking the social order. But though Nature in Lincolnshire was humanized and tidied, and could not speak to Tennyson as the mountains could to Wordsworth, it retained enough wildness to feed his imagination. The Wolds, a bare ridge of chalk hills running through the county from north to south, are nowhere more than a few hundreds of feet above sea-level, but they are high enough above the surrounding plains to give a sense of elevation. Their rounded slopes, covered with springy turf and inhabited solely by sheep, offered him a ready escape into silence, solitude and the exhilaration of wide horizons. To the west the land, more undulating and wooded, stretched away to the next main ridge, the Lincoln Heights, the limestone escarpment crowned and dominated by the three-towered cathedral. To the east it slopes gradually down through fens and salt marshes to the North Sea. Here, if you add the snowdrifts which lie on the Wolds in winter, and the bleak north-east winds that scour them, you already have the sources of many a Tennysonian word-picture. Tennyson became one of the greatest of all masters of description—in English poetry perhaps the very greatest; he would manage effects of every kind from tropical luxuriance to Alpine sublimity. But Lincolnshire was his imaginative homeland, and at the heart of it lay the Rectory garden at Somersby, with its velvet lawns, its lilacs, elms and cedars, and, winding through it

> 'the brook that loves
> To purl o'er matted cress and ribbed sand,
> Or dimple in the dark of rushy coves.'
> [*Ode to Memory*, IV.]

Yet there was very little of Somersby in his earliest poetry. Tennyson had already written a great deal of verse before he went up to Cambridge in 1827. At that time his chief poetic models were Thomson, Gray, Byron, Moore and Scott, and amongst older poets Spenser, Shakespeare and Beaumont and Fletcher. In the third decade of the nineteenth century the names of Shelley and Keats, and even Wordsworth, meant little to the world at large, and in the little world of Somersby next to nothing. 'Romanticism' was in the air, but its essence was taken to lie in Scott's mediaevalizing, Byron's posturing, the Arabian Nights and the gorgeous East, in Ossian or in Malory—in all this, rather than in the natural magic, the realizing imagination, of Wordsworth or Coleridge. The *Poems by Two Brothers* (1826) sing of Bassorah and Nadir Shah, of Mithridates and Alexander, the Druids, or Charles XI of Sweden; of Persians and Greeks, Turks, Spaniards and Peruvians; of Jerusalem and Babylon—and little enough of Lincolnshire. Indeed these poems must have been the Gondal and Angria of the Tennyson parsonage, for the Rectory at Somersby, like the parsonage at Haworth, was no haunt of ancient peace; it was terribly overcrowded, the Doctor was becoming a nervous dipsomaniac, and there were violent scenes and painful tension. From the midst of this chaos the young people, imaginative to the finger-tips, dreamed their way out into a world of their own making. We have Tennyson's own word for it, however, that he had already at this time written better things, but had deliberately left them out of *Poems by Two Brothers* 'as being too much out of the common for the public taste'. And it was certainly as a dedicated spirit that he regarded himself when he entered Trinity College, Cambridge, in 1827.

II. Cambridge

Cambridge meant far more to Tennyson than it ever meant to Wordsworth, Coleridge or Byron. It formed his mind, widened his interests, introduced him to current thought and founded lifelong friendships. Yet all that Cambridge did for him it did, so to speak, unofficially. This was still Unreformed Cambridge, a Cambridge where Mathematics was still the prescribed avenue to honours, and where those who were not mathematical were left to do pretty much what they pleased. And for budding poets this is not at all a bad thing. Some years ago, at the Wordsworth Centenary celebrations at Grasmere, I was introduced to an audience (by an Oxford Professor) as a representative of the University which had done nothing for Wordsworth. I replied that if Cambridge had done nothing for Wordsworth it had therein shown its accustomed wisdom, since 'nothing' was the best thing it could have done for him or any poet. What it did for Tennyson it did by simply being Cambridge, that is, a beautiful place of ancient colleges filled with young men who educated each other in their spare time. In Tennyson's day the whole business of learning the best that was being thought and said in the contemporary world was left to the undergraduates themselves. It was left in very capable hands, at any rate if one belonged to the right set—and Tennyson was elected, at the end of his second year, a member of the famous Society of the 'Apostles'. This Society had been founded by John Sterling and F. D. Maurice for the purpose of discussing all the leading questions of the time (and of all times). It was indeed an era of intellectual, social and political ferment; a time of awakening and questioning. A whole generation of revolution and war had passed, shaking and challenging all traditional assumptions and foundations; and a new set of men, representing new social levels and with a new kind of seriousness—men no longer inheriting the eighteenth century outlook—were facing the problems of a new age. Almost all that the University officially presented to those who longed to solve the riddle of the painful earth was Paley's *Evidences*, that embodiment of the unimaginative good sense of the older world. But the Apostles, fired with the new ardour released by the Revolution and by Romanticism, glanced from earth to heaven, ranging over such topics as: The Origin of Evil, The Derivation of Moral Sentiments, Prayer and the Personality of God, Have Shelley's Poems an Immoral Tendency? Is an Intelligible First Cause deducible from the Phenomena of the Universe? Is there any Rule of Moral Action beyond General Expediency?—and the like; debating, too, on politics, and reading the modern philosophers from Hobbes to Bentham and Kant.

It is significant, and typical of the distinction between Oxford and Cambridge, that whereas the Oxford Movement was Catholic and reactionary, looking back to the

Early Fathers and the High Church divines of the seventeenth century, the Cambridge group was on the whole
progressive and liberal—more disposed, in fact, to come to
terms with new thought than to defy it. Oxford took its
inspiration from Hurrell Froude, Newman, Keble and
Pusey; at Cambridge the paramount influences were those
first of Bentham and then of Coleridge. To say this is to say
something which requires more space than is here available,
and I have touched upon it in a previous volume.[1] Here it
must suffice to remark that wherever Coleridge's influence
was felt, it acted as a seminal force, not conveying systematic
doctrine, but quickening and warming both heart and head,
revealing the shallowness of the unenlivened understanding,
and calling men back to an awareness of spiritual reality.
From Coleridge his disciples learnt that within us there are
spiritual faculties—whether called Reason or Imagination
—whereby spiritual things may be discerned, and that the
enquiring spirit may be combined with the spirit of reverence. From him they learnt the lesson, most needed by the
nineteenth century, that new truths could be confronted and
welcomed, without loss of older meanings.

The introduction of Coleridge to the Cambridge circle
was the work of John Sterling, and above all of F. D.
Maurice, the most distinguished of the Coleridgeans, who
later, through his 'Broad Church' reconstruction of theology
and his 'Christian Socialism', became a central and much-
discussed figure in nineteenth century thought, and one
revered to this day for his spiritual insight and personal
saintliness. Maurice had come up to Cambridge in 1823
from a middle-class dissenting family, and had by then
already felt the Coleridgean influence which led him, in the
Apostles Society, to attack Benthamism, and later to join the
Church of England and to conceive his leading idea of unity
in diversity within the Kingdom of Christ. In a letter to
Gladstone, Arthur Hallam wrote that

> 'the effect which he has produced on the minds of many at Cam-
> bridge by the single creation of that Society of "Apostles" (for the

[1] *Nineteenth Century Studies* (1949), Chs. I and V.

spirit though not the form was created by him) is far greater than I can dare to calculate, and will be felt, both directly and indirectly, in the age that is upon us'.[1]

It was certainly so felt by Tennyson, for he owed to the Apostles not only some of his deepest friendships but also the framework within which, for good or for ill, he was to develop his thought and his art. It was in this circle that he became familiar with the poetry of Wordsworth, Shelley and Keats, and began to take his lifelong interest in science. Here, too, he met—amongst others—R. C. Trench (later Dean of Westminster and Archbishop of Dublin); Richard Monckton Milnes (afterwards Lord Houghton), editor and biographer of Keats; James Spedding, editor of Francis Bacon; the Lushington brothers; W. H. Thompson, afterwards Master of Trinity; and above all Arthur Hallam. I say 'above all', because although their friendship lasted only five years it left upon Tennyson a deeper mark than any of the others. There must, one would think, have been something very extraordinary about Hallam, or Tennyson must have been a highly abnormal young man, for Hallam's early death, sad and unexpected as it was, to have affected him as it did—setting him upon those Elegies which, seventeen years later, were put together and published as *In Memoriam*. Probably both conjectures are correct. Hallam's remaining work suggests little but youthful promise, but he impressed all who knew him as a youth of brilliant powers and sweet disposition. When we find Gladstone, sixty years later, still speaking of him as supreme amongst his Eton contemporaries, we need not wonder that Tennyson succumbed to his charm. For Hallam possessed everything that Tennyson lacked: a buoyant and sanguine temper, nimbleness of mind, ready eloquence, a sociable disposition, a happy and wealthy home-background, a confident religious faith, and—not least important—a high appreciation of Tennyson's poetic gifts. What we hear of Tennyson as an undergraduate reveals him as uncouth, provincial, rather morose and unapproachable, given to despondency and to much brooding

[1] Quoted by Hallam Lord Tennyson in his *Memoir* of Tennyson (1899 ed.), p. 36.

over the misery at home and his own loss of simple faith. To such a youth, Hallam's combination of intellectual brilliance with good breeding and affectionate admiration was irresistible, and it is no wonder that Tennyson idolized him. It must also be remembered, however, that Tennyson did not spend seventeen years bemoaning the loss of a College friend; the Elegies, which gradually accumulated during those years amidst many other works, became with him a habit or resource, and acquired more and more the character of a poetical journal or intimate record of his own spiritual pilgrimage.

iii. Early Poems

It is no part of my present purpose to speak at length of *Poems Chiefly Lyrical*, published in Tennyson's third year at Cambridge (1830), or of *Poems by Alfred Tennyson* (1832). It was the first of these volumes which sustained the rough-and-bluff manhandling of "Christopher North", and the second which was blasted in the *Quarterly* by J. W. Croker, to whom Tennyson was simply Keats hatched over again and hatched worse. 1833 was Tennyson's black year, for only five months after the *Quarterly* article came the death of Arthur Hallam. Tennyson was nearly crushed by the double blow, and published no further volume for ten years. But, though silenced, he was not stunned. Almost at once he began the Elegies, and throughout those dim years he was building up the great poem which was, at last, to win the hearts of the Victorian public and establish him as their representative poet. Before passing on, however, I must observe that the 1832 volume contained the best work of Tennyson's early romantic period: *Œnone*, *The Lotos-Eaters*, *The Palace of Art*, *Mariana in the South*, *The Lady of Shalott* and *A Dream of Fair Women*. Up to this time Tennyson's verse, for all its grace and melodiousness, had lacked some necessary ingredients of what we call great poetry, and it was indeed this lack which caused the dissatisfaction so often felt and expressed about it by his contemporaries. Shall we say that it lacked weight of substance, that it was unimportant, that there seemed no absolutely compelling reason

why it should have been written? It had been shadowy,
dreamlike, remote from 'the broad and common interests of
the time and of universal humanity'.[1] So is *Kubla Khan*, it
may be said. True, but Tennyson had not shown the preternatural visionary power which gives mystery to that poem.
Instead, there had been an affected diction, a preciosity of
tone and an effeminacy or fastidiousness of feeling. So far,
he had escaped from life on the viewless wings of poesy. But
there were strong influences urging him in the opposite
direction, reminding him of the need to have 'a conscience
and an aim'. The thought of his mother must often have
reproached him with a sense of his ineffectiveness, and to
this was added, we know, the influence of the Cambridge
Apostles. ' "Tennyson," said Trench to him once, in the
Trinity days, "we cannot live in art." '[2] And another friend,
Venables, told him that an artist should seek that which is
both ideal *and* real in the minds of the people, and seek it in
'the convergent tendencies of many opinions' on religion,
art and nature, of which Tennyson, in his view, could be the
exponent and unifier. Some have thought that, in thus in-
flicting upon Tennyson a sense of mission to his age, his
friends were doing him irreparable harm, and that his true
vocation lay precisely in the lyric communication of the
evanescent, the shadowy or the sombre. Whatever truth
there may be in this (and there is some, though less than used
to be supposed), I think that Tennyson's 1830 manner, if
persisted in, would have led him nowhere. If he had never
published anything more, he would have been remembered,
if at all, as a third-rate (or fifth-rate?) late romantic minor
poet. He had, however, reached the point where he knew
that he must say, with Wordsworth:

> 'Farewell, farewell, the heart that lives alone,
> Housed in a dream, at distance from the kind,'

and with Keats:

> 'And can I ever bid these joys farewell?
> Yes, I must pass them for a nobler life,
> Where I may find the agonies, the strife
> Of human hearts.'

[1] *Memoir*, p. 104.   [2] *Ibid.*, p. 100.

Tennyson could not at that time have realized how central in Keats's thought was the distinction between the poet and the dreamer, or how constantly he had struggled to surpass his own 'exquisite sense of the luxurious', and become one of the 'great miserable poets of humanity'. But his own development was leading towards such insights, though it was not until after Hallam's death that deep distress had humanized his heart and he became a great poet indeed. *The Palace of Art* is Tennyson's "Chamber of Maiden-Thought", in which at first he sees 'nothing but pleasant wonders', but which 'becomes gradually darkened' by thoughts of the 'misery and heartbreak, pain, sickness and oppression' of the world. Dr Leavis has truly observed of *The Palace of Art* that it typifies Tennyson's predicament: 'the explicit moral of the poem', he says, 'is that withdrawal will not do; but when he comes to the moral his art breaks down: the poetry belongs to the palace'.[1] One other thing remains to be said of the 1832 poems (in view of what follows below), which is that we find Tennyson here, as constantly afterwards, in possession of the Wordsworth–Coleridge secret: the gift of exact observation combined with the imaginative power of modifying or intensifying the object observed, so that it becomes a symbol of the observer's mind and feeling.

> 'And like a downward smoke, the slender stream
> Along the cliff to fall and pause and fall did seem.'

This secret was the choicest gift of romanticism to English poetry, and Tennyson inherited and exploited it to the utmost—though with him the eye was often preponderant over the imagination, so that his felicities sometimes appear decorative rather than organic.

iv. *The Two Voices*

After the consuming fires of 1833, Tennyson did not have long to wait for new Phoenix-wings. Already before the end of that year he had not only begun the Elegies, but had written (besides much else) *The Two Voices* and *Ulysses*. Of

---

[1] *New Bearings in English Poetry* (1932), p. 16.

The Two Voices, which shows the mood in which he faced
despair and change, I want to speak briefly now. It is a
meditation on the theme of To be or not to be, and fore-
shadows much of *In Memoriam*. The despairing voice tempts
him with the thought of suicide:

> ' "Thou art so full of misery,
>   Were it not better not to be?" ' '

The other voice, the Will to Live, propounds one classic
argument after another, but the tempter scornfully exposes
the vanity of each.

> ' "Let me not cast in endless shade
>   What is so wonderfully made" '—

You? wonderfully made? So is the dragon-fly, which
emerged today from its chrysalis:

> ' "An inner impulse rent the veil
>   Of his old husk: from head to tail
>   Came out clear plates of sapphire mail." '

But man is no creature of the moment; he is the crowning
work of Nature. What? does the boundless universe contain
within its 'hundred million spheres' nothing higher than
man?—and in any case, what is one individual amongst so
many others? But the general progress of man, the advance
of knowledge, will go on: am I to miss all this? The scale is
infinite; there is never any final attainment. But I had hoped
to do some good to my fellow-men, and

> ' ". . . having sown some generous seed,
>   Fruitful of further thought and deed,
>
>   To pass, when Life her light withdraws,
>   Not void of righteous self-applause,
>   Nor in a merely selfish cause—
>
>   In some good cause, not in mine own,
>   To perish, wept for, honour'd, known." '

Ah yes! the dream of youth, 'the stirring of the blood', soon
to be followed by 'the check, the change, the fall', when

'pain rises up, old pleasures pall'. Finally, to Hamlet's deter-
rent argument that perhaps death is only the prelude to
worse miseries hereafter, the tempter replies that it ends all.
Think of the lessons of a dead man's face, or of how, above
his grave—

> ' "High up the vapours fold and swim:
> About him broods the twilight dim:
> The place he knew forgetteth him." '

In resisting all this negation Tennyson takes his stand,
however uncertainly, upon the intimations of immortality,
the inklings of spiritual reality, which visited him at rare
intervals, and which later on became the main positives of
In Memoriam:

> 'That heat of inward evidence
> By which he doubts against the sense
>
> . . . . .
>
> He seems to hear a Heavenly Friend
> And thro' thick veils to apprehend
> A labour working to an end.
>
> . . . . .
>
> Heaven opens inward, chasms yawn,
> Vast images in glimmering dawn,
> Half shown, are broken and withdrawn.
>
> . . . . .
>
> Moreover, something is or seems,
> That touches me with mystic gleams,
> Like glimpses of forgotten dreams—
>
> Of something felt, like something here;
> Of something done, I know not where;
> Such as no language may declare.'

The ending of this poem is curious, and has been thought
sentimentally Victorian, yet it seems to me psychologically
true. Such inward arguments cannot end in rational demonstration and conviction: they can only be outgrown, put
aside, replaced by a change of mood or scene, better health
and spirits, a renewed sense of the true proportions of things.
The Book of Job, the archetype of all arraignments of the
moral order of the universe, ends, not with any intellectual

solution of Job's problem, nor with any proffered comfort, but with the voice of God answering out of the whirlwind: 'Where wast thou when I laid the foundations of the earth?' Or again, the Psalmist's injunction, 'Be still, and *know* that I am God', may not satisfy the rational enquirer or the agnostic, but it seems to be, in the last resort, the only kind of answer. Tennyson, therefore, in my view, should not be blamed, as he has sometimes been, for failing to find a solution where no solution exists; nor should he be accused of wishful thinking when he asserts, what from Pascal and others we receive with respect, that the Heart has its reasons of which Reason knows nothing. The ending of *The Two Voices* admittedly falls far short of the Book of Job; it is sweet and domestic, where the Hebrew poem is sublime. But the endings have this in common: they silence rebellious thoughts, not by logic, but by modulation into a new emotional key. What happens in Tennyson's poem? He opens a window, looks out and perceives that it is a Sunday morning; the bells are ringing, and he sees the people walking to church. Just as the Ancient Mariner unconsciously broke his spell by blessing the water-snakes, so in Tennyson's heart a gush of love springs up, and the 'bitter voice was gone'.

> '. . . in that hour
> From out my sullen heart a power
> Broke, like the rainbow from the shower,
>
> To feel, altho' no tongue can prove,
> That every cloud, that spreads above
> And veileth love, itself is love.'

What some critics have found sentimental or ludicrous in this ending, however, is not so much the whole conception (though even to mention Sunday morning makes some people wince), as the following close-up of a churchgoing family:

> 'One walk'd between his wife and child,
> With measured footfall firm and mild,
> And now and then he gravely smiled.

The prudent partner of his blood
Lean'd on him, faithful, gentle, good,
Wearing the rose of womanhood.

And in their double love secure
The little maiden walk'd demure,
Pacing with downward eyelids pure.

These three made unity so sweet,
My frozen heart began to beat,
Remembering its ancient heat.'

Now, if this makes you smile, or squirm, or feel sick, ask yourself why it should be so. Perhaps Tennyson had no right to be comforted by such a spectacle; he ought to have shot himself immediately at the sight of so much hypocrisy? Or is it that the picture of domestic bliss is too impossibly sweet and smug?—the husband too pompous and 'manly', the wife too clinging and dependent, the child too priggish? These people are too conventionally pious and good; they also accept traditional standards, the existing order, too unthinkingly. To be honest and real they should not have been going to church to absorb religious opium; marriage is not sacred; men are not 'grave'; the symbol of womanhood is not a rose but a cabbage or an orchid; little girls don't want parental love, are not 'pure'—and so on. Such presuppositions, or something like them, must, I think, be present in the minds of those who cannot stomach this passage, and I do not deny that they have some weight. Some, but nothing like as much as they were supposed to have, say, thirty years ago. It is no longer necessary or fashionable to treat every Victorian period-piece, as such, with sneers and derision. We can now not only credit Tennyson with sound insight in the mode of his psychotherapy, but we can further grant, I suggest, that a happy family of churchgoers on a Sunday morning in 1833 is a symbol not necessarily or inherently absurd.

The Two Voices, then, concerns us partly because it shows how far Tennyson's inward conflict had proceeded before he had read Lyell's *Geology* or Chambers's *Vestiges of Creation*,

TENNYSON

and long before the heyday of Darwin, Huxley and Tyndall. It is also interesting because it shows Tennyson using his art, not to embellish a dreamworld, but to communicate experience. The same is true, in a different sense, of *Ulysses*, and that is why these two poems, unlike most of his previous and some of his later writing, have a head of pressure behind them; something is there which demands and compels utterance. In *Ulysses* the sense that he must press on and not moulder in idleness is expressed objectively, through the classical story, and not subjectively as his own experience. He comes here as near perfection in the grand manner as he ever did; the poem is flawless in tone from beginning to end: spare, grave, free from excessive decoration, and full of firmly controlled feeling.

v. *The Princess:* 'Jewels Five-Words Long'

I am not concerned here to discuss why Tennyson should have chosen Women's Higher Education as the subject of his first long poem, *The Princess* (1847), nor to appraise that poem as a whole. I merely want to use it as the occasion for a few remarks on his 'jewels five-words long'. The blank verse of *The Princess* is flexible enough to convey tones varying from the up-to-date colloquial through the mock-heroic to the veritable grand manner. In some of Tennyson's work there is an incongruity between the stately Virgilian manner and the trivial or prosaic matter, but in *The Princess*, where romance, burlesque, loftiness and urbanity, mediaevalism and modernity are fused together, and the whole set in a Victorian park where a village fête is going on, this incongruity is appropriate enough. It is true in general that (as a writer in *The New Spirit of the Age* expressed it) Tennyson walks the common daylight in his singing-robes; he is 'silver-voiced' when he asks you to pass the salt, and says good-morning to you 'in a cadence'. We may admit that he is too consistently the conscious artist, and often applies more and richer decoration than his theme will bear. But *The Princess* is large enough and fantastic enough to allow him to load its every rift with ore. And this he did; he poured

71

into it the rich stores of observation and meditation which had been accumulating for years. He put into it, to begin with, those wonderful lyrics which are supposed to be sung by the ladies, to give the narrators breathing-spaces between the cantos. I call them 'wonderful' in the strictest sense, because I think we do, each time we encounter them, catch our breath in astonishment. Suddenly, unaccountably, the labouring artificer—of whom we are usually so conscious in reading Tennyson—vanishes from sight, and these perfect creations come into being before us, seeming to spring, not from the poet himself, but, like flowers, from a hidden root of their own. The best of them, significantly enough, are the most tenuous in 'meaning'; they come nearest of all his works to being what used to be called 'pure' or 'sheer' poetry —if by that was meant verbal music, incantation or a pattern of images. They affect one like Chopin's Preludes, signifying nothing but themselves. Their perfection suggests that in them, where Tennyson most completely loses himself, he was in another sense most himself—in other words, that his most distinctive poetic gift (though not the one that gives him a place in a book like this), was that of a spell-binder. Donne, as we have been reminded *ad nauseam* for the past thirty years, could certainly spin tougher threads of argument and wit in verse, but when it comes to rendering delicacies of sentiment or atmosphere, rarefied and evanescent, he is, beside Tennyson, nowhere. Nor should we expect it to be otherwise: this was the special gift of the nineteenth century, as Donne's was of the sixteenth-seventeenth, and neither need be cried up at the expense of the other.

Another distinctive nineteenth century excellence, possessed pre-eminently by Tennyson, was (as I have said, and as everyone knows) the habit of accurate observation of Nature, and the power to produce what might be called definitive renderings of it. Though these felicities occur everywhere in Tennyson, they are so abundant in *The Princess* that we may well examine some of them at this point. We know, from a letter written in 1882,[1] that at least

---

[1] See *Memoir*, pp. 214 ff.

from his twenties Tennyson was in the habit, as he says, of 'chronicling in four or five words or more whatever might strike me as picturesque in Nature'. Just as Turner, he goes on, 'takes rough sketches of landskip, etc., in order to work them eventually into some great picture', so he stored up phrases and lines for future use, keeping them in mind without writing them down, forgetting many, but often (like Wordsworth) remembering the exact occasion which suggested those that remained. Thus:

> 'A full sea glazed with muffled moonlight'

was suggested by 'the sea one night at Torquay. . . . The sky was covered with thin vapour, and the moon behind it.' Then comes a simile from *The Princess*, of which he quotes only a fragment: here is the whole of it (Ida is overwhelmed with shame and grief after her defeat)—

> '. . . as one that climbs a peak to gaze
> O'er land and main, and sees a great black cloud
> Drag inward from the deeps, a wall of night,
> Blot out the slope of sea from verge to shore,
> And suck the blinding splendour from the sand,
> And quenching lake by lake and tarn by tarn
> Expunge the world.'

This, he says, was suggested by 'a coming storm seen from the top of Snowdon'. Another simile from *The Princess* describes Cyril's erratic behaviour:

> '. . . as the water-lily starts and slides
> Upon the level in little puffs of wind,
> Tho' anchor'd to the bottom, such is he—'

'Water-lilies in my own pond, seen on a gusty day with my own eyes': his insistence here on personal observation is part of a complaint against critics who try to trace every image in a new poem to some older literary source, or to any source rather than Nature. 'Here is another anecdote', he continues,

'about suggestion. When I was about twenty or twenty-one I went on a tour to the Pyrenees. Lying among these mountains before a waterfall that comes down one thousand or twelve hundred feet I sketched it (according to my custom then) in these words:

> Slow-dropping veils of thinnest lawn.

When I printed this, a critic informed me that "lawn" was the material used in theatres to imitate a waterfall, and graciously added, "Mr T. should not go to the boards of a theatre but to Nature herself for his suggestions." And I *had* gone to Nature herself. I think it is a moot point whether, if I had known how that effect was produced on the stage, I should have ventured to publish the line.'

There is a precision, a finality, about these descriptive sketches by which one can usually recognize them as taken from Tennyson's mental stock of Nature-notes, and though sometimes they appear to be lapidary work, 'beauties' applied from outside, they are often so appropriate as to be highly expressive. The following example shows him at his best, I think; it is clearly taken from observation either in the Pyrenees, the Alps, or the English Lakes, and is used in *The Princess* to describe an effect following a furious speech of Ida's:

> '... thereat the crowd
> Muttering, dissolved: then, with a smile, that look'd
> A stroke of cruel sunshine on the cliff,
> When all the glens are drown'd in azure gloom
> Of thunder-shower, [she said ...:]'

Can any explanation be given for the success of this and similar passages? Why do we feel them at once to be 'right' and 'true'? We might answer, first, that they are examples of Coleridge's esemplastic power, whereby separate images are linked together through some point of real likeness. They are not fanciful or conceited comparisons, like Crashaw's description of Mary Magdalene's eyes as 'portable and compendious oceans', or Butler's comparison of the dawn to a boiled lobster turning from black to red. Such disparates have no affinity in Nature; they are yoked together by the violence of fancy. But affinities in Nature, or effects illustrated *from* Nature, are precisely what concern Tennyson; when he describes A in terms of B, it is because

B will release a cluster of associated ideas, images and responses which are relevant to A and will illuminate it and become one with it. Thus in 'A stroke of cruel sunshine on the cliff': *cruel* sunshine—why 'cruel'? Because it is ironical, promising what it will not fulfil; the cliff basks for an instant in a bliss which will be extinguished at once by the storm-cloud. 'Stroke' reinforces this tantalizing and transitory quality, because it conveys the notion of a sudden shaft of light, striking and at the same time caressing the cliff through a break in the clouds. The rumble of the next two lines completes the effect. Now transfer this image to the smile of the angry princess, as she checks her stormy passion for an instant. All the associations that have been evoked are relevant, and, immediately attaching themselves to the princess, they realize for us her expression and the whole scene.

The 'stroke of cruel sunshine', then, is an example of a visual, natural image used to illustrate something less concrete: the effect of an angry woman's smile. A poet will take his illustrations from what he unconsciously assumes to be more immediately apprehensible, more habitually present to the mind, than the object to be rendered. Some poets, for example Byron or Shelley, in describing a stormy sun-ray, might have compared it with the smile of an angry woman. But Tennyson's chamber of imagery is hung with sketches from Nature, all very real to him (and to most later nineteenth century readers); it is therefore they which give reality to less tangible objects, not vice versa. In the line

'Slow-dropping veils of thinnest lawn'

we have a simple example, in which one tangible substance is compared with another. How strange, how unlike water in its usual forms, is that cascade dropping down the thousand-foot mountain ledge! How shall we give an idea of its strangeness, conveying the sense that it seems no longer like liquid in rapid, sparkling motion, but like a solid substance—though of finest texture? Texture! yes, that's it of course; some fabric woven to airy thinness and transparency. Muslin? No—too coarse, and not refined enough in its use, either. Gauze? perhaps *too* transparent, and not white enough. What is that stuff that bishops wear—lawn! the very thing: fine-spun, white, delicate (you could pay out lengths of it over a counter, and it would drop slowly, in folding veils, just like that waterfall)—and, because worn by bishops, refined and even celestial in its associations.

I must not be beguiled from my main theme by Tennyson's *embarras de richesses*. I will work back to it (I have never really been far from it) by asking why these 'jewels', these faithful renderings of Nature, give pleasure—if I may assume that they still do, to some people? Most of these curious felicities in Tennyson (or other poets) depend for their effect upon metaphor or simile; the question thus broadens into an enquiry about the philosophy of metaphor. Why are we pleased (if we are) when a waterfall is shown to resemble lawn, when the Pleiades are likened to a swarm of fire-flies tangled in a silver braid, or when a smile becomes a stroke of cruel sunshine? Critics, from Aristotle to Coleridge and onwards, have spoken of our delight in imitation, and of the principle of similitude in dissimilitude, but they have not explained (as far as I am aware) whence the delight springs. I suspect that we are here facing something ultimate, some unanalysable fact about the fabric of our minds, which can only be 'explained' in terms of itself—that is, cannot be explained at all, but merely illustrated. Why does pleasure please? We can only say that we do, as a fact of experience, take pleasure in noting resemblances, correspondences and analogies, and that from this fact spring not only our delight in the arts but also our zest for scientific classification and philosophical systems. We need to impose coherence, order or significance upon the flux of experience, and whatever in metaphor, allegory or world-picture suggests a unity, discerns or creates connexions, implies a pattern or a linkage where before there seemed mere meaningless disconnexion —whatever does this, gives relief and a sense of mastery.

Even if we grant all this we have still to account for the preponderance in Tennyson (and much of nineteenth century poetry) of *natural* imagery—of images, I mean, from Nature rather than from action or thought or reading. This may seem an otiose question, yet poets of former centuries, even when describing natural phenomena, had seldom striven with such earnestness to find the inevitable, the unimprovable word or phrase. The notion, or rather the unexpressed presupposition, that a chief part of the poet's task is to observe Nature intently and render her faithfully, was the special contribution of the nineteenth century. It begins to appear in the previous century, of course; I have puzzled pupils and even colleagues before now by showing them unassigned passages which they took for Tennyson, but which were in fact by Thomson. But the phenomenon of a poet collecting his material by ranging through the world receptive to every sight, sound, smell or touch, his mind continually on the stretch fitting words to things, never satisfied until he has fixed them definitively, and never more certain, than when he has done so, that he has fulfilled his poetic function—this is something belonging to the nineteenth century. Tennyson exulted when he had found one of his jewels, and smacked his lips as he smoothed, filed and polished it to perfection:

'By the long wash of Australasian seas . . .'

'Dead claps of thunder from within the cliff . . .'

'Laburnums, dropping-wells of fire . . .'

' . . . her hair
In gloss and hue the chestnut when the shell
Divides threefold to show the fruit within.'

But why? Is it so important, then, does it matter above all else, that a poet should reproduce Nature so accurately, so lovingly, and so deftly? Donne would not have thought so. If he refers to the moon, for example—

'O more than moone
Draw not up seas to drown me in thy sphere'—

it is with no thought of its romantic glamour. Donne's moon throws no 'long glories on the level lake'; it is there as a celestial body which, like his mistress, has powers of gravitational attraction. Similarly his violet (in *The Ecstasie*) brings no message of spring; it is there as a moral emblem for lovers (if I transplant your soul into mine, and vice versa,

both will flourish better). Dryden was pleased when he had
written, say—

> 'The weary waves, withdrawing from the fight,
> Lie lulled and panting on the silent shore'—

and pleased, not because he had rendered something seen,
but because he had successfully incorporated in English
verse an image from Statius which seemed 'proper to the
subject'.

It was, of course, the Romantic poets, and above all
Wordsworth, Coleridge and Keats, who had set the example.
They had set it, not only by their skill in chiselling the
perfect phrase:

> 'Clothed in the sunshine of the withering fern . . .'

> 'The moonlight steeped in silentness
> The steady weather-cock . . .'

> '. . . the moon lifting her silver rim
> Above a cloud, and with a gradual swim
> Coming into the blue with all her light . . .'

—not only by this, but by establishing a new conception of
the function of poetry and of the poetical character. The
world lay around us, 'an inexhaustible treasure, but for
which, in consequence of the veil of familiarity and selfish
solicitude, we have eyes that see not, ears that hear not, and
hearts that neither feel nor understand'. It was for the poet
to be 'a priest to us all Of the wonder and bloom of the
world'; through the deep power of joy he is to see into the
life of things, and make us share his insight by 'disimprison-
ing the soul of fact'. Tennyson inherited this conception of
poetry, or rather he unconsciously absorbed it through the
pores of his skin. He did not need to justify to himself or to
others his own propensity for making verbal transcripts
from Nature. In doing this he was being faithful to his
calling; each time he had fixed to perfection some aspect of
sky, cloud, sea or flower, he had brought men a step nearer
to the soul of all things. For there was, I think, a religious,
or at least a pantheistic, assumption beneath all this: Nature
was God's handiwork, his vesture, or his symbolic language;

to study it, then, was not an aesthetic indulgence but a solemn duty, a discipline and a vocation. The poet's satisfaction in his own successes, therefore, was like that of the natural scientist. It was more than the craftsman's or naturalist's joy in his own skill; it was a sense, also, that he had transmitted to his fellow-men a fragment of God's truth. This feeling persisted in Tennyson long after he had ceased to find in Nature the clearest evidence of God's power and love. Its influence pervades the whole nineteenth century, and is still evident (for instance) in Thomas Hardy, for whom Nature, though divested of its divinity, yet remained an object of fascinated attention. Let us remember that this was the century, on the one hand of Turner and Ruskin, and on the other of Darwin and Huxley. Tennyson had in him ingredients of both landscape-painter and field-naturalist.

vi. *In Memoriam*

If 1833 had been Tennyson's black year, 1850 was his *annus mirabilis*. That year, *In Memoriam* was published, and a fortnight later he was married to Emily Sellwood, after a broken engagement which had dragged on for twelve years. And as if this were not enough to atone for all that Tennyson had endured of neglect, disparagement, bereavement and loneliness, Wordsworth died, leaving vacant the Laureateship at the very moment when Tennyson, with the immense success of *In Memoriam*, had become a national institution.

The success and influence of *In Memoriam* illustrate its truly representative quality. The Victorians loved it, and were moved by it, because it dealt seriously and beautifully with the very problems that most concerned them: problems arising from the gradual fading-out of the older spiritual lights in the harsh dawn of a new and more positive age. For *In Memoriam* (it need hardly be said) is far from being a continuous lament over Arthur Hallam. It begins, of course, with the bereavement, with personal grief and lamentation, and with the inevitable questionings about the soul's survival in a future life. Gradually the immediate sorrow recedes, giving place to poignant recollection, and then to more general meditations on man's place in Nature and the impact of science upon religious faith. As in *The Two Voices*, a mood of reconciliation, even hope, is at last reached and the reasons of the heart are vindicated against the reasonings of the intellect. It is needless and beside the mark to look for any greater unity or closer pattern in the poem than this. Tennyson gave a semblance of design to it by rearranging many of the sections and by introducing recurrent Christmases. But it remains a series of elegiac poems strung upon the thread of the poet's own life and following the curve of his development. It is in fact Tennyson's intimate spiritual journal of those years, and it succeeds largely *because* it lacks a more formal structure. Its desultory, informal character ensures its freedom from bardic posturings or routine gestures; the various sections come straight from Tennyson's heart, and were—as he calls them—'brief lays, of sorrow born', or

> 'Short swallow-flights of song, that dip
> Their wings in tears, and skim away.'

This meant that Tennyson's lyric power, the greatest of his gifts, was allowed full play, and we get therefore something very unusual: a long poem free from epic pomp, and built up, like a coral-reef, entirely from living organisms. Moreover, in this poem we find all Tennyson's distinctive graces in fragrant blow together. His artistry is at its height, every verse and line being wrought as near perfection as he could make it; yet such is the pressure of emotion, so compelling the need for utterance, that artificiality is avoided. Similarly, *In Memoriam* is the richest of all repositories of the five-word jewels, exquisite landscapes, renderings of the shifting panorama of the seasons; but these are here employed as vehicles and symbols of the poet's changing moods and share in his imaginative life: they never strike us, as often elsewhere (especially in the *Idylls of the King*), as decoration mechanically and coldly applied from without.

The problems confronted in *In Memoriam*, though forced upon Tennyson by personal experience and by the spirit of his age, are neither local nor ephemeral; they are universal, in that they are those which are apt to beset a sensitive and meditative mind in any age. Has man an immortal soul? Is there any meaning in life? any purpose or design in the world-process? any evidence in Nature, in philosophy or in the human heart, for a beneficent Providence? These issues are dealt with by Tennyson, not in the manner of a thinker —whether philosopher, theologian or scientist—but in the manner of a well-informed modern poet: that is, in the manner of one who, though not ignorant of what the specialists are saying, cares for their results only insofar as they are felt in the blood, and felt along the heart, affecting there the inmost quality of living.

There is another significant point about the way in which Tennyson faces experience in this poem: he faces it, virtually, as a soul unprovided with Christian supports. In spite of the Prologue, 'Strong Son of God, immortal Love' (which was in fact composed at the end), *In Memoriam* is not a distinctively Christian poem. The doubts, misgivings, discouragements, probings and conjectures which make it humanly moving could not have existed in a mind equipped with the Christian solutions. It is well to remember, sometimes, how much in literature as a whole presupposes a suspension, not of disbelief, but of belief. Most of literature lives on the level of Nature, not of grace. And thus *In Memoriam* is not concerned with the impact of the Zeitgeist upon Christian doctrine or apologetic, nor does it proffer Christian consolation. It goes behind Christianity, or passes it by, confronting the preliminary question which besets the natural man, the question whether there can be any religious interpretation of life at all. What made the poem acceptable even to the Christian reader in the Victorian age was that having, though with diffidence and humility, vindicated the believing temper, accepted the reasons of the heart, Tennyson had opened a door which gave access to the Christian territory.

Those who mistake Tennyson for an 'escapist' might ponder the following remark of A. C. Bradley:

'. . . with the partial exception of Shelley, Tennyson is the only one of our great poets whose attitude towards the sciences of Nature was what a modern poet's ought to be; . . . the only one to whose habitual way of seeing, imagining, or thinking, it makes any real difference that Laplace, or for that matter Copernicus, ever lived'.[1]

From his earliest manhood Tennyson breathed the atmosphere of scientific theory and discovery, and throughout his life his meditations were governed by the conceptions of law, process, development and evolution—the characteristic and ruling ideas of his century. Of course, the challenge of science to religious orthodoxy was no new manifestation peculiar to the century. Copernicus had challenged it by destroying the geocentric world-picture; the mechanico-materialism of the seventeenth and eighteenth centuries had undermined the miraculous elements of Christianity. Nevertheless the middle decades of the nineteenth century are rightly felt to be the *locus classicus* of the science-and-religion conflict; and that, perhaps, for two main reasons. First because, to the older idea of immutable law operating throughout the physical universe in the inorganic sphere, there was now added the idea of inexorable development proceeding within the organic world, moulding and modifying living species. Secondly, because this great idea, arriving upon the scene in a century of cheap printing and a vastly augmented reading public, soon advanced outside the studies of philosophers and noblemen—to which 'advanced' thought had hitherto been largely confined—and reached the average man, the sort of man who had generally been in possession of a simple conventional faith.

The first aspects of science that interested the young Tennyson seem to have been astronomy (in particular the nebular theory, propounded by Laplace in 1796) and embryology. Wordsworth, in an oft-quoted passage of the Preface to Lyrical Ballads, had predicted that poetry would eventually be able to absorb the results of science and carry them alive into the heart; Tennyson fulfilled that prophecy in Wordsworth's lifetime. Here is his poetic version of the nebular theory (it is the exordium of Professor Psyche's lecture in *The Princess*):

[1] *A Miscellany* (1929), pp. 30-1.

'This world was once a fluid haze of light,
Till toward the centre set the starry tides,
And eddied into suns, that wheeling cast
The planets: then the monster, then the man.'

It will be noticed that he does not stop at the planets, but carries the development on to man, conceiving the whole process as one. But years before *The Princess* he had written, and deleted from the published version, the following stanzas for *The Palace of Art* (1832):

'Hither, when all the deep unsounded skies
  Shudder'd with silent stars, she clomb,
And as with optic glasses her keen eyes
  Pierced thro' the mystic dome,

Regions of lucid matter taking forms,
  Brushes of fire, hazy gleams,
Clusters and beds of worlds, and bee-like swarms
  Of suns, and starry streams.'

Two more of the excised stanzas run thus:

'"From shape to shape at first within the womb
  The brain is moulded", she began.
"And thro' all phases of all thought I come
  Unto the perfect man.

All nature widens upward. Evermore
  The simple essence lower lies,
More complex is more perfect, owning more
  Discourse, more widely wise."'[1]

Here we see not only the conception of biological evolution but supporting evidence for it taken from the new science of embryology, which taught that the brain of the foetus passed through all the previous phases of evolution, recapitulating in brief the whole history of the species. It is recorded of Tennyson that, right back in his undergraduate days, he once propounded, at a Trinity discussion, the theory that 'the development of the human body might possibly be

[1] Quoted in *Memoir*, p. 101.

traced from the radiated, vermicular, molluscous and verte-
brate organisms.'[1]

But it was from geology that Tennyson received the most
decisive shock. We know that for some months in 1837 he
was 'deeply immersed' in Charles Lyell's celebrated *Principles of Geology* (1830-33). What was there in this book to
disturb him or any other reader? Its main thesis was that the
present state of the earth's crust is to be accounted for, not,
as in Cuvier's theory, by a series of catastrophic changes, but
by the continuous operation, through immense tracts of
time, of the natural forces still at work (erosion, gradual
earth-movement, sedimentation, etc.). This sounds innocent
enough, but the sting of it was that it presupposed for the
earth a vastly greater age than was allowed for in the accepted biblical chronology, and thrust far back, if not out of
the picture altogether, the notion of divine creation and
superintendence. First cooling gases, then aeons of erosion:
what, then, of the Seven Days' creation, Adam and Eve, and
the Flood? Secondly, Lyell went on to show that in the
course of these gradual changes species after species of
living creatures had become extinct through inability to
adapt themselves to changed environments. 'The inhabitants
of the globe', says he,

> 'like all the other parts of it, are subject to change. It is not only
> the individual that perishes but whole species.'
>
> 'None of the works of a mortal being can be eternal. . . . And
> even when they have been included in rocky strata, . . . they must
> nevertheless eventually perish, for every year some portion of the
> earth's crust is shattered by earthquakes or melted by volcanic fires,
> or ground to dust by the moving waters on the surface.'[2]

This teaching, though it might have no direct bearing upon
the doctrine of immortality, seemed to weaken its probability, and certainly weakened any alleged support derivable
by analogy from Nature. Worse still, it seemed hard to

---

[1] Quoted by Sir C. Tennyson, *op. cit.*, p. 83.
[2] Quoted by E. B. Mattes, *In Memoriam* (New York, Expository Press, 1951),
pp. 58 ff. This dissertation is an excellent guide to the sources and structure of the
poem, and I owe much to it in this section of the present chapter.

reconcile with the belief that 'God is love indeed, and love Creation's final law'. What, according to Lyell, has become of the Heavenly Father without whose care and compassion not one sparrow falls to the ground?

Before quitting Lyell's *Geology*, it is worth noting that Lyell himself was quite willing to profess belief in the *fact* of divine activity, provided that science were left free to investigate and demonstrate the mode of it. This was the formula adopted (quite rightly) by the nineteenth century reconcilers of science and religion in general. Lyell was astute enough, moreover, to have thought out a suitably insinuating manner of approaching the orthodox:

> 'If you don't triumph over them, but compliment the liberality and candour of the present age, the bishops and enlightened saints will join us in despising both the ancient and modern physico-theologians. . . . I give you my word that full *half* of my history and comments was cut out, and even many facts; because . . . I . . . felt that it was anticipating twenty or thirty years of the march of honest feeling to declare it undisguisedly.'[1]

It was, of course, all very well to take this line, and to say: "Science the enemy of religion? Not a bit of it, my dear sir! We're not denying that God does all this, we're merely showing you how he does it." I say, 'all very well', because there were many who felt that a God who moved in such a very mysterious way was not the God of their fathers. Some found it more comforting to ascribe to him the attribute of non-existence. Others, of whom Tennyson was one, felt (or came to feel) that the whole spectacle of Nature was somehow irrelevant to faith. Even in the early days, at one of the Apostles' debates at Cambridge, he had voted 'No' on the question 'Is an Intelligible First Cause deducible from the Phenomena of the Universe?' And later, he is reported to have said, of the wonders disclosed by the microscope, 'Strange that these wonders should draw some men to God and repel others. No more reason in one than in the other.' This attitude distinguishes Tennyson, and others of this period, not only from Wordsworth but from that line of

---

[1] Quoted *ibid.*, p. 57.

thinkers who, from the seventeenth century onwards, had been demonstrating the Wisdom of God from the Creation. I suspect that it was also at variance with his own sub-conscious feeling.

However, Tennyson read other books in which a scientific attitude was combined with more explicit reassurances. Mrs Mattes has shown that in October 1843 he possessed a copy of Herschel's *Preliminary Discourse on the Study of Natural Philosophy* (first published 1830). She quotes these typical extracts, illustrating the optimistic gloss which Herschel put upon the grim story of geology.

> 'Is it wonderful that a being so constituted [i.e. man] should first encourage a hope, and by degrees acknowledge an assurance, that his intellectual existence will not terminate with the dissolution of his corporeal frame but rather that, in a future state of being . . . endowed with acute senses, and higher faculties, he shall drink deep at that fountain of beneficent wisdom for which the slight taste obtained on earth has given him so keen a relish?'

> '. . . we cannot fail to be struck with the rapid rate of dilatation which every degree upward of the scale, so to speak, exhibits, and which, in an estimation of averages, gives an immense preponderance to the present over every former condition of mankind, and, for aught we can see to the contrary, will place succeeding generations in the same degree of superior relation to the present that this holds to those passed away.'[1]

In short (if we can pick our way through the verbiage), man is rapidly getting bigger and better, and after all a future life seems quite probable—anyway, let's believe it!

About a year later (November 1844) Tennyson wrote to his publisher Edward Moxon:

> 'I want you to get me a book which I see advertised in the *Examiner*: it seems to contain many speculations with which I have been familiar for years, and on which I have written more than one poem. The book is called *Vestiges of the Natural History of Creation.* . . .'

This book (as was pointed out by Mr W. R. Rutland in a

---

[1] *Ibid.*, p. 77.

very instructive essay called "Tennyson and the Theory of Evolution", over fifteen years ago[1]) contains so many passages which seem to be paraphrased in *In Memoriam* that we cannot doubt its consonance with Tennyson's own thought, and in some particulars its direct influence. Hallam Tennyson has a footnote in his *Memoir*: 'The sections of "In Memoriam" about Evolution had been read by his friends [i.e. in MS.] some years before the publication of *The Vestiges of Creation* in 1844.'[2] But as Mrs Mattes points out, this note does not say which sections, and her evidence indicates that the Epilogue, at least, was not written before 1844. However, only those (if there are still any) who think that Darwin invented Evolution in 1859 will be surprised to find that it is anticipated by Robert Chambers in *Vestiges*, or that Tennyson had anticipated them both. Romanes said that 'In "In Memoriam" Tennyson noted the fact [of Natural Selection], and a few years later Darwin supplied the explanation'.[3] The truth is that the idea of continuous unfolding, development or 'evolution' had been in the air since the latter part of the eighteenth century, being foreshadowed for example by Kant, Goethe and Lamarck. What Darwin did was to collect evidence, not for the fact of evolution, but for the mode of its operation.

Many readers found *Vestiges* disturbing; not so Tennyson. Its harsher implications were already familiar to him, and its consolations were to him truly reassuring. We can form an idea of both these aspects from the following passages (both quoted by Mr Rutland in the above-mentioned essay):

'We have seen powerful evidence that the construction of this globe and its associates, and inferentially of all the other globes of space, was the result, not of any immediate or personal exertion on the part of the Deity, but of natural laws which are the expressions of His will. What is to hinder our supposing that the organic creation is also a result of natural laws, which are in like manner an expression of His will?'

'The Great Ruler of Nature has established laws for the opera-

[1] *Essays and Studies by Members of the English Association,* 1940.
[2] *Op. cit.,* p. 186.   [3] *Ibid.,* p. 186.

87

tion of inanimate matter, which are quite unswerving, so that when we know them we have only to act in a certain way with respect to them in order to obtain all the benefits and avoid all the evils connected with them. He has likewise established moral laws in our nature, which are equally unswerving, and from obedience to which unfailing good is to be derived. But the two sets of laws are independent of each other. . . . It is clear, moreover, from the whole scope of the natural laws, that the individual, as far as the present sphere of being is concerned, is to the Author of Nature a consideration of inferior moment. Everywhere we see the arrangements for the species perfect; the individual is left, as it were, to take his chance amidst the mêlée of the various laws affecting him.'

Man is thus part of the animal or organic creation, and subject to its laws. Yet Chambers has this reflection to add:

'It may be, that, while we are committed to take our chance in a natural system of undeviating operation, and are left with apparent ruthlessness to endure the consequences of every collision into which we knowingly or unknowingly come with each law of the system, there is a system of Mercy and Grace behind the screen of nature, which is to make up for all the casualties endured there, and the very largeness of which is what makes these casualties a matter of indifference to God. For the existence of such a system, the actual constitution of nature is itself an argument. . . . Thinking of all the contingencies of this world as to be in time melted into or lost in the greater system, to which the present is only subsidiary, let us wait the end with patience, and be of good cheer.'[1]

And lastly, this, which parallels the conclusion of *In Memoriam*:

'It is startling to find an appearance of imperfection in the circle to which man belongs, and the ideas which rise in consequence are no less startling. Is our race but the initial of the grand crowning type? Are there yet to be species superior to us in organization, purer in feeling, more powerful in device and act, and who shall take a rule over us? . . . There may be then occasion for a nobler type of humanity, which shall complete the zoological circle on this

---

[1] Rutland, *loc. cit.*, p. 19; Mattes, *op. cit.*, p. 80.

planet, and realize some of the dreams of the purest spirits of the present race.'[1]

It was, then, in the context of such ideas as these that *In Memoriam* was composed. But, needless to say (I hope it is needless), we have not 'accounted for' the poem by mentioning some of the books that Tennyson was reading at the time. If *In Memoriam* were merely a versification of such trite reflexions as I have been quoting, it would be of little more account than they. This consideration applies in general to all philosophical poetry, poetry with a 'message'. Readers (and Victorian readers were especially prone to this) often discuss such poetry as if its doctrine were something detachable, something which could be expressed in prose and presented as its essence or inmost meaning. True, it *can* be so presented, but in that case the 'message' of *In Memoriam* (for instance) could as well be learnt direct from Lyell, Herschel or Chambers. It is not that the 'thought' is unimportant in this or other reflective poetry; the point is that it is important in a different way. If its importance were equivalent to that of its prose counterpart, I should not be devoting this attention to Tennyson now. Instead, I should only be entitled to say something like this: 'Lyell, Herschel, Chambers and Tennyson all considered that, while there was no direct evidence for a life after death, the evidence against its probability was not sufficient to preclude any reasonable man from believing in it if he found it comforting.' But, in fact, Tennyson's statement of this great thought has generally been felt to be worth more than that of the other three authors. Why? not because he 'means' anything different, but because he means it from a far greater depth and in a far richer context. Meaning in poetry, as we all know, is far more complex than meaning in logical statement; it operates through image, symbol, rhythm, suggestion and association, and therefore calls forth from us a far more complete response—'complete' in that the emotions, imagination and sensibility are involved as well as the intelligence. A poem, like a piece of ritual, *enacts* what a credal statement merely

[1] Rutland, *loc. cit.*, p. 23; Mattes, *op. cit.*, p. 80.

propounds; "this", says the poem in effect, "is a tract of experience lived through in the light of such-and-such a thought or belief; this is what it feels like to accept it". As Professor I. A. Richards has said, a poet is usually more valuable to us when he is feeling something than when he is 'feeling that' something. I think it likely that what, for Tennyson, chiefly kept alive the heart in the head was the influence of Carlyle, working upon a soul prepared by a Christian upbringing and not unacquainted with flashes of mystical insight.

Perhaps the reader may find it convenient to have before him here a few of the stanzas (familiar though they be) which show most clearly how Messrs Lyell, Herschel and Chambers appear when felt along the heart:

LV

.   .   .   .   .

'Are God and Nature then at strife,
   That Nature lends such evil dreams?
   So careful of the type she seems,
So careless of the single life;

That I, considering everywhere
   Her secret meaning in her deeds,
   And finding that of fifty seeds
She often brings but one to bear,

I falter where I firmly trod,
   And falling with my weight of cares
   Upon the great world's altar-stairs
That slope thro' darkness up to God,

I stretch lame hands of faith, and grope,
   And gather dust and chaff, and call
   To what I feel is Lord of all,
And faintly trust the larger hope.

LVI

"So careful of the type?" but no.
   From scarped cliff and quarried stone
   She cries, "A thousand types are gone:
I care for nothing, all shall go.

"Thou makest thine appeal to me:
    I bring to life, I bring to death:
    The spirit does but mean the breath:
I know no more." And he, shall he,

Man, her last work, who seem'd so fair,
    Such splendid purpose in his eyes,
    Who roll'd the psalm to wintry skies,
Who built him fanes of fruitless prayer,

Who trusted God was love indeed
    And love Creation's final law—
    Tho' Nature, red in tooth and claw
With ravine, shriek'd against his creed—

Who loved, who suffer'd countless ills,
    Who battled for the True, the Just,
    Be blown about the desert dust,
Or seal'd within the iron hills?

No more? A monster, then, a dream,
    A discord. Dragons of the prime,
    That tare each other in their slime,
Were mellow music match'd with him.

O life as futile, then, as frail!
    O for thy voice to soothe and bless!
    What hope of answer, or redress?
Behind the veil, behind the veil.'

In these two Sections (LV and LVI) we have Tennyson
feeling the first shock of Lyell and Chambers (or of the
interpretations they stand for). Nature seems to deny the
law of love, and man is (in Mrs Mattes's phrase) 'a prospective fossil'. After faintly trusting the larger hope,
Tennyson sinks to even dimmer depths of perplexity; hope
seems to vanish, truth is for ever hidden behind the veil, and
he vainly longs for Hallam's reassuring voice. However, in
a later Section (CXVIII) he makes a new synthesis of his
former thoughts; above all, he unites in one comprehensive
view what Chambers separates: physical and moral law:

CXVIII

'Contemplate all this work of Time,
  The giant labouring in his youth;
  Nor dream of human love and truth,
As dying Nature's earth and lime;

But trust that those we call the dead
  Are breathers of an ampler day
  For ever nobler ends. They say,
The solid earth whereon we tread

In tracts of fluent heat began,
  And grew to seeming-random forms,
  The seeming prey of cyclic storms,
Till at the last arose the man;

Who throve and branch'd from clime to clime
  The herald of a higher race,
  And of himself in higher place,
If so he type this work of time

Within himself, from more to more;
  Or, crown'd with attributes of woe
  Like glories, move his course, and show
That life is not as idle ore,

But iron dug from central gloom,
  And heated hot with burning fears,
  And dipt in baths of hissing tears,
And batter'd with the shocks of doom

To shape and use. Arise and fly
  The reeling Faun, the sensual feast;
  Move upward, working out the beast,
And let the ape and tiger die.'

Man is the product of the natural law, but he must now take conscious part in the evolutionary process, transferring it from the physical to the moral level. Moreover, this very obligation strengthens the probability that the process does not end with physical death, but that the dead are breathers of an ampler day.

Since I am concerned here not exclusively with Tennyson's thoughts and honest doubts, but also with certain aspects of his poetry as such, I will refer to a few more passages of *In Memoriam* which seem relevant. The first illustrates not only the quality of Tennyson's musings on the tragic ironies of circumstance, but also the difference between a prosaic and a poetic statement of the same 'thought'. What, in Chambers, reads: 'the individual is left, as it were, to take his chance amidst the mêlée of the various laws affecting him', becomes in Tennyson's poetry:

'O father, wheresoe'er thou be,
    Who pledgest now thy gallant son;
    A shot, ere half thy draught be done,
Hath still'd the life that beat from thee.

O mother, praying God will save
    Thy sailor,—while thy head is bow'd,
    His heavy-shotted hammock-shroud
Drops in his vast and wandering grave.' [vi.]

The next Section is an example of something I have mentioned: Tennyson's use of his descriptive power, not to decorate, but to enact, realize or symbolize a mood. The mood is that of loss and dereliction, and this is communicated through a picture of London at its dreariest:

'Dark house, by which once more I stand
    Here in the long unlovely street,
    Doors, where my heart was used to beat
So quickly, waiting for a hand,

A hand that can be clasp'd no more—
    Behold me, for I cannot sleep,
    And like a guilty thing I creep
At earliest morning to the door.

He is not here; but far away
    The noise of life begins again,
    And ghastly thro' the drizzling rain
On the bald street breaks the blank day.' [vii.]

The series dealing with the return of Arthur Hallam's remains by ship to England contains several signal examples of the same power. The moods vary from the 'calm despair' of XI, which is rendered through an autumn landscape seen from a Lincolnshire hilltop, to the feverish agitation of XV:

'To-night the winds begin to rise
   And roar from yonder dropping day:
   The last red leaf is whirl'd away,
The rooks are blown about the skies;

The forest crack'd, the waters curl'd,
   The cattle huddled on the lea;
   And wildly dash'd on tower and tree
The sunbeam strikes along the world:'

Note here the deftness with which Tennyson secures his effect with the minimum of significant details; a windy autumn sunset is realized with the utmost economy and compression. The winds 'roar from yonder dropping day': that tells us that the wind is westerly, and prepares us for the appearance, from beneath the cloud-rim, of the angry ray from the setting sun, which 'strikes along the world', apparently 'dashed' there by the wind itself. The rooks, whose return to their rookery at dusk is normally a slow procession, are 'blown about the skies', hence we feel the wind that buffets them. And all this *is* Tennyson's mood: it is not there simply as an exhibition of virtuosity. A little further on he speaks of

'. . . yonder cloud
   That rises upward always higher,
   And onward drags a labouring breast,
   And topples round the dreary west,
A looming bastion fringed with fire.'

The last line of this, especially, is a fairly obvious jewel from the Nature-notes, yet it escapes frigidity by becoming a powerful symbol of Tennyson's smouldering unrest and sense of impending sorrow.

From about the second Christmas, the 'low beginnings of content' begin to sound faintly; joy in Nature reappears, and a mood of wistful recollection becomes habitual. This sense of rebirth is conveyed with magnificent power in Section LXXXVI (composed at Barmouth, perhaps in 1839), in which the coalescence of subject and object, Nature and feeling, is complete:

'Sweet after showers, ambrosial air,
    That rollest from the gorgeous gloom
    Of evening over brake and bloom
And meadow, slowly breathing bare

The round of space, and rapt below
    Thro' all the dewy-tassell'd wood,
    And shadowing down the horned flood
In ripples, fan my brows and blow

The fever from my cheek, and sigh
    The full new life that feeds thy breath
    Throughout my frame, till Doubt and Death,
Ill brethren, let the fancy fly

From belt to belt of crimson seas
    On leagues of odour streaming far,
    To where in yonder orient star
A hundred spirits whisper "Peace".'

Romantic? Sentimental? Perhaps, but not if 'sentimental' means full of unmastered or ill-ordered feeling. Romantic certainly, if by that we mean overflowing with powerful emotion expressed in natural imagery. It is none the worse for that. Indeed, I think we have here a poetic structure as subtly articulated as any of Donne's, though it is made up of sense-impressions and feelings rather than of thought or impassioned wit. To begin with, Tennyson shows true imagination, in the Coleridgean sense, in detecting the correspondence between his subjective state—recovery, renewal after sorrow—and a particular manifestation of weather experienced on the Welsh coast: the relenting of the elements at the close of day after rain. The clearance of the sky and the liberation of his soul are made one and the same; absolution and remission are shed abroad simultaneously throughout the visible scene and within his own heart. The process actually goes on within these four verses, which move steadily onwards, with the majestic march of the retreating clouds, unbroken by any pause between the quatrains. To achieve such a sweep in a series of four-lined stanzas is itself a *tour de force*, but the triumph consists mainly in the linking of the various elements of observation and feeling, the fusing of outer and inner. Tennyson's virtuosity, his victory over his own stanza-form, appears strikingly in the continuity of the flow, and above all in

'... slowly breathing bare
The round of space, ...'

where the passage across what is normally a break gives precisely the required sense of steady clearance, the word 'bare' acquiring double force from its own exposed position. Nature breathes again after storm, and the clearing breeze which sweeps through sky and wood is also the new life which penetrates his frame, releasing and tranquillizing his imagination. The deftness with which the symbols of peace are assembled together in a composite structure at the end, producing at once a completed picture of that particular scene, and also a sense of calm of mind, all passion spent, is worthy of admiration. If there are any criteria which would not allow this to be great poetry, so much the worse for the criteria.

I referred above to the quasi-mystical intuitions which from time to time visited Tennyson. One of these is described in Section xcv, which commemorates a summer night at Somersby. The passage thus relates to an occasion before 1837 (when the family left the Rectory), but it may well have been composed later. Evidently the experience sank deep, for G. G. Bradley, alluding to August 1842, wrote:

'I was greatly struck by his describing to us on one singularly still starlit evening, how he and his friends had once sat out far into the night having tea at a table on the lawn beneath the stars, and that the candles had burned with steady upright flame, disturbed from time to time by the inrush of a moth or cockchafer. ... I do not know whether he had already written, or was perhaps even then shaping, the lines in "In Memoriam" which so many years afterwards brought back to me the incident.'[1]

[1] Quoted by Mattes, *op. cit.*, p. 120.

TENNYSON

The Section is worth quoting, not only for its climax, but for
its setting:

> 'By night we linger'd on the lawn,
>   For underfoot the herb was dry;
>   And genial warmth; and o'er the sky
> The silvery haze of summer drawn;
>
> And calm that let the tapers burn
>   Unwavering: not a cricket chirr'd:
>   The brook alone far-off was heard,
> And on the board the fluttering urn:
>
> And bats went round in fragrant skies,
>   And wheel'd or lit the filmy shapes
>   That haunt the dusk, with ermine capes
> And woolly breasts and beaded eyes;
>
> While now we sang old songs that peal'd
>   From knoll to knoll, where, couch'd at ease,
>   The white kine glimmer'd, and the trees
> Laid their dark arms about the field.'

The others departed one by one, leaving him alone with the
night and with his own thoughts. A hunger seized his heart
for Hallam, and he took out and read some of his dead
friend's letters:

> 'And all at once it seem'd at last
> The living soul was flash'd on mine,
>
> And mine in this was wound, and whirl'd
>   About empyreal heights of thought,
>   And came on that which is, and caught
> The deep pulsations of the world.'

And came on that which is: Wordsworth had said 'And I have
felt A presence', or 'Rapt into still communion that transcends The imperfect offices of prayer and praise'; so poets
from time to time try to communicate the incommunicable.
But no one who has ever felt this oneness with the real, this
contact with 'that which is', can ever after remain long in
unbelief or half-belief, or fail to see life steadily and whole.

The following Section (xcvi) is interesting, if only because it contains the oftenest-quoted phrase in Tennyson:

> 'There lives more faith in honest doubt,
> Believe me, than in half the creeds.'

This is his reply to someone (blue-eyed and sweet-hearted, so presumably Emily Sellwood?) who had told him doubt was 'Devil-born'. No; Hallam's example proves the contrary:

> 'He fought his doubts and gather'd strength,
> He would not make his judgment blind,
> He faced the spectres of the mind
> And laid them: . . .'

The object of Faith is a Power that dwells in darkness and cloud as well as in light, and a man who has never doubted cannot possess that tensest kind of faith which consists, not in doubt's non-existence, nor even in its annihilation, but in believing in despite of it, and dwelling in 'tracts of calm from tempest made'.

Section cxiv deals with the Carlylean (pre- and post-Carlylean as well) theme of the superiority of 'Wisdom' over mere 'Knowledge'; knowledge may advance, but without reverence and charity it will be sterile. Akin to this in thought is cxx, where he rejects the kind of 'science' which is content with reducing man to the level of Nature:

> 'I think we are not wholly brain,
> Magnetic mockeries; . . .
>
> .   .   .   .   .
>
> Not only cunning casts in clay:
> Let Science prove we are, and then
> What matters Science unto men,
> At least to me? . . .'

Tennyson held that we are more than the matter of our bodies and brains, thus he was not worried by explanations of our animal origin; the value of an end-product was not, for him, affected by knowledge about its beginnings.

We come at length to Section cxxiv, where, at the

climax of the poem, Tennyson states the faith he has attained. For a man of his upbringing, a man so awake to spiritual reality and so mystically inclined, a believing attitude was inevitable and necessary. But, as we have seen, it was not achieved without conflict, or by putting out the eyes of the mind. What especially gives Tennyson his representative quality, and also earns him our respect, is that to the best of his ability he kept pace with all new truths, and, much as he longed for religious assurance, would accept none unless it was compatible with them. It was thus that he came to base his faith on what seemed the only invulnerable foundation: the needs and affirmatives of the heart.

> 'That which we dare invoke to bless;
>   Our dearest faith; our ghastliest doubt;
>   He, They, One, All; within, without;
> The Power in darkness whom we guess;
>
> I found Him not in world or sun,
>   Or eagle's wing, or insect's eye;
>   Nor thro' the questions men may try,
> The petty cobwebs we have spun:
>
> If e'er when faith had fall'n asleep,
>   I heard a voice "believe no more"
>   And heard an ever-breaking shore
> That tumbled in the Godless deep;
>
> A warmth within the breast would melt
>   The freezing reason's colder part,
>   And like a man in wrath the heart
> Stood up and answer'd "I have felt".'

'I found Him not in world or sun': in spite of his impassioned and lifelong attention to Nature, and his incomparable success in rendering her, it was not there, not in the classic evidences of wisdom and design in the universe, that he found God. I mentioned his remark about the microscopic world—how strange it seemed to him that its wonders should either strengthen or weaken faith: he found Him not in 'insect's eye'. We recall that even at Cambridge he had voted 'No' at a College discussion on the question 'Is an

Intelligible First Cause deducible from the Phenomena of the Universe?' And if not in Nature, certainly not in metaphysical cobweb-spinning. Because, rejecting these former props of orthodoxy, Tennyson fell back upon the inward evidence, the reasons of the heart, he has been accused, like other believers of his and other times, of wishful thinking. This is perhaps not the place to discuss such a question; I would only remark that in taking up this position Tennyson was in accord with some of the profoundest insights of the ages, and of his own age in particular. From the time of David, through St Anselm with his '*crede ut intelligas*', Pascal with his 'this then is faith, God known in the heart, not proved by the reason', down to Coleridge and Carlyle and Kierkegaard, there had been a recognition that faith is not a matter of rational demonstration; that were it so, it would cease to be faith—i.e. a matter of religious duty, a vital commitment—and become compulsory knowledge; and that its acceptance means an act of the will: a plunge, a venture, or what is now sometimes called 'an existential choice'. If we remember all this, we may be less ready to despise Tennyson—as some of his critics have done—for coming to rest in a similar affirmation. If a man persisted in believing that the earth was flat, or that it rested in space upon the horns of a bull, and the bull upon the shell of a tortoise—if he obstinately clung to these views simply because he felt them in his heart to be true, we should rightly consider him eccentric, and possibly mad. But the shape and position of the earth are matters of empirical observation and mathematical calculation, whereas religious belief is not. In this sphere, the writ of the rational understanding does not run, and we are permitted—no, enjoined—by our experience as responsible moral agents to commit ourselves to those hypotheses without which the good life becomes difficult and, as some find, impossible. Whether or no the reader agrees with this, I hope he will at least allow that Tennyson's position commands respect.

Very characteristically, he added a qualifying stanza to those above quoted, feeling, no doubt, that he might seem to have triumphed too easily over the voice which said "believe no more":

'No, like a child in doubt and fear:
    But that blind clamour made me wise;
    Then was I as a child that cries,
But, crying, knows his father near.'

And here let me draw attention to what seems to me the
most remarkable of Victorian comments on Tennyson. It is
by Henry Sidgwick, who, having resigned his Trinity
Fellowship on account of 'honest doubt', and spent the rest
of his life fluctuating between faith and agnosticism, was
peculiarly well qualified to offer an opinion. There are two
comments recorded in the *Memoir of Henry Sidgwick* (1906);
the first, written in his Journal for February 10, 1887, is
this:

> 'Perhaps a certain balancedness is the most distinctive character-
> istic of Tennyson among poets. . . . Perhaps this specially makes
> him the representative poet of an age whose most characteristic
> merit is to see both sides of a question. Thus in *In Memoriam* the
> points where I am most affected are where a certain *retour sur soi-
> même* occurs. Almost any poet might have written,
>
> > And like a man in wrath the heart
> > Stood up and answered, I have felt.
>
> But only Tennyson would have immediately added:
>
> > *No*, like a child in doubt and fear.'[1]

The second is a much longer passage; it was written nearly
ten years later, after Tennyson's death, for the use of Hallam
Tennyson in his *Memoir* of his father. Here are some relevant
extracts from his letter to Hallam:

> 'To begin, then: our views on religious matters [i.e. Sidgwick's
> own and those of his like-minded contemporaries] were not, at any
> rate after a year or two of the discussions started in 1860 by *Essays
> and Reviews*, really in harmony with those which we found sug-
> gested by *In Memoriam*. They were more sceptical and less Chris-
> tian. . . . And this sceptical attitude has remained mine through life;
> while at the same time I feel that the beliefs in God and in im-
> mortality are vital to human well-being.
>
> 'Hence the most important influence of *In Memoriam* on my

[1] *Henry Sidgwick, A Memoir*, by A. S. and E. M. S. (1906), pp. 468-9.

thought, apart from its poetic charm as an expression of personal emotion, . . . lay in the unparalleled combination of intensity of feeling with comprehensiveness of view and balance of judgment, shown in presenting the *deepest* needs and perplexities of humanity. And this influence, I find, has increased rather than diminished as years have gone on, and as the great issues between Agnostic Science and Faith have become continually more prominent. In the sixties I should say that these deeper issues were somewhat obscured by the discussions on Christian dogma, inspiration of Scripture, etc. . . .

'During these years we were absorbed in struggling for freedom of thought in the trammels of a historical religion: and perhaps what we sympathized with most in *In Memoriam* at that time, apart from the personal feeling, was the defence of "honest doubt", . . . and generally the *forward* movement of the thought.

'Well, the years pass, the struggle with what Carlyle used to call "Hebrew old clothes" is over, Freedom is won, and what does Freedom bring us to? It brings us face to face with atheistic science: the faith in God and Immortality, which we had been struggling to clear from superstition, suddenly seems to be *in the air*: and in seeking for a firm basis for this faith we find ourselves in the midst of the "fight with death" which *In Memoriam* so powerfully presents.

'What *In Memoriam* did for us, for me at least, in this struggle was to impress on us the ineffaceable and ineradicable conviction that *humanity* will not and cannot acquiesce in a godless world.

'The force with which it impressed this conviction was not due to the *mere intensity* of its expression of the feelings which Atheism outrages and Agnosticism ignores: but rather to its expression of them along with a reverent docility to the lessons of science which also belongs to the essence of the thought of our age.

'I remember being struck with a note in *Nature*, at the time of your father's death, which . . . regarded him as pre-eminently the Poet of Science. I have always felt this characteristic important in estimating his effect on his generation. Wordsworth's attitude towards Nature was one that, so to say, left Science unregarded. . . . But for your father the physical world is always the world as known to us through physical science: the scientific view of it dominates his thoughts about it; and his general acceptance of this view is real and sincere, even when he utters the intensest feeling of its inadequacy to satisfy our deepest needs. Had it been otherwise,

had he met the atheistic tendencies of modern Science with more
confident defiance, more confident assertion of an Intuitive Faculty
of theological knowledge, overriding the results laboriously reached
by empirical science, I think his antagonism to those tendencies
would have been far less impressive.

'I always feel this strongly in reading the memorable lines . . .
[here he quotes the two stanzas ending

> '. . . the heart
> Stood up and answered "I have felt".']

'At this point, if the stanzas had stopped here, we should have
shaken our heads and said, "Feeling must not usurp the function of
Reason. Feeling is not knowing. It is the duty of a rational being
to follow truth wherever it leads."

'But the poet's instinct knows this; he knows that this usurpation
by Feeling of the function of Reason is too bold and confident;
accordingly, in the next stanza he gives the turn to humility in the
protest of Feeling which is required (I think) to win the assent of
the "man in men" at this stage of human thought:

> No, like a child . . . etc.

.   .   .   .   .

> And what I am beheld again
>   What is, and no man understands;
>   And out of darkness came the hands
> That reach through nature, moulding man.

'These lines I can never read without tears. I feel in them the
indestructible and inalienable minimum of faith which humanity
cannot give up because it is necessary for life; and which I know
that I, at least so far as the man in me is deeper than the methodical
thinker, cannot give up.'[1]

No better illustration could be found, I think, of that
poised uncertainty of the devoutly inclined agnostic mind, to
which *In Memoriam* made so strong an appeal. At the same
time Tennyson's deeply religious nature, and the intensity of
his longing for assurance, could not but reach the hearts of
his Christian readers also, even though with them a touch of
pity would mix itself with their sympathetic response. For

[1] *Ibid.*, pp. 538 ff.

when all was said, Tennyson had *not* found that degree and kind of certainty which revealed religion, through dogma and Church, claimed to give. The Churchman R. H. Hutton (editor of *The Spectator*) wrote in 1892:

> 'There was an agnostic element in Tennyson, as perhaps in all the greatest minds, though in him it may have been in excess, which kept re-iterating: "We have but faith, we cannot know", and which, I should say, was never completely satisfied even of the adequacy of dogmatic definitions which his Church recognized . . . He finds no authoritative last word such as many Christians find in ecclesiastical authority. . . . The generally faltering voice with which Tennyson expresses the ardour of his own hope, touches the heart of this doubting and questioning age, as no more confident expression of belief could have touched it. The lines of his theology were in harmony with the great central lines of Christian thought; but in coming down to detail it soon passed into a region where all was wistful, and dogma disappeared in a haze of radiant twilight.'[1]

The Prologue to *In Memoriam* was the last Section to be written (1849). It was written to show the Christian world (and Emily Sellwood in particular) how far Tennyson could, with perfect sincerity, go in the direction of Christianity. Some of its phrases (I have italicized them) show the truth of R. H. Hutton's comment:

> 'Strong Son of God, immortal Love,
>   Whom we, that have not seen thy face,
>   By faith, and faith alone, embrace,
> *Believing where we cannot prove;*
>
> .   .   .   .   .
>
> Thou *seemest* human and divine,
>   The highest, holiest manhood, thou:
>
> .   .   .   .   .
>
> *Our little systems* have their day;
>   They have their day and cease to be:
>   They are but broken lights of thee,
> And thou, O Lord, art more than they.
>
> *We have but faith: we cannot know;*'

Yet even this dissatisfied the fastidious Henry Sidgwick: 'I

---

[1] *Aspects of Religious and Scientific Thought* (1901), pp. 406 ff.

have always felt that . . . the effect of the introduction does
not quite represent the effect of the poem. Faith, in the
introduction, is too completely triumphant.'

The Two Voices had ended, as we saw, with Sabbath calm
and domestic bliss; *In Memoriam* ends with a marriage-song,
addressed to Edmund Lushington and Tennyson's sister
Cecilia. It was, for more reasons than one, an appropriate
conclusion. Hallam had been engaged to another of his
sisters, and the approaching wedding of Cecilia enabled
Tennyson to end on the desired note of hope and rebirth, all
thoughts turned towards the future. By a happy stroke of
synthesis, too, he was able to link the marriage, and its
hoped-for offspring, not only with Hallam but also with the
main evolutionary drift of the whole poem—even with that
old thought of embryonic development which had interested
him long before he had read *Vestiges*; and, finally, with the
Victorian dream of progress and a loftier race:

'A soul shall draw from out the vast
And strike his being into bounds,

And, *moved thro' life of lower phase* [my italics]
Result in man, be born and think,
And act and love, a closer link
Betwixt us and the crowning race

Of those that, eye to eye, shall look
On knowledge. . . .
        .   .   .   .   .

No longer half-akin to brute,
For all we thought and loved and did,
And hoped, and suffer'd, is but seed
Of what in them is flower and fruit;

Whereof the man, that with me trod
This planet, was a noble type
Appearing ere the times were ripe,
That friend of mine who lives in God,

That God, which ever lives and loves,
One God, one law, one element,
And one far-off divine event,
To which the whole creation moves.'

CHAPTER III

J. A. FROUDE
(1818-1894)

1. Early Life

FROUDE'S literary career was one of the stormiest of the nineteenth century, almost every one of his principal works arousing dispute, and bringing down obloquy and recrimination upon the author's head. His first novel was bought up by his father to put it out of circulation; his second was publicly burned at his own Oxford College. His main life's work, the *History of England*, was the object of persistent and unexampled detraction by E. A. Freeman in *The Saturday Review*; his *Life of Carlyle* and his edition of the *Reminiscences* produced a furore of which the echoes have not long died down. And yet for most people today, probably, Froude has already become one of 'England's Forgotten Worthies'. His robust, freethinking Protestantism is unfashionable today; his passionate ardour both in advocacy and in censure, his sureness where we are doubtful, and his ambiguity where we demand certainty, all estrange him from the contemporary mind. It is a pity, for more than one reason. His prose, for example, excels—at its best—that of nearly all his contemporaries; it is lucid without dulness, vivid without eccentricity, ringing without brassiness, noble without pomposity and imaginative without excessive purple. The defect of these same qualities leads him sometimes, especially in his early writings, into the melodramatic, the sugared and the lachrymose; the influence of Carlyle, too, is at times painfully evident in his youthful work. But the wonder is that so devoted a disciple caught so little of the master's manner; after *The Nemesis of Faith* his style is his own, and it is for the most part extremely good.

But the other chief reason why Froude is worth remembering is also my reason for including him in the present book. Like F. W. Newman—though in other ways so greatly unlike him—he is a type-figure of the nineteenth century, illustrating in his own development the course of one of its main currents: the drift towards religious liberalism. Yet he illustrates it in a way peculiar to himself. He does not, like Newman, beat out his path to freedom by laborious study, subtlety and learning; he does not droop on tired wings like Clough, nor sail out blandly into enlightenment like Jowett or Arnold; nor does he use the ice-axe of Leslie Stephen or the eighteenth century armoury of John Morley. Swift, eager and essentially simple, he finds himself buffeted between two contrary winds of doctrine, flutters despairingly for a while, then yields himself for ever to one of them. Not himself a spiritual pathfinder, he is dependent upon outside strength; following first one guide, then the other, he marks for us, with peculiar distinctness, the tendency and direction of their leadership. First John Henry Newman, then Carlyle: these, in his view the two most greatly gifted men of their time, successively claimed his allegiance; Newman only for a few troubled years, Carlyle for the steady remainder. Others beside him, like Clough, had felt the pull of Tractarianism and swung away; others, like Matthew Arnold, had admired both Newman and Carlyle for a time, then gone their own way; no one except Froude, I think, came to rest so speedily, and remained so permanently, on the side of Carlyle. Perhaps in the eyes of many today this will brand him as a second-rate mind, and indeed he was not—as I have said—an intellectual pioneer. It is a sign, no doubt, of his simplicity and candour that he was able, under Carlyle's protecting wing, to recover something of his childhood's faith, in however changed a form. Not that he was ever a mere replica of Carlyle in miniature; he never, for example, departed from the Church of England although he renounced its Orders. But to the historian of nineteenth century ideas Froude is inevitably a figure of special interest, not merely as evidence of what Carlylism meant, but above all because in him, more clearly than elsewhere, we can watch the point where the cross-currents meet and divide. For this reason chiefly, and also because enough has already been written about his major works, I am going to devote most of what follows to the novels and other writings of his early and transitional period (1845-50).

I have already hinted at a similitude in dissimilitude between James Anthony Froude and Francis Newman. In one important biographical point the similarity is exact: they were both younger brothers of leading Tractarians. Each grew up overshadowed by an elder brother of greater genius and more dominant personality than his own, and the direction of each life was probably set by the need—first unconscious, then conscious—to resist that influence. The difference was that whereas J. A. Froude, the more sensitive and impressible, resisted his brother Hurrell only to fall (briefly, indeed) under the first enchantments of J. H. Newman, Francis Newman—partly through the accident of his earlier birth—escaped the Tractarian influence altogether. Another accidental resemblance may be noted: both were able, at a vital stage of their early manhood, to compare the neo-Catholic movement with evangelical Protestantism in Ireland, very much to the disadvantage of the former.

Scattered through Froude's writings there are a number of passages, some semi-fictitious and some purely autobiographical, from which with due care we can form a fairly accurate idea of his childhood and youth. We are compelled, indeed, to read between the lines and exercise whatever intuition we possess, for sometimes—as in *Shadows of the Clouds* (1847)—he blackens the picture, and at other times —as in *The Nemesis of Faith* (1849)—he sentimentalizes it. Or again, as in *The Oxford Counter-Reformation* (1881), he reads back into it the wisdom of his maturity. It is clear, however, that the main formative influences were his father, Rector of Dartington and Archdeacon of Totnes, his brother Richard Hurrell, and beyond and around these, the way of life in a remote country parish in the early nineteenth century. He was the youngest of a family of eight; his mother, Margaret *née* Spedding (aunt of James Spedding the Baconian), died before he was three, and five of her children followed soon after—for the family was consumptive. For an impression of Archdeacon Froude we must strike a balance between the account of 1881, written when Froude was inclined to see only the best side of his early training, and that of 1847, written when he was smarting under the lash of paternal misprision. From the standpoint of 1881 Froude senior stood for all that was sound and healthy in the old, 'unawakened' High Church before its constitution was undermined by Tractarian physic. The best parsons of those days were like the Pastor in *The Excursion*, or like the Archdeacon himself, who, says Froude, was 'a continually busy, useful man of the world, a learned and cultivated antiquary, and an accomplished artist'. He was far too preoccupied with his duties as landlord, farmer and ecclesiastical administrator to bother his head about the apostolical succession, or baptismal regeneration, or the spiritual growing-pains of his own gifted children. Yet he had in him that imaginative streak which, transmitted to his youngest son, appeared as narrative and descriptive power of a high order, and which in himself issued in drawings which were admired by Ruskin. Religion in the old Church of his father's time (so Froude in later life writes approvingly) 'meant, essentially, doing our duty'. It meant learning the Catechism, working hard, and striving to attain an honourable position in the world. 'The creeds were reverentially repeated, but the essential thing was practice', 'moral obedience to the will of God'.[1] The Church had 'drifted into the condition of what I should call moral health'—that is, it encouraged the assumption that religion was

'not to be itself an object of thought, but a guide to action. Life was a journey in which there were many temptations and many pitfalls. Religion was the lanthorn by which we could see our way on the dark road. Let the light be thrown on the road, and you will see your way. Keep your eyes fixed on the light itself and you will fall into the ditch. The Christianity of my childhood was the light to our feet and the lamp of our ways, perhaps the ideal conception of what religion ought to be.'[2]

Perhaps this 'ideal conception' was something that

---

[1] *Short Studies in Great Subjects*, iv, pp. 239-42.
[2] Quoted from the "Unpublished Fragment" [of Autobiography], by Algernon Ce il, *Six Oxford Thinkers* (1909), p. 163.

Froude afterwards read back into the past, for it is evident that the 'lamp' often burned very dim. It was not bright enough to prevent Hurrell Froude from terrorizing his baby brother by the process known in the family as 'funny tormenting'—which included such diversions as holding him by the heels and stirring the muddy bed of a stream with his head, throwing him into deep water 'to make him manly', and freezing his blood with tales of a frightful fiend called Peningre, which inhabited a hollow behind the house. It may be plausibly guessed that Anthony might in later life have taken more kindly to Tractarianism, if Hurrell's methods of bringing up his motherless younger brother had been a trifle less mediaeval.

At the age of nine he was sent to a private school at Buckfastleigh, where he showed such precocity that he had read through Homer twice before he was eleven. But this was a false dawn, to be followed by the dark night of his four years at Westminster. So close to Froude's own story, in all its main points, is the biography of 'Edward Fowler' in *Shadows of the Clouds*, that we may safely take the account of Edward's schooldays as a true record of his own. It is a tale which would horrify us even more if we were not already painfully familiar with conditions at the pre-Arnoldian Public Schools. The boy suffered every kind of bullying and brutality. Though physically unfit (he had a hernia at this time), he was mercilessly fagged and beaten; he was forced to incur debt for older boys; he had his clothes stolen, had his face burned with glowing cigar-ends, was made to swallow brandy, and so forth. Being weakly and deficient in courage at that age, he became demoralized and took to skulking, lying and malingering. Worst of all, there was no lovingkindness at home to fall back upon. The Archdeacon, in spite of his 'ideal conception of what religion should be', was a stern father, and took the view that boys deserved what they got (a principle amended later by his son to read 'exactly the treatment they receive from you they will deserve'). In any case he was 'a busy practical man of the world, far too much employed in being of active service to it to be able to spare time in attending minutely to peculiari-

ties in the disposition of his children'.[1] The boy was evidently no good; his clothes had been stolen? more likely he
had pawned them to pay his debts and then lied about it. So
at fifteen he was removed from school—a deliverance which
might have been his salvation had he not returned 'in disgrace', like some Prodigal Son, to a home where the Elder
Brother's views prevailed, and where there were no kind
words or tears of forgiveness from the Father.

However, though there was no softening touch upon his
heart, and though his ignominy was deliberately kept fresh
by a variety of petty humiliations, Anthony did enjoy a good
deal of benign solitude. Gradually, his lonely wanderings
through the Devon countryside and his deep draughts of
Spenser and Gibbon in his father's library began to restore
him body and soul. In time this taste for reading attracted
his father's attention; perhaps, after all, the lad might have
in him the makings of something better than a tanner's
apprentice. At any rate, to a tutor he was sent, and in 1836
(at the age of eighteen) he went up to Oriel.

In order to understand his mood and behaviour at Oxford,
his overwrought nerves and his chaotic intellectual growth,
there is something else to be remembered. Hurrell Froude
had died of consumption only four months before, and two
of his married sisters followed a few months later. There was
no particular reason why Anthony should escape the family
scourge, and in fact he was at this time expecting to die soon.
Small wonder, then, if he was content for a while to bask
idly in the sunshine of life, and taste the joys of emancipation, before that cloud grew bigger than a man's hand.
Froude was never a rake or anything approaching it; he was
just rather lazy and extravagant for a while, and who can
blame him? The wonder is that, plunged straight into an
easy-going, spendthrift set after the rigours of his boyhood,
he remained as steady as he did. Meanwhile that black cloud
approached no nearer: was it even possibly moving away?
In its place, however, came two emotional winds from
opposite quarters, which caught him between them and
changed his whole course. The first was a love-affair begin-

[1] *Shadows of the Clouds* (1847), p. 36.

ning at a vacation reading-party (1839) and leading to an engagement. Froude, transported with the new joy of loving and being loved, threw off his idleness and began to work like a demon for a good degree. Within six months the girl's father, mistrusting this youthful suitor, and probably suspecting him to be in debt, broke off the engagement. Froude was in despair, yet struggled on with bitter stoicism and managed to get a Second, as Hurrell had done before him.

The other was John Henry Newman. The strength of Newman's hold upon him is shown not only in the place allotted to him in Froude's early novels but in the affection and reverence with which Froude, anti-Tractarian as he became, continued to speak of him to the end of his life. Froude, as a boy, had heard Tractarian chatter bandied about at home by Hurrell and his vacation visitors. It was no startling Oxford novelty to hear the Reformation, which he had been brought up to honour, branded as a great schism, a broken limb badly set; or to hear Cranmer condemned as a traitor, and Latimer as a vulgar ranter. The thing that was strange to Froude, and irresistibly fascinating, was to meet with somebody who was not only a Christian and a Catholic, but also good and kind. Newman took notice of this younger brother of Hurrell Froude, and introduced him to the 'reading set'. He may have done much more. If we may credit the relevant passage in *Shadows of the Clouds*, Froude (*alias* Edward Fowler) went to Newman in his 'dark hour', as to a father confessor, and laid bare his soul to him. 'He left me with a feeling for him I never had for man. He pressed my hand in his, and dropped tears on it,—yes, tears. Yes, Arthur, . . . he told me my sins, and he wept for me.'[1] Whether or no this incident actually took place, it is certainly true to Froude's feeling about Newman, and expresses the ideal relationship between them as the younger man saw it. What we do know for certain is how Newman's personality, his purity and unworldliness, and above all his sermons, affected Froude.

'I believe no young man ever heard him preach without fancying

[1] *Ibid.*, p. 157.

that some one had been betraying his own history, and the sermon
was aimed specially at him.'[1]

These words are ascribed to 'Markham Sutherland', the
sceptical hero of *The Nemesis of Faith*, but they are exactly
corroborated by Froude more than thirty years later, when
he says (speaking *in propria persona*):

> 'No one who heard his sermons in those days can ever forget
> them. . . . He seemed to be addressing the most secret consciousness
> of each of us—as the eyes of a portrait appear to look at every person
> in a room.'[2]

One of the most striking of Froude's recollections (illustrating the effect a great preacher can produce when he
really believes what he says) is that of a sermon in which
Newman was describing some of the incidents of our Lord's
passion:

> '. . . he then paused. For a few moments there was a breathless
> silence. Then, in a low, clear voice, of which the faintest vibration
> was audible in the farthest corner of St Mary's, he said, "Now, I bid
> you recollect that He to whom these things were done was Almighty
> God." It was as if an electric stroke had gone through the church,
> as if every person present understood for the first time the meaning
> of what he had all his life been saying. I suppose it was an epoch in
> the mental history of more than one of my Oxford contemporaries.'[3]

At once fascinated and perplexed, strongly drawn to the
man but repelled by the doctrine, Froude stayed on a while
at Oxford taking pupils. 'While in fact we were only Newmanites, we fancied we were becoming Catholics.'[4] With an
almost guilty exhilaration he watched Newman sapping the
foundations of the old Protestantism, examining the logic
of unbelief 'with a kind of pleasure, as hitting our adver-
saries to the death and never approaching us at all', admitting
the strength of Hume and the weakness of Campbell and
Paley. The magnetism of Newman 'took us all his own way;
all, that is, who were not Arnoldized'[5]—a phrase which

[1] *The Nemesis of Faith* (reprinted in Scott Library, 1904), p. 157.
[2] *Short Studies*, iv, p. 283.
[3] *Ibid.*, p. 286.   [4] *Nemesis*, p. 138.   [5] *Ibid.*, p. 149.

suggests that if, like Clough, Matthew Arnold, Stanley and the rest, Froude had been at Rugby instead of Westminster, he might have been spared much spiritual conflict. His was an *anima naturaliter arnoldiensis*; unlike Clough, he would have been fortified rather than enervated by the Doctor. As it was, he had to make the difficult passage from Dartington Rectory via Newman to Carlyle under his own canvas.

Soon afterwards came another unsettling—and, as it proved, decisive—experience: a tutorship in the family of the Rev. Mr Cleaver, Rector of Delgany in Ireland. In the family of this Evangelical clergyman he found what seemed to him the very model of true, practical Christianity. What was more, he found a noble and Christ-like Protestantism, 'flying the colours', like a military garrison, in the midst of a decadent and priest-ridden Catholicism. In Oxford, history had seemed to be on the side of Catholicism; it was the 'movement party' which claimed the dedicated lives. Here in County Wicklow it was just the reverse; here were the facts which justified the Reformation. 'Modern history resumed its traditionary English aspect.'[1] In the home of Mr Cleaver he found none of the vulgarity, cant or illiberality sometimes associated with evangelicalism; he found, instead, true holiness of life conjoined with cultivation of mind; 'serious subjects were lighted up as by an ever-present spiritual sunshine'. Nowhere had he met with people in whom 'the spirit of Christ was more visibly present'.

> 'And this was Protestantism. This was the fruit of the Reformation we had been learning at Oxford to hate as rebellion and to despise as a system without foundation.'[2]

Whatever might be the "Notes of the Church", he concluded, 'a holy life was the first and last of them; and a holy life, it was demonstrably plain to me, was no monopoly of the sacramental system'.[3]

It was while Froude was in Ireland that Tract XC appeared (1841), in which Newman had put upon the Thirty-Nine Articles as Catholic a construction as he thought

---

[1] *Short Studies*, iv, p. 297.
[2] *Ibid.*, p. 296.   [3] *Ibid.*, p. 302.

they could bear. Cleaver was horrified at what he considered the dishonesty, the treachery of Newman. And Froude, not by any means for the last time, found himself defending Newman against such charges; at least he knew for a fact, however much he resisted Newman's trend, that Newman was not 'insidious', but 'the most transparent of men'. This crisis brought the Irish visit to an end, and Froude, returning to Oxford at the beginning of 1842, first won the Chancellor's Prize for an essay on Political Economy, and was then elected to a Devonshire Fellowship at Exeter College.

The next seven years were years of inward conflict and heart-searching; they are mirrored in *Shadows of the Clouds* and *The Nemesis of Faith*, and the quality of their rebelliousness and *weltschmerz* can be indicated when we come to examine those ill-starred works. Froude remained, throughout this time, at the meeting-place of the cross-currents: reading Carlyle, Emerson, Goethe, Lessing, Neander, Schleiermacher, Spinoza and *Vestiges of Creation*, and yet at the same time preparing for ordination and writing (at Newman's request) a *Life of St Neot* for Newman's series of English Saints. Why did he undertake this latter task—a task so contrary, one would suppose, to the bent of his mind? No doubt he was flattered by this mark of Newman's continued confidence, and attracted by the prospect of historical research. But beyond this he had an impulse, not yet exhausted, to see things as Newman saw them; to leave no possible claim in the Newmanite case unexamined and unallowed for. It is permissible here to refer to *Shadows of the Clouds*, since 'Edward Fowler' is there made to excuse himself for doing the very same thing. In a fictitious letter dated June 1843 'Fowler' says:

'But for these lives I certainly do wonder Newman should have asked me to help him with them. Newman, with his profound knowledge of human nature, and who had so lately given me a proof how well he knew me. . . . It was impossible I could really feel towards them as he did, or believe the stories I was to have the relation of.'[1]

[1] *Shadows*, p. 184.

'Fowler' did it, he says, simply as an exercise in throwing himself into Newman's way of viewing things, and well aware that Newman would have considered this to be dangerous levity. As an exercise in Newmanism the *Life of St Neot* undoubtedly failed of its purpose. As Froude burrowed further and further into his source materials he was dumbfounded by their fabulousness and the credulity of their authors.

> 'The order of nature, whether always unbroken or not, is generally uniform. In the lives of the Christian saints the order of nature seems only to have existed to give holy men an opportunity of showing their superiority to material conditions.'[1]

Thus St Patrick lighted a fire with icicles, changed a Welsh brigand into a wolf, and floated across the Irish Sea on an altar stone; 'I thought it nonsense'. He had to admit that in some states of mind the distinction between objective and subjective truth disappears; accordingly he adopted, in this *Life*, a sceptical view of history.

> 'Even ordinary history,' he wrote, 'except mere annals, is all more or less fictitious; that is, the facts are related, not as they really happened, but as they appeared to the writer; as they happened to illustrate his views or support his principles.'

If this is so, what then is to be expected of mediaeval lives of Saints?

> 'Their Lives,' he goes on, 'are not so much strict biographies, as myths, edifying stories compiled from tradition, and designed not so much to relate facts, as to produce a religious impression on the mind of the hearer.'[2]

What Newman thought of this contributor is not (to my knowledge) recorded. The effect it had upon Froude himself is known: it disgusted him with the supernatural as a historical category, and, through disillusionment about saintly miracles, suggested doubts about the Gospel miracles too.

[1] *Short Studies*, iv, p. 157.
[2] Quoted by W. G. Hutchinson, Introd. to *Nemesis*, pp. xix-xx (1904).

Froude took deacon's Orders in 1845, the very year of Newman's secession. From what he has written about 'Markham Sutherland's' hesitations before taking Orders, and from what we know of his reading at this time, it is certain that he took the step with great misgiving. He never proceeded to priest's Orders, and would doubtless have renounced his deacon's Orders within a few years if the law had then allowed it. He had to wait until 1870, when Bouverie's Act legalized the renunciation.

From the enchantments of mediaeval hagiography it was a relief to turn, as Froude did next, to Spinoza, the first great saint of modern rationalism, in whose world all was order, law and love. A strong infusion of Spinozism entered Froude's blood-stream at this time, and left effects that endured. By the side of Spinoza's sublime conception of the *amor intellectualis Dei*—that submission of the mind to truth, and of the affections to the divine will, which brings with it inward calm, self-command and the deep power of joy— how paltry, how superficial, seemed all the topics of the minute philosophers, the vapourings of the evangelicals, and the incantations of the Tractarians! From *Shadows of the Clouds* we might infer that what Froude first gained from Spinoza was a deeper awareness of the laws which mould and govern character and determine conduct, and hence a more tolerant judgment of human error. But his article in the *Cambridge and Oxford Review* (October 1847) takes us further. Here he exhibits Spinoza as a saintly prototype of all who have fought against bigotry, stupidity and super-stition; further, Spinoza is a type of the human mind itself in its highest modern development, and the source of the 'purest and loftiest religious philosophy' which has flowed out over Europe. Once again a Jew had 'turned the current of the world's thought, and re-directed the religious destinies of mankind'. Emile Saisset (whose French translation of 1842 was one of the works reviewed by Froude in this article) had called Spinozism 'a tendency' of the human mind; 'Yes,' says Froude, 'it is *the* tendency of *the* human mind,—what all great philosophers and all great religions have struggled towards from the beginning until now, and been only powerful as they have partaken of its fulness.'[1] What attracted Froude was the loftiness of Spinoza's character and the beauty of his practical teaching. For his metaphysics, for his demonstration of God, he had little use; he could never believe in a God so proved. But he believed in God already without the proof, so he could perfectly accept Spinoza's inferences. Religion depends on 'obedience of life', not on 'speculative consistency'; its sphere is the conscience, not the intellect. So, although Spinoza's logic 'proves' nothing except to the already convinced, Froude is in complete accord with his moral attitude:

> 'The love of God is the extinction of all other loves and all other desires. To know God, as far as man can know him, is power, self-government, and peace. And this is virtue, and this is blessedness.'[2]

Spinoza counted for much in the lives of many nineteenth century freethinkers and liberals. It was very fortifying to know that this mighty thinker and great saint had already, two hundred years before, 'demythologized' religion as fully as any Victorian progressive could desire.

ii. *Shadows of the Clouds*

The year 1847 saw the publication not only of the article on Spinoza but also of *Shadows of the Clouds*. This carelessly printed novel, which appeared under the pseudonym 'Zeta', is mainly a thinly disguised transcript of Froude's own experience at home, at school, in love and at Oxford. Froude's biographer, Herbert Paul, takes it unquestioningly as straight autobiography. Froude's father the Archdeacon also evidently took it as autobiography (though doubtless he felt it to be a distortion of the truth)—for he was indignant enough at the exposure of himself to buy up and suppress the book as far as he could. One may think him justified on more general grounds, for it is not a book that much enhances one's respect for the author. It was clearly written in

---

[1] *Cambridge and Oxford Review*, October 1847, p. 427.
[2] *Short Studies*, i, pp. 386-7 (first published in *Westminster Review*, *July* 1855).

order to rid his bosom of the perilous stuff that clogged it: rankling indignation about his misery at Westminster, resentment against his father for misunderstanding and undervaluing him, and unassuaged grief at his frustration in love. Perhaps it helped him to resolve his inner conflict, but it is not—as a true work of art can be and often is—in itself a resolution of disharmony, an escape into the impersonal. One may say that it would have been better unpublished. Yet it is of interest for our present purpose, if only for the light it throws on Froude's early experiences and on the contents of his heart (hardly of his head) at the time of composition.

It is not necessary to summarize its contents in any detail, and I have already referred to it in speaking of Froude's school and home life—here described (with *dis*advantages) as 'Edward Fowler's'. After reading the *Spinoza* one can see how he is applying Spinozism, however superficially, to the problems of parenthood and upbringing. 'Canon Fowler' is condemned for always acting on general principles, as that boys are inherently likely to deserve severe treatment, and for never studying the actual specimen of boyhood before his eyes and striving to understand what forces were at work upon him and within him. Neither the Canon nor the Rev. Mr Hardinge (father of Edward's beloved) took account of the causes affecting character; they allowed of no degrees of praise or blame: all was white or black. Thus, when Hardinge learns that Edward has run into debt at Oxford and concealed the fact, he acts immediately according to crude notions of 'right' and 'wrong', and without true (Spinozistic) understanding; he breaks off the engagement and makes his daughter renounce Edward for ever. From this point onward there is mounting melodrama. Emma Hardinge, half crazed with grief, decides to sacrifice herself (and the undistinguished Mr Allen, her second suitor) by accepting the Rev. Mr Barnard, described as a 'religious cipher' ('only a Christian, not a man'), because her father favours him. This inoffensive and boring gentleman, surprised and gratified, hurries on the marriage-date without a qualm, while Froude, impersonating a Victorian melodrama-audience, shouts

'Open your eyes, Barnard. Fool, fool, can you not see the abyss into which you are plunging?' There is finally an *éclaircissement* scene of great pathos, in which Papa, intervening at the last minute, kneels down by his daughter, and, 'great tears streaming down the old man's cheeks', adjures her by all that she holds sacred not to do this terrible thing. She yields, and soon afterwards (at her father's request) consoles herself with Mr Allen.

Fowler not unnaturally thinks her fickle, and retires to Torquay, in a mood of Spinozistic resignation, to die gradually of the Froude family complaint. He hastens his end by plunging into the sea to rescue a drowning child who—need it be said?—turns out to be the son of Emma and Allen. Emma comes to thank him, tells him all, and then attends him in his last illness, with the full approval of Henry Allen. From the ethereal and highly wrought sentimentality of these final scenes a few points of interest can be isolated. Edward's mood is not that of a Christian death-bed; he is unnaturally composed, unimpassioned, without heart. He expects from God only what is good, including reformatory punishment as may be necessary, but not eternal punishment which cannot improve him. Surviving friends should conquer their grief by reflecting that their loss is discipline, and by learning (from Spinoza) to see all things 'as they are in God'. The only necessary articles of religion are God and Duty; give these up, and immorality follows. But the same is not true of the other 'articles'. Edward's poise is such that he can love and honour both Newman and Carlyle, and some of his most vehement language, as we have seen, is poured out in Newman's defence. Somebody tells him of a newspaper attack on Newman; '"Yes," Edward said, "let them hoot on; they have driven out their Coriolanus, and these are their triumph shrieks. Let them see to it he does not come again in power; and no Virginia [*sic*] and Volumnia to beg him back again."'[1] Homage to Carlyle (indirect though it be) takes the form of a terrible piece of pantheistic rant from Jean Paul, in a style recalling the more embarrassing passages of *Sartor* ('"In the star-sown heaven at night thou

[1] *Shadows*, p. 156.

hast beheld one-half of the Infinite, and by day the other"',
etc., etc.), which Edward asks to have read to him. 'These
beautiful words were his passing bell.'

iii. *The Nemesis of Faith*

The Nemesis of Faith (1849) is a much more interesting
book; for the historian of nineteenth century ideas, it is even
an important book. It is important because it depicts a
typical nineteenth century predicament—a personality torn
to pieces by the conflicting claims of conscience and intellect,
authority and reason, Tractarianism and liberalism. It contains one of the best extant analyses of the Oxford Movement as it struck a sensitive, open-minded and receptive
contemporary; it also expresses vigorously that very liberalism which was its enemy. Indeed, the meaning of the
book, its main drift, is very hard to isolate. Froude's outlook
is not yet integrated; he follows one hint, then another; his
head is with Spinoza or Carlyle, while his heart is with
Newman. Even this statement needs qualifying, for his
'heart' seems to have been divided between Newman and the
idealized Church of his childhood; moreover, part of what
was with Newman was 'head' rather than 'heart'. Carlyle,
wagging his beard disgustedly over the book, pronounced
that 'a man should consume his own smoke' (a maxim not
always scrupulously observed in his own work). Froude
himself called it 'a cry of pain', and he told Kingsley that he
had 'cut a hole in his heart' and written with the blood. The
'moral' of the book, if it has one, would seem to be that
'doubt' leads to immorality; yet the story is not told in such
a way as to make this seem convincing. Perhaps a better clue
to its main 'message' is this phrase from the book itself:

> 'Woe to the unlucky man who as a child is taught even as a
> portion of his creed what his grown reason must forswear.'[1]

Let us look into this book somewhat closely, and try to
pick our way through its numerous contradictions and
ambiguities.

[1] *Nemesis*, p. 136.

First, then, we have 'Markham Sutherland', a second *alias* of James Anthony Froude, hesitating on the brink of Holy Orders. He hesitates because of his religious doubts, and we are certainly made to feel that the doubts are not only honest but the outcome of clear thought, true insight and scorn for all cant and hypocrisy. Sutherland cannot conscientiously declare that he unfeignedly believes all the canonical writings of the Old Testament, for example. He cannot believe that God was ever, as represented in the Old Testament, the patron of 'one small section of mankind', or that the Persians, Greeks and Romans were all outcasts. 'No, Arthur,' he says (for the early part of *The Nemesis* is written in that most irritating of conventions, the epistolary), 'this is not God. This is a fiend.' Nor does the doctrine of eternal punishment commend itself to him; even if Christ did use such a phrase (and for this we have only the testimony of ignorant or prejudiced men), it would be madness to 'build theories of the everlasting destiny of mankind on a single vehement expression of one whose entire language was a figure'. Froude here, and elsewhere, shows himself possessed of that famous solvent of bibliolatry—the distinction between literature and dogma. Speaking of biblical 'inspiration', for instance, he remarks that this admirable metaphor had become 'petrified into a dogma'. The Bible is its own evidence, insofar as it is pure and holy; some things in it, however, seem neither pure nor holy, but because they are there we must believe them on some other kind of evidence. On what, then? on the witness of the Church. 'The Church proves the Bible, and the Bible proves the Church—cloudy pillars rotating upon air—round and round the theory goes, whirling like the summer wind-gusts.' Froude adopts the bold 'liberal' strategy of 'honouring' the Bible as a human document, and reprimanding the bibliolaters for 'dishonouring' it.

Fretted by these and other doubts, Sutherland looks back yearningly to the 'simple faith' of his childhood, and evokes most nostalgic memories. Yet we are to understand that his whole predicament is due to the unwise admixture, in his religious upbringing, of mythological tares with the wholesome wheat of 'pure Christianity'. Presumably, then, the simple faith had really been a subtle snare. At any rate, he now desires to preach not the Christian religion but 'the religion of Christ': the poor man's gospel, the message of forgiveness, reconciliation and love; 'oh, how gladly would I spend my life, in season and out of season, in preaching this'. His ideal parson would be a slum-worker, bringing the peace of God to the downtrodden by teaching them the love of God and of their neighbour, and teaching it not as theology but as heart-knowledge, knowledge proved upon the pulses. He may use Bible language when it confirms this, but he must also share the outlook and understand the day-to-day experience of the workers, and make another Bible for them out of that. One of his chief distresses is the failure of most parsons to come anywhere near this ideal. He finds the clergy, as a body, 'fatally uninteresting'. One reason for this is their worldliness and careerism; another is of an opposite kind: the Church is (apart from its glittering prizes) an ill-paid profession, and only attracts 'the refuse of the educated'. 'Not more than one in fifty takes Orders who has a chance in any other line.'

Sutherland's uncle the Dean treats his doubts as a disease, and gives him the same advice as Keble gave to Thomas Arnold, namely, not to 'sit still and think' but to plunge into parish routine and cure the malady by action. He does so, but soon finds himself scattering the good seed on very stony ground. Neither the hardened poor on the one hand, nor the 'fashionable loungers' on the other, seemed to be at all ready to receive the gospel of reconciliation and love. Sutherland found it hard to believe in the alleged 'immortal souls' of the many and the mediocre who were too dull to love good or hate evil. But, what was more serious, he offended the orthodox and the respectable by not marrying one of them, by not supporting the numerous religious societies, and above all by certain sinister gaps in his preaching. At last he fell victim to a dark conspiracy; he attended a dinner-party at which, by a preconceived plan, he was to be 'drawn' and made to commit himself on the subject of the Bible Society. Of course he would take the Chair at a forthcoming meeting?

He declined, and when pressed for his reasons blurted out some terrible indiscretions about the madness of disseminating amongst the heathen, without necessary interpretation, a book which when ignorantly read can be made to justify all manner of heresies, crimes and follies. ' "It is as I told you," remarks his clerical questioner; "the enemy is in our midst." '

Soon after this he is sent for by the Bishop, and there follows a tense interview in which Sutherland pours out his heart and mind. The Bishop, with grave kindness, charges him with never once, during his year's service, having preached a single sermon 'which might not have been a Socinian's'. He had not taught Socinianism, but he had avoided all mention of the Incarnation and the Atonement. Sutherland, in reply, embarks on a harangue which would shock no modern Churchman but which then meant the end of his ministry. The Incarnation was a doctrine which arose naturally enough in an age when the imaginative world-picture was very different from our own, and when heaven was conceived as a locality between which and the earth there was constant two-way traffic of gods and men. As for the Atonement, he cannot see that 'justice' is done by transferring punishment from the guilty to the innocent. He can see how, historically, the doctrine evolved from men's primitive sacrificial ideas and their instinct to persecute saints, but he cannot accept it as 'plain prose', that is, as a factual account of something which has happened once and for all, and something which was predetermined before the world began. The Bishop listens to all this more in sorrow than in anger, prays to be 'taken away from the evil day', and weeps over the young apostate—who at the sight weeps also. But of course Markham must give up his ministry.

At this point Froude also gives up all attempt to preserve continuity; the epistolary narrative now collapses into observations by 'Arthur' (or an impersonal voice), interspersed with extracts from Sutherland's 'papers'. It makes no difference who is speaking—whether it be 'Arthur' anticipating Hardy: '[Nature] has brought beings into existence who have no business to be here; . . . whose life is only suffering;

and whose action is one long protest against the ill foresight which flung them into consciousness'; or Sutherland himself anticipating Matthew Arnold: 'In Christianity, as in everything else which men have thrown out of themselves, there is the strangest mixture of what is most noble with what is most . . . I shrink from the only word'; or asking why it is thought 'wicked' to be an unbeliever, and replying that it is because 'an anathema upon unbelief has been appended as a guardian of the creed'; or remarking that 'from being the example of devotion, [Christ] is its object; the religion of Christ ended with his life, and left us instead but the Christian religion'; or, in Spinozist–Godwinian fashion, reasoning away 'sin' as a chimaera.

In the next seventy pages, headed "Confessions of a Sceptic", we have what is virtually an early draft of Froude's later and much better-known essay, *The Oxford Counter-Reformation* (1881). It cuts right across the flimsy structure of fiction, but it is the most interesting section of the book. Froude's unresolved conflict appears in his lamentations on the theme of 'the things that I have felt I now can feel no more' (thus he adapts Wordsworth). What things? The religious sentiments of childhood, the sanctities and affections of home, the joys of a lost Paradise and Golden Age. Intellectually he is rejecting this simple faith, yet sentimentally he yearns for it with a Byronic 'sad and weary longing'. He does not seem to admit the possibility of any development or maturing of belief; there is either Paradise, or else Paradise Lost—'the blighted juices fly trembling back into the heart', etc. He utters the solemn warning quoted above: 'Woe to the unlucky man who as a child is taught even as a portion of his creed what his grown reason must forswear', yet he finds in the 'early unreasoning reverence' (for the Bible) the real source of our faith. 'We start on our reasonings with foregone conclusions; and well for us that we do so, or they would certainly lead us a different road.' Well for those, that is to say, who have not been led, as Froude has, along that 'different road'. Froude's trouble is that he cannot, like F. W. Newman, boldly advance along it, strong in the conviction that he is being obedient to a heavenly vision; he is dogged by the fear that 'infidelity' is necessarily wicked. His dilemma is hopeless: his rejection of falsehood is surely God-given, yet there is no faith except the simple one which includes falsehood. Believe impossibilities, or go to the dogs! thus the problem presented itself to his troubled soul, and any who today may underestimate the anguish of this condition—an anguish known to many nineteenth century doubters—may guess at it if (making due allowances for a rhetorical lachrymosity distasteful to the present age) they will consider a passage like this:

> 'Ah! you who look with cold eyes on such a one, and lift them up to Heaven, and thank God you are not such as he,—and call him hard names, and think of him as one who is forsaking a cross, and pursuing unlawful indulgence, and deserving all good men's reproach! Ah! could you see down below his heart's surface, could you count the tears streaming down his cheeks, as out through some church-door into the street come pealing the old familiar notes, and the old psalms which he cannot sing, the chanted creed which is no longer his creed, and yet to part with which was worse agony than to lose his dearest friend; ah! you would deal him lighter measure.'[1]

Or was there, perhaps, a way out of the dilemma after all —the way of Newmanism? Certainly Newman spoke to his condition at this time with almost irresistible authority; it was precisely to the victims of 'liberalism' that Newman was addressing himself. 'Reason was not the whole of us, and alone it must ever lead to infidelity.' The cry 'the Bible only' was absurd, since 'if the Church was mistaken, why must the Bible be true?' Froude writes with awe of Newman even while disagreeing with him: such as he are the 'one sole evidence that there is more in "this huge state" than what is seen. . . .' It is no wonder that Froude felt the spell of this teacher who was using reason, even scepticism itself, to establish faith.

> 'Confessedly Christianity was mysterious; the mysterious solution of a mysterious world; not likely to be reasonable. If once we began accommodating and assimilating, shrinking from that diffi-

___
[1] *Ibid.*, pp. 116-17.

culty, and stretching our creed to this, expanding liberalism would grow stronger by concessions. . . .'[1]

Moreover, 'Sutherland' learned to look upon the world's ignoble scene in the light of Newman's pure spirituality. 'What a sight must this age of ours have been to an earnest believing man like Newman . . .!'—a thoughtless and ignorant clergy, thinking only of carriages, lazy sofas and prebendal stalls, denouncing the world yet living in it; a sluggish Church, worm-eaten with Erastianism and worldly wisdom, and lacking the spiritual authority of Rome!

> 'Long-sighted men [the Tractarians] saw now that Christianity itself had to fight for its life, and that, unless it was to die in England as it had died in Germany and France, something else than the broad, solid English sense must be instilled into the hearts of us.'[2]

Arguments against Catholicism now seemed to be merely arguments against 'Christianity itself', and the Reformation had been, after all, 'the most miserable infatuation'. The Reformers, in denying the authority of the Church's witness, and falling back upon individual judgment and private interpretation, had 'cut away the only support on which Revelation could at all sustain itself'.

> 'To wean the Church from its Erastianism into militancy, where it might at least command respect for its sincerity—to wean the bishops from their palaces and lazy carriages and fashionable families, the clergy from their snug firesides and marrying and giving in marriage: this was the first step. Slowly then to draw the people out of the whirl of business to thought upon themselves— from self-assertion, from the clamouring for their rights, and the craving for independence, to almsgiving, to endurance of wrong, to the confessional—from doing to praying—from early hours in the office, or in the field, to matins and daily service: this was the purpose of the Tract movement. God knows, if Christianity be true, a purpose needful enough to get fulfilled.'[3]

'Sutherland' could even declare that if we believed in the reality of sin as Newman did, we should choose from among

---

[1] *Ibid.*, p. 162.   [2] *Ibid.*, p. 166.   [3] *Ibid.*, p. 168.

the various forms of religion 'that one where the sacraments are most numerous and most constant, and absolution is more than a name, and confession is possible without episcopal interdictings'. Man is a fallen creature, in need of redemption; perhaps then—why not?—a 'peculiar body of people' had from the beginning been the 'channels of peculiar grace', inspired and divinely guided. Catholicism is a preternatural system, which by definition treats the world as a place of trial and temptation; Protestantism is everywhere developing, through Socinianism, into Pantheism, until the 'fact' is becoming 'an idea merely'.

Newman's reward for trying to infuse into the Church a severer tone and doctrine was to be denounced as a Cassandra. He 'left the falling house, not without scorn'. 'But', adds 'Sutherland', 'I had left him too, before this.' Why? I have already suggested reasons why Froude himself could never have gone all the way with Newman, deeply as he always revered him. To 'Sutherland' he ascribes certain historical considerations which also told strongly upon himself: the Tractarians taught us to hate the Reformation, yet in the sixteenth century the Church *had* become a 'huge system of fraud, trickery and imposture'. The Counter-Reformation was a belated attempt by a guilty Church to set its house in order. Since the Reformation the Catholic nations have declined and the Protestant nations have progressed; the Catholic Church since then has produced no great scientist, statesman, philosopher or poet. Historical criticism and science have 'tended to invalidate the authority of histories to which the infallible Church has committed herself'. In Catholic countries the personal character of the people is generally 'poor and mean', largely owing to the demoralizing effect of priestcraft.

Meanwhile, Carlyle was beginning to press in upon 'Sutherland' from the other flank, offering him theocracy without Christianity, certainly without dogma. The *French Revolution*, which he read about three years before Newman's secession, taught him that 'two men may be as sincere, as earnest, as faithful, as uncompromising, and yet hold opinions far asunder as the poles'. Here was the medicine

J. A. FROUDE

for his mind's disease; and, while he was hesitating to quaff it, Newman preached a sermon in St Mary's which decided him. It contained a discussion on Science and Revelation, in the course of which Newman suggested a sceptical re-conciliation between the scriptural and the scientific cosmo-logies: science says the earth moves, Scripture says the sun moves, 'and we never shall know which is true till we know what *motion* is'. 'Sutherland' revolted against this attempt to save 'Revelation' by evading its plain and obvious meaning:

'No; once for all, I felt this could not be. If there were no other way to save Scripture than this, then, in the name of plain sense and honesty, let Scripture go.'[1]

The concluding section of the book, though it is fiction once more and contains some truly imaginative writing, is unsatisfactorily tacked on. It is in the Radcliffe–Godwin convention: luscious, vehement, rhetorical and sentimental. Moreover, the final tragedy has no real connexion with Faith or with Nemesis. Sutherland, after his *débâcle*, goes off to recuperate for the winter by the shores of Como, where, with 'his books and his pen', he finds peace (and presumably a modest competence). Unfortunately, in addition to his writing equipment, he has a flute which 'obeys him as its master', and by playing this on the lake one dreamy May evening he captivates the heart of an unhappily married Englishwoman. The pair proceed in due course to fall violently, hopelessly and platonically in love. Mr Leonard, the husband, is complaisant and generally absent, while Helen's little Annie adores her new 'papa'. There are 'weeks of intoxicating delirium', but at last one fatal evening Annie, during a romantic moonlight boating-excursion, gets wet, catches pneumonia and dies. Awakened thus from their dream, the lovers are driven opposite ways: Markham inter-preting the disaster as a judgment for his unlawful love, Helen as a judgment for her 'sin' in having married Leonard. They part melodramatically, Helen to a convent and Mark-ham to find a secluded and picturesque spot in which to commit suicide. From this particular fate he is rescued in

[1] *Ibid.*, p. 174.

129

the nick of time by Newman, who, thinly disguised as 'Mr Frederick Mornington', appears miraculously on the scene just as Markham is raising the deadly phial to his lips. Succumbing once more to the commanding personality of Mornington, whose 'voice so keen, so preternaturally sweet', had thrilled him at Oxford in past years, he allows himself to be whisked away to a monastery, where he repents and submits to the Church. He finds here, however, no lasting peace, for his doubts soon return, and he dies eaten up with remorse—not for what he has done, but for what he has not done.

What exactly, then, was the 'Nemesis of Faith'? An honest doubter need not necessarily fall in love with another man's wife; the circumstances of Markham's later life are arbitrarily selected and do not spring inevitably from his lack of faith. The *dénouement* lacks convincingness because Froude has not yet found his own way out. As his reviewer in *Fraser's* said, the book is essentially hopeless and negative; its conclusion means that there is no alternative between Romanism and suicide, and no real peace in the former.[1] The very phrase 'Nemesis of Faith' is ambiguous. This same reviewer, for instance, takes it to mean 'Faith's revenge on those who stray from her'; thus Markham suffered just punishment for neither sticking to his simple faith nor following Newman. On the other hand the phrase could also mean 'Retribution for believing the wrong things'; according to this view Markham deteriorated when and because he discovered that his faith had been partly fabulous. The latter seems nearer to Froude's own notion. 'Faith', he says, 'ought to have been Sutherland's salvation—it was his Nemesis— it destroyed him.'[2] It destroyed him because from the beginning it had been partly a false faith; it had been mixed up with old-wives' tales in childhood; and the effort of shaking off the falsehoods had weakened his whole moral being. Froude's difficulty, when he wrote the book, was that he could not yet clearly see his way to a faith which was neither 'simple' nor Roman, but simply true.

[1] *Fraser's Magazine*, May 1849, pp. 552-3.
[2] *Nemesis*, Pref. to 2nd ed. (p. lv in *op. cit.*).

'The faith which is avenged upon Markham', the *Fraser* re-viewer justly says, 'is nothing but a mere unquestioning passive reception of dogmas, connected with home recollections of "the still, calm Sunday", with its best clothes and tiresome services; the "secret" of which lies in the "early unquestioning reverence" for the Bible resulting from "our mechanical treatment of it".'

Froude has also partly seen through the pseudo-faith of Tractarianism, but is yet so entangled with it that he can represent it as the only alternative to doubt or suicide. With all this uncertainty the reviewer contrasts the faith of Luther in God's grace, adding that the 'vengeance' of *this* sort of faith upon unbelief is 'not suicide nor the convent—but reconciliation, forgiveness, blessing, life'.[1] The book shows that man cannot live without Faith, but does not show by what Faith he can live.

The Nemesis of Faith was a scandalous book in 1849, and it ended Froude's Oxford career. A copy of it, belonging to one Blomfield, was publicly burned in the Hall of Exeter College by the Sub-Rector, William Sewell—a circumstance of which Blomfield later complained: 'I lost my *Nemesis of Faith*,' and 'I think I lost "Faith" in my college tutor, for at least he should have recouped costs (3s. 6d. I believe was the book's price), or presented me with one of his own books, e.g. Sewell's *Christian Morals*.'[2] It disgusted freethinkers as well as the orthodox, because in the story it is freethought that appears to incur and to deserve the retribution. Even the reviewer in *Fraser's*, sympathetic and admiring though he mostly was, regretted that the book had been published, did not recommend its indiscriminate perusal, and in short thought its publication a 'sin, not to be justified or palliated, but to be repented of'. Nevertheless a second edition was called for, and Froude's Preface to this shows that his conscious mind was on the 'liberal' side, although the book seemed to have shown Nemesis lurking in that quarter. In that Preface he compares his attitude to Hebrew 'myth-ology' with Plato's to Greek. Markham falls, he continues,

[1] See *Fraser's, op. cit.*, pp. 555 ff.
[2] Hutchinson, Introd. to *Nemesis* (1904), p. xxv.

'as he would not and need not have fallen if the seeds of religion, which had been sown in his childhood, had been able to grow up freely, and had not been so mixed with fable and falsehood, so twisted and entangled into system, that his heart had bled to death in the effort of delivering himself'. More and more he speaks in the tones and accents of Carlyle: what can make us really men but faith in Him who alone *is?* 'We seek for God, and we are sent to find Him in the words and thoughts of other nations and other ages about Him—which are no longer His glorious garment, but a curtain which conceals Him.' This age has outgrown the Greek, Roman and Scandinavian mythologies, the *Acta Sanctorum,* and witchcraft stories, but it still clings to the Bible. We think our duty to God is not 'to love Him, and to walk in His ways, but to hold certain opinions about Him, to maintain the truth of certain old histories about Him.' The result of this is 'that utter divorce between practice and profession which has made the entire life of modern England a frightful lie'. Finally Carlyle takes, in effect, the pen from his hand, and writes: 'The one great Bible which cannot lie is the history of the human race.'

iv. History

Appropriately, then, it was to history that Froude now turned, and to history that he devoted his life. Resigning his Oxford Fellowship, he fled for refuge to Charles Kingsley, who for two months (at Ilfracombe) protected him from the hostile letters which came by every post. Soon afterwards Froude married Kingsley's sister-in-law, Charlotte Grenfell, and retired to North Wales to begin his life's work. The direction of any man's chief effort is determined by his deepest emotional needs, and Froude's revolt from Tractarianism, reinforced by Carlyle's prophetic impetus, now turned him inevitably towards the sixteenth century. If we may say that Leslie Stephen, for instance, wrote his *History of English Thought in the Eighteenth Century* in order to vindicate his own revolt from orthodoxy, we may also say that Froude wrote his *History of England from the Fall of*

Wolsey to the Defeat of the Spanish Armada in order to undo the work of the Oxford Movement, and to vindicate Carlyle against Newman, himself against his brother Hurrell. The nineteenth century had outgrown the formularies of the sixteenth, but the Reformers, insofar as they stood for truth and honesty against superstition and imposture, could be shown as the prototypes of those who, in the modern world, were fighting against bigotry and reaction. Froude's object was to show that the Reformation, so far from being a regrettable and rather unimportant historical digression, was 'the hinge on which all modern history turned'.[1] The Reformation to Froude, like the French Revolution to Carlyle or the Captivity to the Hebrew prophets, was a signal example of divine judgment working itself out in history. 'One lesson, and only one, history may be said to repeat with distinctness; that the world is built somehow on moral foundations; that, in the long run, it is well with the good; in the long run, it is ill with the wicked.'[2] What Froude and his like craved for in the nineteenth century was a 'positive, manly, and intellectually credible explanation of the world'[3]; the philosophers and critics have 'done for' the claims of modern Protestantism, but in the sixteenth century it had offered just that.

> 'As it was in the first century, so it had been in the sixteenth. Again the truth had been crusted over with fictions. Again the intellect rose in protest, and declared that incredibilities should not be taught any longer.'[4]

We can still, moreover, fear God, honour the Queen and obey the divine will by following conscience—and this became for Froude, returning via Carlyle to Dartington, the whole duty of man and the essence of religion.

It does not fall within my present scheme to speak of Froude's later life, or of his work as historian, biographer and imperialist; I have wished merely to follow him around

[1] Quoted by Herbert Paul, *Life of Froude* (1905), p. 72 (from Froude's *Lectures on the Council of Trent*).

[2] *Short Studies*, i, p. 21 (*The Science of History:* 1864).

[3] From Froude's West Indian Diary, 1886, quoted H. Paul, *op. cit.*, p. 358.

[4] *Short Studies*, iv, p. 355.

the quicksands till he regained firm foothold. I will conclude with a few illustrations of his mature outlook.

'Believe in the Pope! I would as soon believe in Jupiter.' So Froude quotes Thomas Arnold, approvingly, at the beginning of his review of Newman's *Grammar of Assent* (1870).[1] In this essay, written while the Vatican Council was sitting, Froude can still go part of the way with Newman. He is with him while he distinguishes between 'notional' and 'real' assent; with him when he bases faith primarily upon conscience and its accompanying sense of obligation to God; with him still when he shows that belief is not the outcome of logical argument. He parts company when Newman begins to represent the Church's infallibility as a self-authenticating truth, and to suggest that the test of truth is the vividness with which we experience a conviction of truth. He parts company still more decisively when Newman points to the history of the Church as bearing upon it clear marks of the Church's divinity; this releases all the stock Protestant responses: what of the Inquisition? the burning of heretics? the corruption of the monasteries, the venality of the Papacy? etc.

> 'Father Newman identifies Christianity with the complex doctrinal system embodied in the formulas and represented in the constitution of the Catholic Church. We mean by it the code of moral duties which were taught by our Lord upon the Mount, and which, as the type of human perfection, He illustrated in His own character.'

To Newman the spread of Christianity in the beginning seemed explicable only as the effect of miraculous and superhuman powers working from without; Froude thinks we need no miracle to account for it:

> 'The Roman government offered to the devotion of the empire a Divus Nero or a Divus Domitianus. The image of a peasant of Palestine, a being of stainless integrity, appeared simultaneously, pointing to a Father in heaven and requiring men in His name to lead pure and self-sacrificing lives; and if it be true that man is more than a beast, and that conscience and moral sense are a part of his

[1] *Ibid.*, ii, p. 101.

natural constitution, we require no miracles to explain why millions of men and women with such alternatives before them were found to choose the better part.'[1]

One of Froude's most justly celebrated pieces is his *The Oxford Counter-Reformation* (written in 1881, and to be found in Volume IV of *Short Studies on Great Subjects*), from which I have already quoted freely. It is remarkable as auto-biography, as memoir, as a chapter of intellectual history; above all it is remarkable for its warmth of affection towards Newman, though Froude is now sixty-three. Froude had done his work; he had vindicated the Reformation, and he could afford to be magnanimous to its arch-enemy, whom after all he had loved and admired. But he has taken his stand, and in the last section of this essay he dissociates himself finally from Newmanism. He could not have done this more decisively than by selecting for criticism, as he does, the most moving and characteristic passage in the *Apologia*—that by which, if a reader has any sympathy at all with Newman, he is most likely to be swayed. I have quoted (and commented upon) it elsewhere, but this is the part chosen for refutation by Froude:

> 'What shall be said to this heart-piercing, bewildering fact [the mystery of the world's evil; the misery of man without God]? I can only answer, that either there is no Creator, or this living society of men is in a true sense discarded from His presence. Did I see a boy of good make and mind, with the tokens on him of a refined nature, cast upon the world without provision, unable to say whence he came, his birthplace, or his family connections, I should conclude that there was some mystery connected with his history, and that he was one, of whom, from one cause or other, his parents were ashamed. Thus only should I be able to account for the contrast between the promise and condition of his being. And so I argue about the world;—if there be a God, *since* there is a God, the human race is implicated in some terrible original calamity.'[2]

To Froude this view, however impressive, seemed historic-ally false. Would a visitor to this earth from another planet,

---

[1] *Ibid.*, pp. 141-2.
[2] *Apologia* (Everyman ed.), p. 218.

contemplating the present state of the world and taking into account the evolution of the human race, really suppose that man was like a child of which its parents were ashamed? Would he not far rather see him as 'slowly, through conscience and intellect, rising to a knowledge of God'? Moreover, if God is estranged from 'the world', does not the history of the Church, and the state of the Roman Catholic countries, suggest that He is estranged from the Church also?

> '. . . if an institution with such a history behind it is an exceptional instrument to bear witness to God's existence; if it be the voice through which alone He speaks to man, and makes known His nature and His will; then the attempt to understand this world, and what goes on in it, had better be abandoned in despair.'[1]

[1] *Short Studies*, iv, p. 360.

CHAPTER IV

SEPTEM CONTRA CHRISTUM
(*Essays and Reviews*, 1860)

1. Introductory

ALITTLE book called *Essays and Reviews*, written by six parsons and a pious layman, appeared in March 1860. It slipped unobtrusively from the press, yet within a year of its publication the orthodox English world was convulsed with indignation and panic. The Protestant religion, as by law established, had weathered the Gunpowder Plot and the Popish Plot; it had survived the Reform Bill, the *Tracts for the Times*, the Hampden case and the Gorham controversy; but here was something still more alarming—a conspiracy of clergymen to blow up the Church from within. Cries of horror, grief and pain rang from the press and the pulpit; the Bishops protested; the Court of Arches and the Judicial Committee of the Privy Council came into action. The authors of the book were denounced as 'Septem Contra Christum', 'the seven extinguishers of the seven lamps of the Apocalypse', 'the seven champions not of Christendom', and so forth. Yet who now cares? How many persons now living have read *Essays and Reviews*? Some few know of it through the histories and biographies of the nineteenth century; they place it, perhaps, alongside *The Origin of Species* (1859), as one of the blasts then troubling the stagnant waters of orthodoxy; they remember some of the contributors for other reasons: Frederick Temple (Headmaster of Rugby, Archbishop of Canterbury), Mark Pattison (Rector of Lincoln College), and Benjamin Jowett (Master of Balliol). Knox and Vidler, in their *Development of Modern Catholicism*, praise the essayists for their courage, but add that their conclusions are now commonplaces. Why then revive their memory? Surely no dry bones are less susceptible of renewed life than those of a dated theological controversy.

Such, as I meditated this chapter, were the thoughts which chilled and well-nigh daunted me. However, it so happened that in the very week of my discouragement I came across the following pronouncements, one in a daily and the other in a weekly newspaper:

(a) '. . . religion will not arrive at a right approach until it discards myth and unwarranted assumption from its intellectual framework and bases its beliefs on scientific facts and principles.'

(b) '. . . if Christianity is to survive among thoughtful people . . . it must present, on its own behalf, a reasoned case which does not rely on the evanescent emotionalism of an evangelist like Billy Graham, or on the authoritarian dogmas of Rome.'

Now, allowing for the crudities of ephemeral writing, and deducting whatever there may be of animus, we have here a fair statement of the case put forward by the Essayists and Reviewers of 1860, whose main endeavour was precisely to enquire what must be done if Christianity were to survive among thoughtful people. As for 'discarding myth' and basing beliefs on scientific facts and principles, that too, far from being a bright new thought of our own time, was the main theme and endeavour of nineteenth century liberals in general. It is one of the chief purposes of this present book to show how they worked it out. Another is to compare the old liberalism and the new—for, in the teeth of many contrary winds, religious liberalism is raising its head again today. To read the opening pages of Rudolf Bultmann's *Kerygma and Myth*,[1] where he asserts the need for 'demythologizing' the New Testament, and dismisses its 'three-decker' universe as incredible to modern man, is to ask oneself whether all this had not already been said a hundred years ago. It becomes clear, however, on reading further, that the old and the new liberalisms are not identical. The new has evolved spirally from the old, and occupies a position not beside it but vertically above it. Historical reactions, as we have by now learned to expect, never go back to the originals; they are syntheses of thesis and antithesis; old

[1] English translation (S.P.C.K.) 1953.

affinities are revived, but in the light of intervening experience.

In this chapter, then, I propose first to consider *Essays and Reviews* as a document of nineteenth century liberalism, and then to juxtapose it with the 'demythologized' gospel according to Bultmann, hoping in this way to show that the old is not dead, but that the new both presupposes and transcends it.

Lecky, in his *Democracy and Liberty*,[1] wrote:

> 'No change in English life during the latter half of the nineteenth century is more conspicuous than the great enlargement of the range of permissible opinions on religious subjects. Opinions and arguments which not many years ago were confined to small circles and would have drawn down grave social penalties, have become the commonplaces of the drawing-room and of the boudoir. The first very marked change in this respect followed, I think, the publication in 1860 of the "Essays and Reviews", and the effect of this book in making the religious questions which it discussed familiar to the great body of educated men was probably by far the most important of its consequences.'

With *Essays and Reviews* Lecky cites, as influences making in the same direction, the writings of Renan, Buckle, Colenso and Darwin; the infiltration into England of German and Dutch biblical criticism; and the publication (since 1865) of magazines containing *signed* articles on serious issues by men of varied and opposed opinions.

Essays and Reviews was mainly an Oxford manifesto, a new series of Tracts for changed times. It may be taken to represent the delayed action upon Oxford of Thomas Arnold, or the revival of the liberal spirit after its long eclipse by Newmanism. Its main promoter was Henry Bristow Wilson, whose Bampton Lectures in 1851 had been a call for theological freedom and Christian unity, and who after twenty-five years at Oxford had taken a (St John's) College living at Great Staughton in Huntingdonshire. There was no preconcerted plan, except the 'free handling, in a becoming spirit, of subjects peculiarly liable to suffer by the repetition of conventional language, and from traditional

[1] Vol. i, pp. 424-5 (1896).

methods of treatment'. The contributors chose their own subjects and worked independently. The most belligerent Essays were those by Rowland Williams (Vice-Principal and Professor of Hebrew at St David's College, Lampeter) and Baden Powell (Savilian Professor of Geometry at Oxford), but the centre of gravity is to be found in the concluding Essay, "On the Interpretation of Scripture", by that great Oxford liberalizer, Benjamin Jowett (then Regius Professor of Greek, but not yet—by ten years—Master of Balliol). And it is in Jowett's thinking and writing, during the previous decade and after the publication, that the setting of the book is best perceived.

As far back as 1844 Jowett had written:

> 'I feel very deeply that one cannot live without religion, and that in proportion as we believe less, that little, if it be only an aweful [*sic*] feeling about existence, must be more constantly present with us; as faith loses in extent it must gain in intensity, if we do not mean to shipwreck altogether.'[1]

In the 'fifties Jowett was reading Lessing, Schleiermacher, Hegel, Bauer and much other German literature highly compromising to an English clergyman of those days; he was also watching, with mounting disquiet, the steady, inch-by-inch retreat of 'religion' before geology, and the vain attempts to preserve it by making it fill up the remaining interstices of science. Gradually he came to see his own task, and that of his age, in an attempt to cast off the 'incrustations' and bring out the 'eternal import' of religion, without 'breaking rudely with the past'. This, he never doubted, could be done 'if we could once get out of the pious fraud line', and if we could ignore those who, cowering behind the dykes of the German Ocean, would fain keep knowledge at one level here when it had already reached a higher in Germany. As time passed, and especially when the prosecutions against the essayists came on, Jowett spoke more and more plainly. 'Sooner or later the Church of England will find it impossible to subsist as a fabric of falsehood and

---

[1] To B. C. Brodie, December 23, 1844 (*Life and Letters*, by E. A. Abbott and Lewis Campbell, 1897 ed., vol. i, pp. 114-15).

fiction.' At all costs we must 'reconcile intellectual persons to Christianity', for

'In a few years there will be no religion in Oxford among intellectual young men, unless religion is shown to be consistent with criticism.'[1]

'I am sorry that the Clergy are so determinedly set against all the intellectual tendencies of the age. . . . The real facts and truths of Christianity are quite a sufficient basis for a national Church, but they want to maintain a conventional Christianity into which no one is to enquire, which is always being patched and plastered with evidences and apologies.'[2]

To reconcile Christianity with criticism, to show its compatibility with the intellectual tendencies of the age, and thus to reconcile 'intellectual persons' with Christianity: these may fairly be taken as the aims of *Essays and Reviews*. With these phrases in mind, then, let us briefly examine the essays in turn.

1. The first essay, "The Education of the World", by Frederick Temple (Headmaster of Rugby, afterwards Archbishop of Canterbury), is an expanded version of a sermon which, when delivered, had raised no stir. It will stir no emotion in a modern reader save one of boredom, though Samuel Wilberforce scented enough heresy in it to make him tremble for the faith and morals of the Rugby boys. Temple, as is not unnatural in a headmaster, sees the history of mankind as an educational process, and enlarges interminably on this analogy—dividing history into stages corresponding to Childhood (obedience to Law and precept), Youth (preponderance of the affections over the understanding; need for an Example to follow and imitate), and Manhood (Action by Principle, the meaning of which is understood). To this education of the world certain races or countries have made distinctive contributions, Greece supplying courses on Logic and The Beautiful, Rome on Law and Government, Judaea on Righteousness, and Asia on Otherworldliness and the Immortality of the Soul.

---

[1] To Dean Elliot, February 8, 1861 (*ibid.*, p. 345).
[2] To the same, April 1, 1861 (*ibid.*, p. 348).

The strategy in all this is to induce the assumption that the history of man has been one long upward and onward process, that each successive stage has been an 'advance' on the previous one, and that in these latter days of adult maturity we may perhaps begin to put away a few (carefully selected) childish things. Having established his historical framework, and having secured from his readers a favourable response to the implication of an 'evolutionary' Ascent of Man, Temple can begin to be—very mildly—outspoken. For instance, because there has been no more 'revelation' since apostolic times, the claim to infallibility, 'still maintained by a portion of Christendom, has been entirely given up by *the more advanced section*' (my italics). Also, 'many of the doctrinal statements [of the Early Church] are plainly unfitted for permanent use'. Since the Reformation the main lesson to be learnt has been 'to modify the early dogmatism by substituting the spirit for the letter, and practical religion for precise definitions of truth'. Nowadays, the Creation must be read alongside Revelation. Yet the paramount need of our time is the thorough study of the Bible, the defining of what it does and does not teach, the limits of its 'inspiration', the degrees of its authority. We are to go forward fearlessly, undaunted by geology, and unabashed by the discovery of errors, interpolations or forgeries in the text. The knowledge of these will merely remove the false glosses which have been foisted upon it by 'human interpretation'.

2. The head and front of the book's offending was felt by many to lie in the essay of Rowland Williams on "Bunsen's Biblical Researches". Even the mild and tolerant A. P. Stanley was pained by the pugnacity and irritability of its tone. Williams was perhaps not quite a gentleman? at any rate his warm Welsh blood made him a doubtful ally. To Wilberforce and his like it was a shocking thing that a clergyman and theological Professor should deliberately champion a subversive German, and through him the whole infidel crew of Germany. For Williams himself Bunsen was 'a man who in our darkest perplexity has reared again the

banner of truth, and uttered thoughts which give courage to the weak, and sight to the blind'.

For what, then, did Bunsen's work stand? For the widening of the idea of 'Revelation', and the enlightened and reverent application to biblical study of the critical canons applicable to all other ancient documents. 'We cannot', he writes,

> 'encourage a remorseless criticism of Gentile histories and escape its contagion when we approach Hebrew annals; nor acknowledge a Providence in Jewry, without owning that it may have comprehended sanctities elsewhere.'

This, to Wilberforce, meant that no one who 'with Niebuhr has tasted blood in the slaughter of Livy can be prevailed upon to abstain from falling next upon the Bible'. Williams, it is interesting to find, was in possession of a distinction afterwards made much of by Matthew Arnold—that between literature and dogma, or, in more recent terminology, between emotive and scientific language. To our habituated ears and minds Williams's enunciation of this point will merely seem a tentative understatement, for it is in an unemphatic aside that he observes in speaking of biblical interpretation:

> 'Nor should the distinction between poetry and prose, and the possibility of imagination's allying itself with affection, be overlooked.'

Not much 'pugnacity' here, one may reflect, remembering the bulk and persistence, throughout the centuries, of the type of commentary which proceeds as if poetry did not exist, or at least as if it had no possible connexion with religion. However, Williams gathers momentum as he goes on, and speaks in firmer tones when he praises Bunsen for neither repeating 'traditional fictions' about the Bible nor reading it 'with that dulness which turns symbol and poetry into materialism'. After the apostolic age, when intense religious experience forced language to express something of what it had meant, a hardening process set in, 'the fresh language of feeling or symbol being transferred to the domain of logic'. Similarly, certain central facts of the spirit, conveyed in the burning metaphors of St Paul, had been robbed of their immediacy and their awakening power by being discerned, not spiritually, but through the mind of the flesh or the prosaic understanding. So Williams, who has read his Coleridge, advises us to try translating some of these hardened phrases back into moral and spiritual terms: let us interpret 'justification by faith', for example, not as 'a fiction of merit by transfer', but as 'the peace of mind, or sense of Divine approval, which comes of trust in a righteous God'. Or again, let us interpret Christ's Atonement, not as a 'purchase from God through the price of his bodily pangs', but rather as 'Salvation from evil through sharing the Saviour's spirit'.

Like Temple, Williams sees the history of man as a process of divine education. For him, however, the question of questions is whether God has in fact conducted this spiritual training 'within the sphere of nature and humanity', along the lines of his own ordered Providence, or whether by means of supernatural incursions into Nature. He for his part cannot doubt that it has been by the former method, and he sees science, historical enquiry, and the law of growth visible within the Bible itself, as forces working together to bring 'almost uniform accession of strength to the liberal side'.

The battle against uncritical bibliolatry was won so long ago by 'the liberal side' that Williams's ardent partisanship can stir us little today. Such an essay as this, however, is worth reading even now, if only to remind ourselves that most of what became 'worm-eaten with liberalism' was already dead wood. It is salutary to be reminded, as Williams reminds us, of the sort of thing which a Christian was supposed, only a hundred years ago (and much less), to believe about the Bible. As for instance, that 'modern history is expressed by the Prophets in a riddle'; or again, beliefs inherited from the days when Justin could seriously argue that Lot's daughters symbolized the Jewish and Gentile Churches, that the Shunammite Abishag meant 'heavenly wisdom for the honour of David's old age', or that the riches of Damascus and the spoils of Samaria signified 'the Magi and their gifts'. It is interesting to find a writer praising Bunsen, so comparatively short a time ago, for knowing that you can no longer say "David foretold the Exile" simply because it is mentioned in the Psalms, nor refer to "Isaiah" as if the book belonged to one author and one era, nor assume that 'the Maiden's Child of Isaiah vii. 16 was not to be born in the reign of Ahaz, as a sign against the Kings Pekah and Rezin'. But it is not only for scholarship that Williams praises Bunsen; it is for knowing the facts and yet not missing the true witness of the Prophets to the Kingdom of God. The main purport of the essay can be summed up in Williams's own words:

> 'It is time for divines to recognize these things, since with their opportunities of study, the current error is as discreditable to them, as for the well-meaning crowd, who are taught to identify it with their creed, it is a matter of grave compassion.'

3. Professor Baden Powell's essay, "On the Study of the Evidences of Christianity", is a nineteenth century variation on the theme of Hume's Essay on Miracles. He argues that whereas the essentials of Christianity remain the same yesterday, today and tomorrow, its 'external accessories' vary from age to age. Above all, the 'evidences' for it vary in convincingness according to the intellectual presuppositions of each period. Thus in ages when miracles are universally taken for granted, expected and credited, they can serve to support religion; today, they are the principal obstacles to it. Even so recent a theologian as Paley thought that a revelation could only be communicated by miracles; now, we feel that a revelation is most credible when it appeals least to any violation of natural causes. This has come about because, for us today, physical science has set up a new standard of what is antecedently credible. Throughout the realm of Nature, law reigns supreme; yet science must and does recognize that beyond and outside the material order its writ does not run. The concern of Faith is not with material miracles but with spiritual realities.

At this point Baden Powell breaks off to rebuke the bigoted who resist the time-spirit and are consequently unjust to those who do not. Their favourite and most reprehensible line is to attack honest doubters for moral obliquity. But they are themselves guilty of disingenuous paltering over 'evidences', for although they refer you to matters of historical fact as 'evidence' for Christianity, they will not allow the application of the usual historical tests to them. Their alleged 'facts' turn out to be too sacred to be looked into, and Baden Powell suggests that in that case they were not 'facts' in the ordinary sense at all. The apologists must really not try to have it both ways.

Returning to the evidential value of miracles, he argues (following Hume) that from the nature of our 'antecedent convictions' the probability of 'some kind of mistake or deception somewhere, though we know not where, is greater than the probability of the event really happening in the way and from the causes assigned'. This conviction about what is most probable is more decisive than any testimony could possibly be; no amount of testimony could convince us that $2 \times 2 = 5$. 'All evidential reasoning is essentially an adaptation to the conditions of mind and thought of the persons addressed, or it fails in its object.' Thus Christian miracles will not prove Christianity to a Muslim, who believes his own miracles; similarly, as we know, they had no evidential value for the Jews, who thought them diabolical.

It may be safely assumed that, behind the more constructive part of Baden Powell's argument—notably his separation of the spheres of Faith and Science—lies the influence of Coleridge, particularly his distinction between Reason and Understanding. Religion has nothing to do with the Understanding, which is the mind of the flesh and judges according to sense. 'The more knowledge advances,' he says, 'the more it has been, and will be, acknowledged that Christianity, as a real religion, must be viewed apart from connexion with physical things.' If astronomy, geology, archaeology or biological evolution appear as stumbling-blocks, this is due to the encroachment of the Understanding upon the domain of Reason, the faculty by which spiritual reality is spiritually discerned. The reverse kind of encroachment is correspondingly injurious to science; there must be no trespassing either way. I am not simply guessing at Coleridge's influence here. Baden Powell quotes from *Aids to Reflexion* one of its best-known passages:

> '"Evidences of Christianity! I am weary of the word: make a man feel the want of it . . . and you may safely trust it to its own evidence."'

To readers of Chapter I of the present book it may be of interest, too, that he also quotes the question posed by F. W. Newman: whether any moral truth ought to be received in mere obedience to a miracle of sense. Baden Powell's essay is the only one of the seven to refer to Darwin's *Origin of Species* (which appeared the year before). The development theories of Lamarck and the author of *Vestiges*, at first disputed, have now been confirmed by Mr Darwin, who has demonstrated 'the origination of new species by natural causes', and established 'the grand principle of the self-evolving powers of nature'. Powell's approval of Darwin is typical of the liberal-Christian attitude; invulnerable within the battlements of Faith, he can learn from Darwin, with reverent candour, by what processes God has thought fit to work through his servant Nature.

4. The essay of Henry Bristow Wilson, "Séances historiques de Genève: The National Church", gave great offence because it favoured relaxation of Subscription and recommended some 'demythologizing' of the Bible. After a preliminary review of certain recent lectures on Church history at Geneva, Wilson begins to examine, very much in the spirit of Coleridge (whom he quotes) and of Thomas Arnold, the idea of a National Church. This leads him on to confront two main questions of the day—those that chiefly led to *Essays and Reviews* as a whole—the alienation of the People, especially the scientific, literary classes, from the Church, and the need to check and reverse this by widening the Church's formularies in accordance with modern thought. He deplores the situation of the time, in which

thought and speech are free everywhere *except* in the Church. One chief reason for the defection of the educated is the Church's persistence in 'an extreme and too exclusive Scripturalism'. The 'Word of God' is identified with 'the Bible', instead of being sought within it; and the idea prevails that even to *notice* discrepancies—between the Gospel narratives for example, or between Kings and Chronicles—is to 'attack a holy thing'. Wilson argues that in point of fact the VIth Article allows us to accept 'literally, or allegorically, or as parable, or poetry, or legend, the story of a serpent tempter, of an ass speaking with man's voice, of an arresting of the earth's motion, of a reversal of its motion, of waters standing in a solid heap, of witches, and a variety of apparitions'. Distinguishing between different levels of 'truth', Wilson urges that a story may be legendary or mythical and yet symbolize or convey an important spiritual truth. A myth may be a true myth, that is, a true representation in this-worldly imagery of other-worldly realities. These latter phrases are naturally not Wilson's; his own words are:

'We do not apply the term "untrue" to parable, fable, or proverb, although their words correspond with ideas, not with material facts; as little should we do so, when narratives have been the spontaneous product of true ideas, and are capable of reproducing them.'

The Transfiguration, the opening of blind eyes, the feeding of multitudes, the genealogies of Jesus, the angelic appearances at his nativity: these and many other similar things, however questionable they may be as history, are quite as much steeped in spiritual meaning as though they were historically verifiable. Indeed the spiritual meaning is so important that the historical question becomes quite secondary. And so with sacramental teaching: when we hear of a Real Presence in the Holy Communion, or of a psychical change effected on the spot in baptism, we may remember that

'within these concrete conceptions there lie hid the truer ideas of the virtual presence of the Lord Jesus everywhere that He is preached, remembered, and represented, and of the continual force of His spirit in His words, and especially in the ordinance which indicates the separation of the Christian from the world'.

If the human element in Scripture were freely recognized by the orthodox, so much the more freely would the unorthodox recognize its divine element.

On the question of Subscription it is certainly a little disconcerting (as Wilberforce was not slow to point out) to find Wilson, one of the Four Oxford Tutors who had condemned Tract XC for catholicizing the Articles, attempting here, in a few pages of casuistry, to liberalize them by dissolving away such terms as 'allow', 'acknowledge' and the like. We must make allowances here, however, for a touch of irony in Wilson's argumentative strategy; if the Articles and Canons may be made out to be flexible (he is perhaps saying), then this is a game at which liberals can play as well as Newmanites. He is correct, at any rate, in claiming that the Church of England may in fact be doctrinally 'freer' than some of the sects. His real point is that the clergy should now be liberated from the bondage of subscription to the Articles; only thus can the Church be kept truly national, as well as adequate to the present times. The Articles will naturally not be forgotten, but they will be decently enshrined as museum pieces.

I may conclude these remarks with the following quotation, which sums up Wilson's main affirmations:

> 'Jesus Christ has not revealed His religion as a theology of the intellect, nor as an historical faith; and it is a stifling of the true Christian life, both in the individual and in the Church, to require of many men a unanimity in speculative doctrine, which is unattainable, and a uniformity of historical belief, which can never exist.'

5. The essay "On the Mosaic Cosmogony", by C. W. Goodwin (Fellow of Christ's College, Cambridge), in spite of its Cambridge *provenance*, need not be noticed here at any great length, because for us today the argument has died of its own victory. Its main aim is to protest against the attempts of 'theological geologists' like Dr Buckland (in his *Bridge-*

water Treatise), Hugh Miller (in *Testimony of the Rocks*), or Archdeacon Pratt (in *Science and Scripture Not at Variance*) to 'harmonize' Genesis and geology. Such writers have tried to do this, for instance, by inserting whole geological ages between 'the beginning' and 'the first day', by slurring over discrepancies of detail, by supposing that sun, moon and stars were obscured by cloud till the fourth day, by imagining that Moses was reporting a vision which had been given to him, by assuming that 'day' means 'aeon', etc., etc. They have tried to do it, that is to say, by falsifying the obviously simple narrative and sophisticating it out of all recognition. How much better to recognize that the Bible does not impart scientific information! How much wiser, too, to confess our error in presupposing what sort of revelation God ought to have given instead of humbly noting his actual procedure, both in 'revelation' and in nature. We should never have had to sophisticate Genesis if science had not revealed God's truth, and the harmonizers are merely wasting time, and perpetuating false notions. I extract the following passage for its period interest:

> 'Physical science goes on unconcernedly pursuing its own paths. Theology, the science whose object is the dealings of God with man as a moral being, maintains but a shivering existence, shouldered and jostled by the sturdy growths of modern thought, and bemoaning itself for the hostility which it encounters. Why should this be, unless because theologians persist in clinging to theories of God's procedure towards man, which have long been seen to be untenable? If, relinquishing theories, they would be content to enquire from the history of man what this procedure has actually been, the so-called difficulties of theology would, for the most part, vanish of themselves.'

6. Mark Pattison's "Tendencies of Religious Thought in England, 1688-1750", is in a class apart from all the other essays. Unlike the rest, it is a work of original research, and as such has claims to survive in its own right. It is in fact a fragment of a projected work which, had Pattison not been disheartened by the publication of Leslie Stephen's *History*

of English Thought in the Eighteenth Century, might well have rivalled the latter in importance. For us today it is interesting as an early—indeed, in England, a pioneering—effort in a genre since become familiar, I mean the 'history of ideas'. What is more, it was to *religious* ideas that Pattison applied the historical technique, and that at a time when (as Jowett remarked in another context) 'to most persons the very notion that ideas have a history is a new one'. Pattison's essay had less direct relation to the times than any of the seven, but its oblique strategy was more effective. One essential aim of *Essays and Reviews* was to turn certain stagnant ponds of thought into running streams; to break up that spiritual fixity which comes from mistaking assumptions for 'facts'. And a very effective way of doing this is to direct attention to a past age, an age to which one is not committed, and through historical analysis of its notions, to emancipate one's readers imperceptibly from thraldom to their own. Once begin to admit, in this way, that an accepted religious idea has a history, that it can be viewed in its origins and growth and so be *explained*, and you are already no longer under its necessary dominion.

Mark Pattison begins by referring to the current estimate of the eighteenth century—in which even Newman and Carlyle agree—as an age of 'decay of religion, licentiousness of morals, public corruption, profaneness of language . . . an age whose poetry was without romance, whose philosophy was without insight, and whose public men were without character'. The average Anglican, particularly the High Churchman, simply omits that period from his historical idea of the Church. But one cannot write or think history in this way; today is today in virtue of yesterday. We assume, if we are Catholics, that religious ideas are authoritatively 'given'; if we are Protestants, that they are arrived at by 'free enquiry' and judgment of evidence. In neither case do we allow sufficiently for the principle of historical growth; we lack any scientific technique for interpreting religious ideas according to 'the laws of thought'. Yet if we want to understand the position of the Church in our own age we must try to understand the forces which were at work in the previous century.

In the *seculum rationalisticum*, Christianity 'appeared made for nothing else but to be "proved"; what use to make of it when it was proved was not much thought about'. Similarly, 'the only quality in Scripture which was dwelt upon was its "credibility"'. But this evidential approach by-passes the spiritual *content* of revelation; 'evidences stir no feeling'; the mind which 'occupies itself with the "external evidences" knows nothing of the spiritual intuition, of which it renounces at once the difficulties and the consolations'. Yet, despite all this emphasis on evidence, there was hardly a trace of 'honest enquiry into the origin and composition of the canonical writings'. And here we have an example of how Pattison criticizes the nineteenth century obliquely through the eighteenth; we too, like our predecessors, profess to base our belief on historical evidences, but, like them, we are afraid to let those evidences be examined 'in open court'.

Theology in the proper sense 'had almost died out when it received a new impulse and a new direction from Coleridge'. Under the spell of this magician, 'the evidence-makers ceased from their futile labours all at once', and 'Englishmen heard with as much surprise as if the doctrine was new, that the Christian faith . . . was "the perfection of human intelligence"'. But in the eighteenth century it was unconsciously assumed (not explicitly stated) that 'a man's religious belief is a result which issues at the end of an intellectual process'. It is true that, in order to establish *a priori* the necessity of a revelation, you had to devalue 'reason' a little. But not too far, or your whole position was undermined. You followed Locke's *via media*: natural religion (or 'nature and reason') ought in theory to have sufficed for man, but never in fact quite did. Similarly, virtue is and always was its own reward, but could not in practice maintain itself without additional sanctions. 'Faith' is understood to mean, not a 'devout condition of the entire inner man', but intellectual assent to the 'proofs' of God.

This age of coffee-house philosophy was practical in all its aims, and its highest educational objective was the attainment of 'a sound secular judgment'. Indeed the common reason of men was now virtually the supreme tribunal, replacing the Universal Church of the Middle Ages, the Bible of the Reformation, the National Church of Laud, the Inner Light of Quakerism and the transcendental Reason of the Cambridge Platonists. The appeal was to 'reason', indeed, but this meant the 'rational consent of the sensible and un-prejudiced', the judgment of 'the bulk of mankind'. In the Deistic controversy, for example, both parties unconsciously assumed the 'rationalistic fiction', that their respective beliefs were the outcome of candid, impartial enquiry into the evidence. The result of this attitude was a theology which excluded on principle 'not only all that is poetical in life, but all that is sublime in religious speculation'.

'The defect of the eighteenth century theology', Pattison concludes, 'was not in having too much good sense, but in having nothing besides'. Of what use, then, can the study of it be to us in the nineteenth century, when 'nothing is allowed in the Church of England but the formulae of past thinkings'? Precisely this, that whereas for us these fossil thinkings have 'long lost all sense of any kind', the eighteenth century did at least aim at practical results; such theology, such religious faith as it had, it did try to connect with every-day life and conduct. 'The endeavour of the moralists and divines of the period to rationalize religion was in fact an effort to preserve the practical principles of moral and religious conduct for society.' At this point Pattison warns us against regarding the depravity and corruption of the eighteenth century as the *result* of its utilitarian or prudential bias. It may be true, he admits, that when Man is made an end in himself, when he becomes his own Proper Study, you get, not perfection, not even improvement, but spiritual debasement. Yet he invites us to regard the rational and utilitarian teachings of the eighteenth century not as causes, but as efforts to stem the secular tide by the only methods then likely to avail. In all this there is something of the ambiguity which bedevils much thinking about historical causation. Which is to blame, the congregation for ignoring the preaching, or the preaching for having lost the initiative? It might be argued that the Church could have kept the lead if, instead of condescending to a godless world, it had consistently defied it. In praising the Church for adopting the prudential line in the eighteenth century, Pattison is saying —in effect—that having irretrievably lost the lead, it did the best it could by panting after the great world and murmuring to it good advice in its own idiom. To admit this seems to be a surrender to the materialist interpretation of history. And yet Pattison goes on to say that the very failure of the prudential system, as a restraining force upon society, led to the Evangelical and Methodist reaction which, we know, had a considerable measure of success. Its success was due to defiance of the world, not compliance with it. 'The preaching of justification by works had not the power to check wickedness, therefore justification by faith, the doctrine of the Reformation, was the only saving truth.'

And the moral of all this for the nineteenth century? Something like this: You have seen that religious ideas have a history; that, whether as cause or effect, they change with changing times. You have seen, too, that it is possible for a whole era to mistake the true grounds of religious conviction. Ask yourselves, then, whether by any chance you are making that kind of mistake. On what basis is Christianity now supposed to rest?

7. I said above that in the last of the essays, Jowett's "On the Interpretation of Scripture", was to be found the book's centre of gravity. Although Jowett's argument overlaps to some extent that of Rowland Williams, it is set forth with much greater weight, urbanity and self-assurance. It deals with the central issue of the times—the problem of scriptural authority, and although Jowett's contentions are now the accepted axioms of biblical interpretation, it is still instructive to note the obstacles which then confronted him, and the methods he used to overcome them.

Jowett had two special qualifications for his task: classical scholarship, and a profound—if somewhat Olympian—faith in what he believed to be the 'real' truths of Christianity. To which we may perhaps add a serene confidence in his own power to discern what these are. Jowett brought to biblical interpretation a mind schooled by years of wrestling with other ancient texts, and especially by the sustained effort to enter, and to render intelligible in modern English, the mind and world of Plato. He knew, none so well as he, the extreme difficulty of apprehending an ancient as in himself he really was, and the still greater difficulty of interpreting him to a modern reader without distortion—above all, without imputing to him conceptions of later origin. No wonder, then, that when he surveyed the history and the present state of biblical interpretation, he was profoundly disturbed by what he saw. Even in saying this much, I have begged the question Jowett had to demonstrate; I have presupposed that in passing from Plato to the Bible he was passing from one ancient text to others, not indeed of the same kind, but subject to the same canons of interpretation. But—let us not weary of reminding ourselves—this was by no means generally admitted in England then, and Jowett's maxim 'Interpret the Scripture like any other book'—was received by many with horror and indignation. Jowett knew perfectly well that in many ways the Bible is and must be unlike any other book; quite apart from its surpassing spiritual value it cannot be approached in forgetfulness of the unique rôle it has played in Christendom. What Jowett meant was that the Bible is (to put it no higher) worth understanding, and that to reach understanding there simply are no methods in existence other than those used in interpreting Plato. He was in effect using modern scholarship to complete the work begun by the old Reformers—that of penetration to the original bedrock through the stratified deposits of the centuries. To read the Bible 'like any other book' meant simply to recover the original as it really was, forgetting theological afterthoughts. We ask of Plato, for instance, what he actually meant, whereas for centuries we have been asking of the scriptural writers, not what they meant, but what—by allegorical, mystical, rhetorical and other manipulations—they may be made to mean. We introduce into the interpretation of Scripture, as no scholar would do in expounding any other ancient text, the notions of later ages: credal formulations, and the glosses of Fathers and Schoolmen; we 'harmonize' contradictions; we ignore differences of date and authorship; we construe figurative language as though it were logical statement. To get inside the world of Scripture we need a very different approach. We need, first, the usual techniques of scholarship: knowledge of the original meanings of Hebrew and Greek words, of the times in which the texts were composed, and of the ways in which men thought and spoke in those times. We need also to make 'an effort of thought and imagination, requiring the sense of a poet as well as a critic—demanding, much more than learning, a degree of original power and intensity of mind'. Our present disregard of these principles is having a bad effect in religious education; it is demoralizing for the young to feel obliged to apply to the Bible methods of interpretation which they would think it dishonest to apply to a classical author— excusing, reconciling, using multiple meanings or adopting the fancies of the Fathers. 'The mixture of truth and falsehood in religious education'. says Jowett, 'certainly tends to impair, at the age when it is most needed, the early influence of a religious home.'

We now reach the central affirmations of Jowett's essay, which were also those of *Essays and Reviews* as a whole, and of religious liberals and 'modernists' at all times: *'the time has come when it is no longer possible to ignore the results of criticism'.*[1] What next? Fight a rearguard action with the philologists, geologists and biologists, hoping that 'a generation will pass away before we sound a last retreat'? Not a bit of it! What we must do, on the contrary, is to welcome 'the results of criticism', and show that Christianity (properly understood) is in harmony with them. At all costs we must extricate ourselves from the impossible position, into which we are thrust by a timid apologetic, of seeing 'objections to some received views' universally recognized by competent judges as valid, yet feeling obliged to denounce them as the 'objections of infidels'. Nothing could be a greater mischief to the Christian cause than this.

'. . . that in the present day the great object of Christianity should be, not to change the lives of men, but to prevent them from

[1] Italics mine.

changing their opinions; that would be a singular inversion of the purposes for which Christ came into the world. *The Christian religion is in a false position when all the tendencies of knowledge are opposed to it. . . .*[1] No one can form any notion from what we see around us, of the power which Christianity might have if it were at one with the conscience of man, and not at variance with his intellectual convictions.'

It was characteristic of Jowett that he should choose, in trimming the Christian sails to the prevailing winds, the line of *suaviter in modo*, if *fortiter in re*. As a College Tutor, and an academic diplomatist, he was highly skilled in the arts of plausibility and tactful representation; he knew how to lead men on, by gentle insinuation, and without antagonizing them, into positions remote from their own. This is the Jowett who appears so deliciously parodied as 'Dr Jenkinson' in *The New Republic*. It was this Jowett, too, who aroused the suspicions of that inflexible devotee of impossible loyalties, Francis Newman. In a *Westminster Review* article (1859) on "Jowett and the Broad Church", Newman had saluted Jowett as 'the foremost mind in the Anglican Church', and added that in him, 'for the first time, has the learning, fairness, religious sentiment and profound thought of modern Germany been exhibited in an Anglican divine'.[2] He approved highly of Jowett's Commentary on St Paul, and indeed of almost all his words and deeds—except his casuistry: his advice to modern Christians to do as others do, to avoid a morbid conscience, and not to damage their cause by attempting apostolic ethics in the Victorian age. Where meats and moons are concerned compliance may not be ignoble, but what of vital matters like military service or the Thirty-Nine Articles? On Jowett's principles, Newman complains, how could Christianity ever have arisen, or ever have produced martyrs?

Jowett would, indeed, have been the Erasmus and not the Luther of any Reformation. One may contrast his treatment of New Testament quotations from the Old Testament with Newman's. Newman points out, with considerable ferocity,

[1] Italics mine.   [2] Reprinted (abridged) in *Miscellanies*, vol. ii (1887).

that nearly all these quotations are misunderstood or mis-
applied by the New Testament writers. Jowett knows this
perfectly well, but in his anxiety to avoid offence, to edify
while pulling down, he opens the matter after this fashion:
"Misapplications, you say? but why all this asperity? Every
age interprets according to its own best insights, and why
should we insist that the New Testament interpretations
coincide with the original Old Testament meanings? The
truths which the New Testament writers thought they found
in the Old, they had really put there themselves? Oh, dear
me, yes; but consider, my dear sir, what truths these were:
they were truths necessary for the salvation and conversion
of the world!"[1] It is only after this preliminary softening-up
process that Jowett drops, in a bland aside, the observation
which Newman and others made with bitter disillusion:

> 'There are many quotations from the Psalms and the Prophets
> in the Epistles, in which the meaning is quickened or spiritualized,
> but hardly any, probably none, which is based on the original sense
> or context.'

There are here, it will be noticed, certain implications which
do not immediately meet the eye. One is, the quiet abandonment of any theory of 'inspiration' according to which the
scriptural writers were precluded from all error. Another, of
a different kind, is one which might seem inconsistent with
Jowett's main argument; after urging at great length that
we must on no account distort the original meanings by
introducing our own adaptations, he then excuses the New
Testament writers for doing this very thing. Presumably he
regarded them as a privileged class of interpreters, since
their errors happened at the same time to be saving
truths.

It is in the same spirit of sanctified shrewdness that
Jowett recommends his own technique to ordinands. Culti-
vate prudence and tact! 'Much depends on the manner in
which things are said. . . . There is an aspect of truth which
may always be put forward so as to find a way to the hearts of
men.' It would, however, be quite wrong and most unjust to

[1] The argument is his, but the words are mine.

represent Jowett as a sort of spiritual Lord Chesterfield, concerned only with pleasing and accommodating the great world. If his surface was smooth, there was 'a hidden ground of thought and of austerity within'; if he believed little, he believed that little intensely, and the 'little' was everything to him. I purposely omitted, so as to emphasize it now, the most important of his injunctions to ordinands: they are to trust, not only in tact and prudence, but in 'the power of a Christian life'. Similarly he tells intending missionaries not to force the Bible on the heathen as if it were the Koran, sacred in every letter and comma; 'the power of the Gospel resides not in the particulars of theology, but in the Christian life'. Here we have the clue to Jowett's confidence in the possibility of reconciling Christianity with the 'results of criticism'; the thing could be done because the 'eternal import' of Christianity was invulnerable, and would not only survive the removal of 'incrustations', but be strengthened in the process.

And what is this 'eternal import', this 'true basis', these 'essentials', which Jowett was for ever distinguishing from the accretions? It is already clear that he meant 'the Christian life', but we can learn what, in turn, this meant to him by referring to the end of the *Life and Letters*,[1] and noting some of his last thoughts there recorded. The true basis of Christianity is the re-enactment within the soul of the life and death of Christ: death to the world and sin, self-abnegation, rebirth in such union with God as Christ himself had. We shall never return to disproved miracles or outworn dogmas, the 'immortality' of the soul may come to mean its present consciousness of God; the 'personality' of God may pass into 'an idea'. We shall believe in a Christ risen indeed, but not risen in a 'physical' or ghostly sense. Yet the 'essence' will remain, an absolute morality common to Plato and the Gospel. Anyone who devotes himself to the good of others, and takes up his cross, will find no more doubts or difficulties; his faith will depend no longer on 'historical events, the report of which we cannot altogether trust. Holiness has its sources elsewhere than in history'.

See, e.g., vol. ii, pp. 273, 306, 310-18.

At last, a few years before his death, he could speak thus gently but cursorily of the weary old issues:

'I think that I believe more and more in Christianity, not in miracles or hell, or verbal inspiration, or atonement, but in living for others and in going about doing good.'

11. How It Struck Some Contemporaries

I. FREDERIC HARRISON

There may, I think, be something of more than 'period' interest in noting how *Essays and Reviews* struck some contemporaries. I do not propose to rehearse the oft-told tale of the prosecutions: Dr Lushington's judgment in the Court of Arches (June 1862) condemning Williams and Wilson on single points; their suspension from their offices for a year; the appeal to the Privy Council; Lord Chancellor Westbury's reversal of the partial condemnation, described by Bowen as 'Hell dismissed with costs' (February 1884). Instead, I select from the mass of contemporary comment three reviews by men of widely different standpoints: Frederic Harrison (liberal-agnostic or 'positivist'), Samuel Wilberforce (conservative-Anglican) and A. P. Stanley (liberal-Anglican).

Frederic Harrison's review, entitled "Neo-Christianity", appeared in the *Westminster Review* for October 1860. It was his first publication, and reflects all the ardour of his recent conversion to positivist principles. His point of view, in this very able and important article, is sufficiently peculiar to call for a few explanatory biographical words. Harrison, whose long life (1831-1923) spanned two-thirds of the nineteenth century and nearly a quarter of the twentieth, had been brought up amongst High Church influences, and early acquired a strong taste for ritual and a deep affection for the Bible and the Prayer-Book. He could still (in 1907) call the Burial Service 'the grandest piece of tragic poetry in our language (Shakespeare being *hors concours*)', adding that 'even now I take the Evening Service at an Episcopal Cathedral, Catholic or Protestant, to be the most moving

SEPTEM CONTRA CHRISTUM

form of Art ever devised by man'.[1] Harrison entered Wadham College in 1849, and was immediately plunged into the post-Tractarian whirlpool. Most of his College contemporaries came from Anglican parsonages, and most of them were destined for Holy Orders. Theological discussion was incessant. The undergraduates were expected to summarize each week's University Sermon, and the perplexing variety of views thus imbibed seems to have been the first unsettling influence. 'The creed of one Sunday becomes the heresy of the next.' 'I have myself heard in the University pulpit', he says, 'Dean Mansel's agnostic dialectics, Canon Liddon's Catholic homilies on the Divinity of Jesus, H. Bristow Wilson's Lectures on the universal reign of Law in place of Will, Bishop Gore, the late Master of Balliol, Dr Pusey himself, and Richard Congreve, afterwards founder in England of the Positivist Church of Humanity.' At this time he bought a costly Bible, which he says he has kept at his side for fifty-eight years ('I have no book which I value more or open with greater zest'), but he also embarked upon a course of reading which undermined his orthodoxy for life. Beginning conventionally enough with Plato and Aristotle, Dante and Milton, Butler's *Analogy* and Sermons, *The Christian Year*, Coleridge's essays, the religious novels of Newman and Kingsley, and *In Memoriam*, and continuing with the more risky Byron, Shelley and Carlyle, he soon succumbed to the lures of the *Westminster Review* and of Francis Newman, 'whose beautiful nature and subtle intelligence I now began to value'. He read *The Hebrew Monarchy*, *Phases of Faith* and *The Soul*, and, though at first unable to accept Newman's heterodoxy, he was deeply influenced by him. Then Mill, G. H. Lewes, George Eliot and Littré introduced him to Comte, and finally the *Westminster Review*, with its articles on Strauss's *Life of Jesus*, Renan and Bauer, and 'constant essays by Herbert Spencer, W. Call, W. R. Greg, Mill, the two Lewes [*sic*] and Francis Newman opened to us the whole of the critical study of the Scriptures and the Creeds as far as it had gone down to the appearance of Spencer's *Synthetic Philosophy* and C. Darwin's

[1] This and the following quotations are from *The Creed of a Layman* (1907).

161

Origin of Species'. More interesting than this official list of professional 'unsettlers' is Harrison's testimony to the influence of certain other writers, not all of them beyond the pale of orthodoxy:

> 'What moved me far more than the critical assaults of Strauss, or Francis Newman—*a man of a learning and an intellect far superior to that of the Cardinal*,[1] but one who had no clerical *claque* to belaud him—what shook my orthodoxy, was the way in which devout and noble spirits such as that of F. Robertson, of F. D. Maurice, of F. Newman, Theodore Parker, together with followers of Dr Arnold, of Coleridge, and the poets Tennyson and Browning, struck off the fetters of what Carlyle called "the rags of Houndsditch". Maurice, Coleridge, Carlyle, and F. Newman, in different ways and often without intending it, would fill me with horror and shame at many passages of Scripture and many dogmas of the Church which I felt to be profoundly repugnant to morality and even to human nature. I never can forget poor dear old Maurice stammering through the story of Dinah, when that horrible chapter of Genesis came to be read in its turn.'

When studying Law at Lincoln's Inn he used to listen to Maurice's sermons, and they 'demolished what remains of orthodoxy I had'. How was this? According to Harrison, it was because of Maurice's way of riddling some passage of Scripture or Creed, and then saying we ought to accept it after all—'hug our fetters, and revel in our darkness'. At the same time he was plunging into science: Huxley, Tyndall, Robert Owen, Darwin and A. R. Wallace; he was also consorting with the Chapman and Congreve circles, where he personally met Lewes and George Eliot, F. Newman, Spencer, R. W. Mackay and others. 'Saturated' by this time with Mill, Buckle, Spencer and Darwin, he was ready to receive the full impact of Comte, thenceforward his lifelong prophet and high priest.

All through this autobiography Harrison insists that his development was peaceful and continuous; he evolved from High Anglican into High Comtean with no painful break, such as befell other defaulters from simple faith. Like

[1] Italics mine.

George Eliot, he shrank from clean sweeps and from atheism: 'the moral and intellectual tone of what is commonly called Infidelity was always alien to me; and that of positive Atheism was intensely repulsive'. Comte had come to fulfil the Law, not to destroy it. So there was no bitter sense of loss or deception, no searing doubts, no nostalgia. He was not shocked by Colenso on the Pentateuch; he merely wondered how anyone could suppose the Pentateuch to be anything *but* mythical. So far from feeling robbed of anything precious, he enjoyed his Bible (except, presumably, the story of Dinah and the 'many passages' which were profoundly repugnant to morality) more than ever, as 'sublime poetry', 'magnificent allegory' and the like. By this time he needed no Hume on Miracles to convince him of 'the universal reign of Law in the whole range of human experience'; the irrational nature of Miracle was now 'felt as an axiom of thought'.

In the light of the foregoing, how should we expect the twenty-nine-year-old Harrison to be affected by *Essays and Reviews*? Remembering what we have just seen of his development, remembering that though exulting in the dawn of the final (the positivist) Revelation he was still a theist, and still (eclectically) attending Christian worship, should we not have expected him to salute these liberal Christians as kindred spirits? Instead, he attacks them vehemently, and through them, the whole conception of religious 'modernism'.

It was not their 'liberalism' that he disapproved of, but their 'dishonesty' in trying to 'adapt' Christianity to modern thought and yet remain Churchmen. His *Westminster* article "Neo-Christianity" is essentially an ex-Christian's cry of surprise and dismay: "you are stealing our thunder!" he says in effect; "what is the use of our having left the Church if Churchmen themselves are using our arguments?" He gives the essayists due praise for their enlightened views, but tells them in the first place that they do not carry out their own principles far enough to be genuine moderns and positivists, and secondly that they have destroyed their own position. He wants to force them back on to the ground they

have evacuated—that is, on to miracle, biblical fundamentalism, etc. That is the only ground that professed Christians
may logically occupy; abandon this, and they are left with
no real foundation at all. 'Ideological' re-interpretations are
humbug, and mere stress on being good—living an (ethic-
ally) Christian life—will never bind a Church together.
These modernists (Harrison does not use that word) want to
go on using creeds and forms of which they have destroyed the
original meaning, and reverencing a Bible whose authority
they have riddled. This will never do; *Essays and Reviews* is

> 'incompatible with the religious belief of the mass of the Christian
> public, and the broad principles on which the Protestantism of
> Englishmen rests. . . . Just as their instinct repudiated the ingenious
> attempts of the Tractarian writers to build a semi-Romish system
> on the dogmas of our Church; just so it will revolt from any
> attempt, however sincere, to graft the results and the principles of
> rationalism on the popular Christianity of the day.'

The idea that Christianity might be a living organism, with
powers of growth and adaptation to a changing climate, was
quite foreign to the earnest agnostics and positivists of the
time; their favourite image for it (the one that Harrison uses
here) is the 'crumbling edifice', too ruinous to be patched
up, and certainly not to be preserved by sweeping away the
whole of its substructure. What *do* the modernists suppose
Christianity to be? Has it all been a mistaken rendering that
men have been believing so long? These essayists have
altered the whole scheme of salvation; divine rewards and
punishments, the Fall, Original Sin, the vicarious sacrifice,
justification by faith—all are repudiated, together with
prophecy, miracles and 'inspiration'; the Mosaic history
'dissolves into a mass of ill-digested legends, the Mosaic
ritual into an Oriental system of priestcraft, and the Mosaic
origin of the earth and man sinks amidst the rubbish of
rabbinical cosmogonies'. The Headmaster of Rugby reduces
the Hebrew race to the level of the Romans; Rowland
Williams equates the Bible with Livy; Baden Powell eliminates the supernatural altogether.

All this Harrison thoroughly approves: indeed, a few

pages below we find him asserting, himself, that 'he who understands the meaning of law, whether laws of matter or laws of mind, treats with contempt the notion of miracle in either'. What infuriates him is that the residue, after all this purging, should still be calling itself 'Christianity'. There is no middle way; the essayists should either stick to 'the broad principles on which the Protestantism of Englishmen rests' (apparently Harrison's definition of 'Christianity'), or they should come out from among them and be positivists. Often Harrison uses the very same arguments as the essayists, but with the implication that these arguments undermine, not support, their position. For instance, after reading Williams's account of biblical scholarship, he exclaims, 'Was ever literature so provokingly untrustworthy? . . . Is this the world-wide source of life and truth?' The essayists first reduce the Bible to 'poetry' and then ask us to revere it more than other poetry. But why—on their principles? What gives Scripture its canonical numinousness when stripped of its supernatural quality? The essayists had themselves popularized these subversive thoughts; therefore, according to Harrison, they must not call themselves Christians—for Christians are by definition fundamentalists. The *Essays and Reviews* theory of 'inspiration' either includes a vast amount *outside* the Bible, or excludes a vast amount *in* it: a proposition with which Jowett would have heartily agreed. But 'Christians' do not accept such views, therefore Jowett is not a Christian. Or again, what, Harrison asks, has driven 'the most advanced thinkers within the orthodox pale' to make their 'fatal concessions' to the time-spirit? He answers that it is the all-conquering notion of the century, 'the conception of development'. 'Step by step the notion of evolution by law is transforming the whole field of our knowledge and opinion.' 'In the physical and the moral world, in the natural and the human, are ever seen two forces—invariable rule and continuous advance; law and action; order and progress.' Just as Darwin has demonstrated the process of growth according to rigid law in the physical world, so 'the reception given to the book of Mr Buckle has proved that public opinion was ripe for the admission of regular laws in the moral world'. But all this, the reader of *Essays and Reviews* might reflect—perhaps remembering especially Baden Powell's approval of Darwin's 'grand principle of the self-evolving powers of nature' (see p. 147 above)—all this is entirely in accord with the spirit of the essayists themselves; how then can it be turned into an argument against them? Always we are brought back to the same point: such admissions are irreconcilable with a profession of Christianity, a religion committed irrevocably to miraculous breaks in nature and history. The essayists had indeed gone far to eliminate physical miracles, and admittedly their whole programme implied allegiance to the principle of development and its application to religion itself. Yet because they cling to Christianity they must necessarily postulate at least a break in history (the Incarnation), if not in 'nature', whereas 'the whole analogy of history condemns, not merely miraculous events, but stupendous violations of order in the growth of moral and spiritual life'.

In his concluding remarks Harrison makes some points which, on the assumption that Christianity must either be dogmatically conservative or cease to exist, are cogent enough, and might have been put forward by any orthodox opponent of modernism then or now. The essayists, he says, meet the decay of faith in a characteristic way: they acknowledge 'in sad and eloquent words the prevailing antagonism between our intellectual convictions and our religious professions'; they hope 'to mitigate the evil by thrusting the intellectual behind the moral element of the belief'; they sum up the Gospels 'in the practice of the Christian life'. Why not? Because 'no collection of maxims or rules of life can last very long when deprived of dogmatic basis and common intellectual assent':

> 'Once doubt the certainty of the story or the reality of the sacrifice [of Christ], and to what will the preacher appeal? He will be left to the truism, "To be good, for it is good to be good." . . . It 's not this which can bring order out of the intellectual anarchy around us, control the whole moral energy of the present, and heal the deep diseases in societies and states.'

True, the severance of religion and reason is the great evil of our time:

> 'all the tenderer and holier of our ties lead one way; all the stronger and more rational, another'.

What then is the remedy? Not Jowett's remedy, the restatement of religion in terms meaningful to the modern mind; on the contrary, the 'mask of conformity' must go.

> 'Religion, to regain the world, must not only be not contrary to science but it must be in entire and close harmony with science. . . . Its intellectual basis must be broad and unimpeachable. . . . That end will not be attained by our authors, by subliming religion into an emotion, and making an armistice with science.'

Religion, in fact, must be dogmatic, militant, self-assured. Catholicism, then? Ah yes, but Catholicism minus Christianity—which, as everyone knows, means the Positivist Church of Humanity.

2. SAMUEL WILBERFORCE

> 'It is not often that we can agree with our outspoken contemporary, least of all on matters touching the Christian faith; but undoubtedly he is here altogether in the right.'

Thus spake the *Quarterly*, January 1861, of the *Westminster*, October 1860; thus Samuel Wilberforce acknowledged that, for once, he and Frederic Harrison were fighting the same enemy (though from opposite flanks and for opposite reasons). Samuel Wilberforce, Bishop of Oxford since 1844, was indeed a typical exponent of 'the broad principles on which the Protantism of Englishmen rests'; he represented very fairly what Harrison thought a 'Christian' ought to be. Too English and too Protestant to go all the way with Newman, Wilberforce had become the leading champion of moderate but rigid High Churchmanship against the dangerous forces of liberalism. Most people have heard of his participation in the attempt to exclude the liberal Hampden from the Bishopric of Hereford (1847), and everybody has heard of his brush with T. H. Huxley at the British Association meeting (1860); not so many, probably, are familiar with his attack on *Essays and Reviews*.

Wilberforce was a man of ability, and did not misunderstand Harrison's "Neo-Christianity" in the fashion of some of his humbler colleagues, who imagined that if *Essays and Reviews* had given offence even to the *Westminster Review* it must be poisonous indeed. He not only understood it very well, but (as we have just noted) referred to it with approval and quoted from it in his own article. His point of view was that of the average Englishman, that 'no enlightened person should become a clergyman, and that the clergyman who became enlightened and let men know it should be unfrocked',[1] a point of view almost identical with that of Harrison, and incidentally that of Carlyle, whose comment was 'The sentinel who deserts should be shot.' He differs from Harrison only in his ultimate aim, which was to preserve the Church from contagion, whereas Harrison, wanting to see it die of liberalism, resented all attempts to save it by vaccination with the liberal serum.

As Wilberforce sees it, 'infidelity, if not Atheism' is the tendency of the book. The essayists 'endeavour to defend some shadowy ghost of Christianity by yielding up all that has hitherto been thought its substance'. In his 'soapiest' manner he laments 'with the deepest sorrow' that Temple is amongst this godless crew—such a man 'as his past career has made us believe Dr Temple to be'. In Temple's similitude of the education of the human race he sees an oblique denial of the Fall and hence of the Redemption; all history becomes a gradual rise, a progressive improvement. And the Creation narrative: if this is to be dissolved into a mist of 'rationalizing ideology', what becomes of 'For as in Adam all die . . .'? He picks out Rowland Williams as the worst offender, but he finds that Temple, too, subjects Revelation to an alleged 'verifying faculty' within each man's consciousness, whereby he claims to settle 'what is or is not true in the Inspired Record'. Williams had seen the virtue of Abraham in his having *desisted* from the blood-sacrifice demanded by a savage cult, and transferred his allegiance to justice, reason

---

[1] Lewis Campbell, *Life of Jowett*, vol. i, 294.

and love. This interpretation seems to Wilberforce a typical case of subversion: the notion, that is, 'that faith consists in "principles of reason and right", and in disobedience to God's external authority, in order that we may by that disobedience more completely obey what we consider our own reason'.

Summarizing the views of the essayists about biblical 'inspiration', Wilberforce argues (and in so doing condemns the whole tendency of modern biblical scholarship) that the analysis of the Synoptic problem, for example, tends to 'the utter destruction of all notion of inspiration'. The prophets are reduced to 'ordinary moralists'; miracles are declared impossible (but why? they are theoretically credible to any theist); and much of what we had hitherto received as 'the Word of God' is said to include 'legendary matter'—Mr Wilson assuring us that this really makes no special difference. In fine, what we are offered, in place of the old inspired Scriptures, is a 'residuum' embedded in a crust of legends, traditions and poetic licences; a residuum to be variously identified by each intelligent adult in this advanced age. We are to reject most of the Old Testament history, all miracles, all prophecy whether secular or Messianic; and even the 'residuum' is to be thought of as the 'voice of the congregation' rather than as something of unique authority.

Temple prefers practical religion to 'precise definitions of truth'; but the definitions, the dogmas, are the foundation on which the practice rests. This process of 'dissolving into a general halo of goodness all distinct doctrinal truth' is carried further by Jowett, who wants to 'free' us from the Atonement. Others of the essayists discuss the matter 'without that softening haze of Christian sentiment in which Mr Jowett has involved it'. Wilson's peroration about the Future Life leaves us with nothing but a 'poor Buddhist dream of re-absorption into the Infinite', 'a dreamy vagueness of pantheistic pietism, which is but the shallow water leading on to a profounder and darker atheism'.

Harrison's point had been that Christianity was doomed, that it was being superseded by Positivism, and that those who were as clear-sighted as the essayists had no business to be on the sinking ship. Logically, he ought to have applauded them for making it founder more quickly than ever; he prefers, however, to insist upon their 'dishonesty'. It is on this question that Wilberforce joins forces with him most cordially. Though for him, of course, Christianity was assuredly not doomed to founder, yet it never occurred to him, any more than to Harrison, that the liberals, far from scuttling the ship, might be mending holes already made. 'The attempt of the Essayists', he writes, 'to combine their advocacy of such doctrines with the status and emoluments of Church of England clergymen is simply moral dishonesty.' What, he asks, 'was the claim of liberty put forward by the writer of Tract XC, compared with those advanced by the authors of "Essays and Reviews"?' The straightforward English mind was solidly against Newman's 'sapping' of 'honest subscription'; how much. greater, then, will be its suspicion of these essayists. And H. B. Wilson was one of the Four Tutors who had protested aganist Tract XC (we can allow the Bishop this good debating point). Let these essayists beware of the slippery slope! whether they know it or not, they are in a position where it is impossible to remain. *They believe too much not to believe more, and they disbelieve too much not to disbelieve everything*': I italicize this, because Wilberforce has had the skill to compress into an epigram the whole gist, not only of his own case, but of the general case against modernism, whether urged from the Right or from the Left. Religious liberals have always been under fire from both sides at once: from those who believe too much, and from those who believe too little. Do the essayists, Wilberforce asks, really want to remain Christians and to put Christianity on a better footing? Then they ought to see that it is impossible 'to surrender all the objective truths of Christianity and yet to retain its subjective powers'.

Next he makes another of the routine controversial moves, which is to assert that it has all been said before—by the English Deists and the French Atheists. And in Germany the attempt has also been made (unsuccessfully) 'to remove the supernatural from that which is either a system of super-naturalism or a falsehood'. So bluntly, and shall we say

crudely (without definition of the key-words), does the
Bishop pose the alternatives. Further, the essayists ex-
aggerate the disease (the alleged revolt against traditional
Christianity, the effects of biblical criticism, etc.) in order to
extol their own remedy. They assume, unwarrantably, that
no one who 'with Niebuhr has tasted blood in the slaughter
of Livy can be prevailed upon to abstain from falling next
upon the Bible' (cf. above, p. 143). They assume a vast new
increase of knowledge; they assume too readily that criticism
has turned the flank of orthodoxy, and that new defensive
positions must be prepared; they assume [surely with justice?] that their readers will be ignorant of the German
literature of the past hundred years. But already the German
rationalist movement is spent, and is provoking its own
reaction from within. Our own old Deists were the original
culprits; from them the virus spread through Voltaire to
France and thence to Germany: and now these 'advanced'
writers are borrowing *blunted* weapons from the infected
Germans.

After rashly claiming that all the objections they raise are
merely the 'already abundantly repelled objections and
fallacies of German rationalism', Wilberforce ends with the
satisfying reflection that

'these writers will surely exert very little influence on the calm,
sound and essentially honest English mind'.

The Bishops of Winchester, St David's and Oxford, diverse
as their positions are, have already openly condemned them;
perhaps, then, High and Evangelical Churchmen will at last
be united by this common danger.

3. A. P. STANLEY

The review by Arthur Penrhyn Stanley appeared a few
months later in the *Edinburgh Review* (April 1861). After
the heated rhetoric of Harrison and Wilberforce it falls on
the ear with the calming and distancing effect of a Greek
chorus. Stanley, choice product of Arnold's Rugby, was of
all distinguished clergymen the best fitted to deal justly and

mildly with *Essays and Reviews* and what it stood for. He it was who (in 1850) had written in defence of the Gorham judgment that 'the Church of England, by the very condition of its being, was not High or Low, but Broad, and had always included and been meant to include, opposite and contradictory opinions'. Characteristically, he had lent his weight on successive occasions, first against the condemnation of the Tractarians, and then against the condemnation of Hampden. Later he advocated a relaxation in the terms of clerical subscription to the Thirty-Nine Articles. At the time of *Essays and Reviews* Stanley was still Professor of Ecclesiastical History at Oxford and Canon of Christ Church. He was a close and lifelong friend of Jowett's, sharing many of his opinions and activities. Jowett, on behalf of H. B. Wilson, had invited him to contribute to *Essays and Reviews*, but Stanley, who disliked anything savouring of party-spirit, had declined. Nevertheless he came gallantly to its defence in the review we are now briefly to consider.

Strange as it may seem to us now, the row over *Essays and Reviews* had even for a time drowned the noise over Darwin. Stanley was therefore wise to begin by calmly reviewing the history of previous religious panics from the mutilation of the Hermae to the Gorham controversy. Having thus restored our sense of proportion, he turns to more immediate matters—beginning with the two reviews we have just examined. It was Harrison's "Neo-Christianity" which first raised the dust. This article, says Stanley,

> 'evidently proceeded from the hand of a writer who, whilst retaining a certain amount of religious sentiment, repudiated all belief in Christian Revelation, and who combined with a profound ignorance of all that had been written on the questions at issue an almost fanatical desire to inveigle those who stood on more secure positions to the narrow ledge of the precipice on the midway of which he himself was standing.'

Harrison had ended by complaining of the reluctance of the writers 'to abandon all the truths which they most cherished in order to adopt the mixture of Paganism and Catholicism in which the followers of M. Comte have found a refuge'.

And Wilberforce? He, too, displayed or affected complete ignorance of this century's theological literature. Mingling denunciation with misrepresentation, he had described *Essays and Reviews* as 'a conspiracy of clergymen banded together to undermine the Christian faith', and the writers as 'seven infidels, in the disguise of clergymen, asserting that the Bible was a fable, denying the truth of Christianity and the existence of God'. Stanley himself has a few mild, preliminary objections: the book is perhaps too purely negative, and it is not quite clear for what class of readers it is intended. It contains little that is essentially new: we have already had Herder, Schleiermacher, Lücke, Neander, De Wette, Ewald, Tholuck, Olshausen and Hengstenberg; in England, Coleridge first led the way, and Thomas Arnold, Thirlwall, Alford and Milman followed. Half the rising generation, a quarter of the Bishops, and the leading spirits among the clergy as a whole, are aware of these writers and in accord with their principles.

Turning to the essayists themselves, Stanley refers to Temple as a worthy successor to Arnold, and speaks of his years of self-sacrificing work; to Pattison's great distinction as a scholar; to Wilson, whose Bampton Lectures had made a greater impression on the religious mind of Oxford than any others—'if, for a different reason, we except Mr Mansel's celebrated attack on the first principles of theology'. Lastly there is Jowett, who is described by Stanley as, since the Tracts, 'the only man in Oxford who has exercised a moral and spiritual influence at all comparable to that which was once wielded by John Henry Newman. . . . He stands confessedly master of the situation in the eyes of the rising generation of English students and theologians.'

What, then, has all the fuss been about? The general themes of *Essays and Reviews* are, how to study and interpret the Bible; the relative value of the 'external' and 'internal' evidences of Revelation; the relation of dogmatic theology to the Bible and to history. These topics have been exhaustively treated by the critics just mentioned, and the general outcome of their work has been greatly to reduce the importance of the 'external' evidences, which had been so popular in the eighteenth century. The essayists, Stanley suggests, should be thought of, not as denying miracles, but as feeling the 'increasing difficulty' of receiving wonders as the proof of divine revelation rather than the contents of the revelation itself. They are with 'Dean Trench and St Augustine' in preferring to credit miracles for the sake of the doctrines, rather than the doctrines on account of the miracles. They have in short attempted, says Stanley, coming to grips with the central issue,

> 'mistakenly or not—*to place Christianity beyond the reach of accidents*,[1] whether of science or criticism; to rest its claims on those moral and spiritual truths which, after all, are what have really won an entrance for it into the heart'.

He stoutly rebuts the suggestion, made by both Harrison and Wilberforce, that free-thinking or 'enlightened' clergymen should leave the Church; anyone would think, he observes, that 'Truth was made for the Laity and Falsehood for the clergy—that Truth is tolerable everywhere except in the mouths of the ministers of the God of Truth'. The fact is that the formularies of the Church left 'doors . . . wide open to the questions which a later and critical age was sure to raise into high importance'. There are no Articles on Inspiration or on External Evidences, and no definitions of a 'miracle' or of 'prophecy'. ' "Doubt", says Professor Jowett, "comes in at the window when enquiry is denied at the door." '

Probably in twenty years' time the essayists will be seated in High Places (Temple did become Archbishop of Canterbury, and Jowett Master of Balliol); but meanwhile let them continue to build up Christianity by the love and devotion of their lives.

III. 'Neo-Christianity': Then and Now

Nearly a hundred years have passed since Jowett said that 'the time has come when it is no longer possible to ignore the results of criticism', and deplored that Christianity should

[1] My italics.

find itself opposed to all the tendencies of modern thought and knowledge. Has Christianity since then, has it by now, been placed 'beyond the reach of accidents, whether of science or criticism'? Much has happened since then; indeed, it can be argued that the most Himalayan of all historical watersheds separates us from those days. Two world wars, with their accompanying changes and aftermaths, have shaken the old order—political, social and spiritual—within which the old liberals flourished, and upon which they subconsciously relied as the guarantee of stability and peaceful amelioration. The West has been largely—not completely— deliberalized and dehumanized; some say it has been 'unchristened' as well. Liberal humanism does not flourish in an age of contraction, despair and anxiety; it becomes unfashionable at a time when most people are seeking, not for truth or enlightenment, but for authoritative guidance or assurance. Christianity, as we see, has survived not only 'the results of criticism', but also the secular disintegration of this age; indeed, from the eschatological stress of our own time it has derived new strength, self-knowledge and belligerency. In doing so, however, it has sometimes tended on the one hand to become harsh, dogmatic and irrational, and on the other—ignoring 'the results of criticism'—even to return to 'fundamentalism'. It is true that what startled and horrified Wilberforce has become the datum of every modern biblical student, so that in that sense 'liberalism', as I suggested above, has died of its own victory. But has it really been victorious in this field? Not, I think, amongst the rank and file of Christians. Here, we may find old attitudes persisting, though often accompanied by a cheerful assumption —based on ignorance of scholarship or of the text itself— that no amount of 'reducing' can have had any real effect.

This rejuvenescence of Christianity within the last two decades, which is real enough to be attracting attention (favourable or otherwise) in the press, is usually ascribed to the loss of bearings, despair of politics, and a longing for reassurance in a frightening world. It is generally supposed, especially by those outside it, to imply a return to scholasticism and inflexible dogma (as a counterblast to Marxism), or a return to biblical fundamentalism. In either case it is interpreted as an obscurantist movement essentially hostile to liberal-humanism. According to this view, the 'neo-Christianity' of today would be a relapse into Catholicism or Protestantism; it would certainly not be a development along the lines laid down by *Essays and Reviews*. Two observations suggest themselves at this point: first, that Protestantism (of Romanism I do not speak here) could never have recovered its athletic tone without the slimming process inflicted upon it by the nineteenth century liberals. The second observation is that, in the course of shedding accretions and surplus beliefs, Christianity may after all (incredible as it may seem to many or most) have recovered—as Jowett thought possible—its own essential meaning. 'Is it to be held a thing impossible', Jowett had said, 'that the Christian Religion, instead of shrinking into itself, may again embrace the thoughts of men upon earth?' He goes on, 'Those who hold the possibility of such a reconcilement or restoration of belief are anxious to disengage Christianity from all suspicion of disguise or unfairness.' If it could be shown that there are any such today, then liberalism would not have foundered completely in the storms of hostile doctrines, but would have made its way, in however battered a state, into contemporary waters. I suggest that this is so; that there is a liberal Christianity alive today which, though not identical with (say) Jowett's, is an authentic development of it; and that the assumption, commonly made nowadays, of a necessary connexion between liberal-humanism and 'agnosticism' is incorrect. In order to support this view, I will now briefly examine a recent book in which I seem to see the spirit of nineteenth century liberalism alive and vigorous once more, yet wearing a new look appropriate to its twentieth century reincarnation. The book I mean is the one referred to above (cf. p. 138): *Kerygma and Myth*,[1] by Rudolf Bultmann and others, a book of which the general theme is 'the mythological element in the message of the New Testament', and of which the main task is that of 'demythologizing the New Testament proclamation [Kerygma]'.

[1] English translation first published 1953 (S.P.C.K.).

Bultmann's first move, as an English contributor[1] to the volume says, is 'to disarm prejudice by conceding all the anti-mythical objections with dramatic recklessness'. The old three-decker universe, Heaven, Earth and Hell, with its dramatis personae, divine and diabolical, its supernatural events, and its expected dramatic *dénouement*—all this has gone for ever. There was nothing specifically Christian in it; it was simply 'the cosmology of a pre-scientific age'. If the 'Kerygma' involves all this, then it is incredible to modern man, who is 'convinced that the mythical view of the world is obsolete'. All our thinking is now shaped, for good or ill, by science; we cannot and must not split our world-view into halves, reserving one for 'religion' and using the other for everyday life. We believe no longer in 'descending into hell' or in 'ascending into heaven', or in stellar influence, or evil spirits, or the mythical New Testament end-of-the-world, which was expected soon but did not come. The idea of original sin as an 'inherited infection' seems to us 'sub-ethical, irrational, and absurd'; we ask, too, why salvation should take the form of wearing heavenly robes in a realm of celestial light.

At this point, having apparently conceded—in the manner so popular with preachers—all that an infidel could advance, Bultmann pauses to offer earnest advice to pastors. There must be no mental reservations, no private selection or subtraction of which the listeners are not aware; parsons must be absolutely frank with their congregations about what they expect them to accept or reject. 'At all costs the preacher must not leave his people in the dark about what he secretly eliminates.'

Coming next to the definition of terms, Bultmann defines 'mythology' as 'the use of imagery to express the other-worldly in terms of this world and the divine in terms of human life, the other side in terms of this side'. Now, the importance of the New Testament mythology lies not in the imagery itself but in 'the understanding of existence which it enshrines. The real question is whether this understanding of existence is true. Faith claims that it is; and faith ought

[1] Austin Farrer, *ibid.*, p. 212.

not to be tied down to the imagery of the New Testament mythology.' Demythologizing is even forced upon us by the nature of the New Testament itself, where for example man is sometimes represented as determined by cosmic forces and sometimes as an autonomous 'I'. 'Side by side with the Pauline indicative stands the Pauline imperative.'

Now all this might have been said, and was said, by the old liberals of thirty or forty years ago—or should we not rather say, after considering *Essays and Reviews*, a hundred years ago? Bultmann is thinking of Harnack and the *Religionsgeschichtschule* (but we may think of Jowett and his like) when he says that the older liberal theologians were working on the wrong lines; they threw away not only the mythology, but with it the Kerygma itself. They fancied that they could eliminate the 'temporary garb' and yet retain the 'essence'—what Jowett called the 'eternal import', or an 'absolute morality' common to Plato and the Gospel. In one sense this sifting—eliminating the mythological and retaining the essential—is exactly what Bultmann himself is doing; the old liberalism and the new, however, differ over what the 'essence' precisely is. For the old liberals it consisted in the great, timeless, eternal truths which can be apprehended by the purified soul in mystical contemplation at all times, and history is not of paramount importance to religion. The new liberalism faces the fact that the New Testament speaks of an *event*, and that Christ is important less as a teacher than as a person who *is* this event. The "History of Religions School" saw indeed that Christian faith is not equivalent to religious idealism, and that Christian life is not simply a matter of fulfilling one's individual personality or making the world a better place. But they failed to see that in the New Testament the Christian 'detachment' is not mystical but 'eschatological'—is connected, that is, with a final and decisive event in history. Again the Kerygma has vanished; 'they are silent about a decisive act of God in Christ as the event of redemption'.

Bultmann discerns a movement, within the last twenty years, away from 'criticism' and back to a naïve acceptance of the Kerygma; this, he fears, may make the Gospel unintelligible to the modern world. What we have to do, then, is not to abandon liberalism, but to be wiser liberals, liberals on a twentieth century level: 'we cannot dismiss the critical labours of earlier generations without further ado. We must take them up and put them to constructive use'—interpreting mythology instead of eliminating it. We must try to recover the truth of the Kerygma for men who reject mythology, without at the same time forfeiting its character as Kerygma. How can this be done? By an existentialist interpretation, and by this alone. Bultmann means, I think, that the 'understanding of existence' underlying the New Testament myth of redemption, and expressed through it, is still relevant, and can give to modern man 'an understanding of himself which will challenge him to a genuine existential decision'. I suspect that the phrase 'existential decision' would have made Jowett's flesh creep. Its meaning, however, which I take to be a responsible decision about the sort of life one intends to live—would have been very familiar to him indeed, and he would have sympathized with those who a hundred years after him find the word 'existential' exciting, meaningful and 'contemporary'.[1] Anything, even a hideous new word, which can awaken a sense of the reality and momentousness of spiritual issues, would have had his approval. It is better in religion, as probably in the arts too, to say the old things in the ugly and complicated new way and *mean* them, than to go on repeating beautiful old expressions as clichés.

In his next section Bultmann asks what is human existence apart from Faith, that is, apart from an act of self-knowledge, leading to self-commitment (an act of 'existential choice') to unseen realities? Without such Faith, he finds, human existence is merely enslavement to 'the powers of this world'; it means basing one's life on 'the flesh'—that is, on the visible and tangible, which are transitory; it means the pursuit of self-contrived and self-regarding security. The life of faith, on the other hand, means life based upon unseen reality; self-commitment to God in expectation that all will come from his grace, nothing from ourselves. This state of un-

[1] I am told that for several months now it has been less fashionable.

worldly detachment—*not* asceticism, but knowing how to care and not to care—Bultmann calls 'eschatological existence'. This is another 'new-look' phrase, which seems to mean living in the presence, in the awareness and in the light of ultimate issues. To a man who so lives, the 'last things' are contemporaneous, redemption has already been realized; he is already a new creature, and the future has become present.

But life in faith 'cannot be exclusively expressed in indicative terms; it needs an imperative to complete it. In other words, the decision of faith is never final; it needs constant renewal in every fresh situation.' For the Christian, the Spirit which sanctifies, and witnesses within us to spiritual truth, is not the Gnostic or mystic 'immanent possession'; it is 'the possibility of a new life which must be appropriated by a deliberate resolve'. (In this way Bultmann frees 'Spirit' also from mythological implications.)

But further, this faith—this self-commitment and detachment—means, for the New Testament Christian, faith *in Christ*; it only becomes possible through and because of the *event*, which is Christ. Is this 'event' still, perhaps, a piece of mythology? Has our existentialist re-interpretation eliminated the Kerygma, just as that of the old liberals did? To answer this, Bultmann contrasts Christian existentialism with the secular existentialism of Heidegger and Kamlah. According to such thinkers, self-commitment is 'natural' to man; philosophic teaching releases within us the capacity to *become* what we *are*. We can 'become what we are'(i.e. what we 'ought' or 'are meant' to be?) by taking thought: by understanding and reflection. The New Testament agrees with these philosophers, says Bultmann, in teaching that 'authentic life' is only possible because it is already in some sense in existence; but the New Testament does not so address the *homo naturalis*—only the 'redeemed in Christ. The 'natural man' cannot be what he was meant to be. It is not enough to be told about your 'authentic' nature; the actual (as distinct from the theoretical) possibility of realizing it has been lost. Self-commitment is not achieved by one's own efforts, but as a gift from God. Self-assertion leads man to *think* of existence as a prize within his grasp; to think of fair shares of fortune; to indulge in self-pity, and so forth. All this is 'sin'. Sin is overcome, in an acceptable and non-mythological sense, when the love of God meets man and treats him 'as if he were other than he is'. 'At the very point where man can do nothing, God steps in and acts.' 'God has acted, and the world—"this world"—has come to an end' —i.e. 'eschatological existence' has become possible. Faith, it now becomes possible to say, is not just faith in 'abstract' or unseen 'reality'; it is faith in the love of God. And faith in the love of God, unless it is to be mere wishful thinking or subtle self-assertion, means faith in the love of God *as revealed in Christ.*

At this point Bultmann pauses; is there perhaps more demythologizing still to be done? Is not the position summarized in the last paragraph still expressed in mythological language? Anyone who thinks that 'God has acted', for example, is mythological language, is bound to answer 'yes'. One could have wished that here Bultmann had considered more fully two questions: one from an unsympathetic reader who might ask: "At what point in history can it be said that God has *not* acted?" and the other from a sympathizer who might exclaim (with Francis Newman or Dean Mansel), "But surely *all* language purporting to describe God's 'acts', his being and attributes, or even language purporting to describe 'things in themselves' (Nature), is necessarily approximative, figurative, mythical, or mythological?" However, Bultmann's aim is to construct a statement which will not *seem* mythological (and therefore false) to a hard-headed modern man. So he goes on to ask whether the 'event of Christ' is mythical? He replies that it is a unique combination of myth and history: the pre-existent Word with Jesus the carpenter; the historical crucifixion with the 'definitely non-historical' resurrection. Having, as it seems, let slip the last statement almost in a casual aside, as if it were a commonly accepted view, he pauses to apply a little further demythologizing to the Crucifixion and the Resurrection. All the current myths about the Crucifixion (the vicarious sacrifice theories) are a hotchpotch of sacrificial and juridical analogies which have ceased to be tenable for us today.

Belief in the Cross, then, does not mean belief in a mythical external process; it means making the Cross our own, being crucified to 'this world'. The Crucifixion (historical event though it be) is thus inseparable from the (non-historical) Resurrection, which is the New Testament's attempt to convey the meaning of the Cross. Christ's death was itself the victory over the power of death, and did not need any physical resurrection to 'reverse' it. The Resurrection, then, is not to be regarded as 'a miraculous proof capable of demonstration and sufficient to convince the sceptic that the Cross really has the cosmic and eschatological significance ascribed to it'. Bultmann calls 'the legend of the empty tomb and the appearances' 'most certainly later embellishments of the primitive tradition'. Other such miracles are not unknown to mythology. Moreover, if the Resurrection *were* a demonstrable fact, a proved miracle, belief would be compulsory, and would no longer be an act of faith, an 'existential choice'. But in fact the Resurrection is 'far more than the resuscitation of a corpse'—it is an article of faith, an affirmation that *we* are now dead to sin, but alive to God in Christ.

But the question will still be asked, How do we come to believe in the saving efficacy of the Cross? Why does the contemplation of it bring us to the point of making the 'existential choice' of a life which is crucified to the world and sin? Would it do so unless we already believed in the divinity of Christ on other (and probably miraculous) grounds? Is it not a distortion of history to make out that the Resurrection was the New Testament's attempt to express the meaning of the Crucifixion? Was it not rather their belief in a 'historical' Resurrection which led the New Testament writers to interpret the Cross correctly? Bultmann does not deal with problems of this kind, but he has his own answer to the question of how we come to believe in the saving efficacy of the Cross. We believe in it because (or rather, if?) we believe the proclamation, the Kerygma, the summons, the 'word of preaching' contained in the Gospels. Christ meets us here, and he meets us nowhere else. Why does this proclamation challenge us to the decisive existential choice? Because it 'confronts us as the word of God'—which means, I take it, that it carries upon it a divine imprint, and speaks to us with commanding authority. We do not try to 'prove' its truth by historical research; *it* proves *us* by demanding of us an act of self-understanding; it poses us with a demand for decision: are we prepared to understand ourselves as crucified with Christ and risen with him?—that is, to live 'eschatologically'?

Christ 'meets us in the word of preaching and nowhere else'—what does this mean? It means first, presumably, that we need expect to find no 'historical Jesus' behind the New Testament Kerygma, as the old liberals hoped to do. It means, further, that our own conviction is acquired by infection, as it were, from the ardent certainty of St Paul and the evangelists, and from the same certainty as mediated and transmitted by the Church. What certainty? That in Christ God had 'acted', that Christ was an event, *the* event, which has power to constrain us to the saving decision. Bultmann appears to teach that the modern man can be so affected, can hold the faith in his sense, although the certainty of the New Testament and the Church was inseparably bound up with the mythology he discards. We can only be affected by that part of the Kerygma to which the scientific world-view has not rendered us allergic.

All this is very well, but one may be disposed to ask in what respect Bultmann thinks his liberalism superior to that of the nineteenth century modernists? Has he really demythologized the New Testament without himself forfeiting the essence of the Kerygma? What he has left of the Kerygma seems hard to distinguish from, say, Jowett's residuum: that the true basis of Christianity is the re-enactment within the soul of the life and death of Christ—a Christ risen indeed, but not in a physical sense. Stripped of its existentialist jargon, Bultmann's theme is virtually that of *Essays and Reviews*, as expressed for instance by A. P. Stanley in the statement (quoted above, p. 174) that we feel an 'increasing difficulty' in accepting wonders as the proof of divine revelation rather than the contents of the revelation itself. Each century, each generation, must make its affirmations in its own language (whether these affirmations be theological,

183

poetical, musical or architectural), and it is well that Bultmann, though saying little more than was said by Jowett,
should be saying it in the idiom of today. No one will listen
now to Jowett, but Bultmann's twentieth century overtones
and complexities may carry the same message alive into the
hearts of present-day readers. With a few examples of these
overtones I will conclude this chapter.

In the very interesting section of *Kerygma and Myth* called
"Bultmann replies to his critics", he argues that Christianity,
unlike Pantheism, is not an anterior philosophical conviction
that God is 'in all' or 'acts always'. Those who have endured
the hardships of a modern prison camp 'know better than
anyone else that you cannot say *terra ubique domini* as an
explicit dogma; it is something which can be uttered only on
specific occasions in existential decision'. The paradox of
faith is that while it certainly transcends 'the closed weft of
cause and effect' it does so *not* in the manner of mythology,
that is by 'miracle'. The old-fashioned belief in miracle
simply 'surrenders the acts of God to objective observation',
and thus becomes both superstitious and also vulnerable to
the 'justifiable criticisms of science'. But, it may be objected,
if an 'act of God' can only be spoken of in relation to our
own existence, does this not reduce it to the status of a subjective experience? If God is 'no more than an experience in
the soul', how shall we answer those who insist that 'faith
only makes sense when it is directed towards a God with a
real existence outside the believer'? Bultmann, virtually re-
assuming the position taken by Coleridge nearly 150 years
ago, replies: 'That God cannot be seen apart from faith does
not mean that he does not exist apart from it. . . . True, it
is impossible to prove that faith is related to its object. But
. . . it is just here that its strength lies. For if it were susceptible of proof it would mean that we could know and establish
God apart from faith, and that would be placing him on a
level with the world of tangible, objective reality'—a world
in which we are certainly allowed and compelled to demand
proof.

In like manner, 'Scripture' can only be intelligibly called
'the word of God' *when* it evokes religious experience in us.

'That Scripture is the word of God' is not an objective fact susceptible of proof, it is something that *happens*—and 'happens only in the here and now of encounter'. Bultmann does not explain what differentiates the Hebrew scriptures, in that case, from any other scriptures, works of art or natural objects, which may 'evoke religious experience in us'. But he is at his best when he insists that religious knowledge cannot be 'possessed as a timeless truth, for its validity depends upon its being constantly renewed, and upon an understanding of the imperative it involves'. Faith 'needs to be emancipated from a world-view expressed in objective terms, whether it be a mythical or a scientific one'. The conflict between the mythological cosmology of the Bible and the scientific world-view, as long as that conflict exists and has meaning, shows that faith has 'not yet discerned the proper terms in which to express itself; it has not realized that it cannot be logically proven; it has not clearly understood that its basis and its object are identical; it has not clearly apprehended the transcendental and hidden character of the divine activity, and by its failure to perceive its own "Nevertheless" it has tried to project God and his acts into the sphere of objective reality. God withdraws himself from the objective view: he can only be believed in defiance of all outward appearance.' Summing up, Bultmann asserts of his argument that 'starting as it does from the modern world view, and challenging the Biblical mythology and the traditional proclamation of the Church, this new kind of criticism is performing for faith the supreme service of recalling it to a radical consideration of its own nature'. The same could have been said of *Essays and Reviews*, and of much other liberal and agnostic writing of that age.

CHAPTER V

"*MARK RUTHERFORD*"
(William Hale White, 1831-1913)

'A childlike faith in the old creed is no longer possible, but it is equally impossible to surrender it' [*Pages from a Journal*, p. 86].

1. Tanner's Lane

'LOOK', exclaimed Matthew Arnold in a well-known passage of *Culture and Anarchy*, 'look at the life imaged in such a newspaper as the *Nonconformist*; —a life of jealousy of the Establishment, disputes, tea-meetings, openings of chapels, sermons; and then think of it as an ideal of human life completing itself on all sides, and aspiring with all its organs after sweetness, light and perfection!' This, amongst many other things, is exactly what Hale White did in the "Mark Rutherford" novels, and since the Dissidence of Dissent and the Protestantism of the Protestant religion have not figured largely in our previous Studies, let us take a look at them now through his eyes. There are also other reasons why we should consider him; one is his literary excellence. 'L'écriture de Hale White', wrote André Gide in his *Journal* (1936), 'est d'une transparence exquise, d'une scintillante pureté. Il mène à perfection des qualités que je voudrais miennes'; 'his art is made of the renunciation of all false riches'.[1] D. H. Lawrence, thinking more of Hale White's essential integrity (of which his style was the index), praised him three times in his letters: 'How good he is!— so just, so harmonious.' 'I've read the *Revolution in Tanner's Lane*, and find myself fearfully fond of Rutherford. I used to think him dull, but now I see he is so just and plucky and sound. . . .' 'I have always greater respect for Mark Rutherford: I *do* think he is jolly good—so thorough, so sound, and so beautiful.'[2] Above all, he concerns us in these Studies as an embodiment of the Puritan spirit adrift in the Age of

[1] Quoted by Catherine Maclean, *Mark Rutherford* (1955), pp. 222, 292.
[2] *The Letters of D. H. Lawrence*, pp. 81, 82, 179.

Agnosticism. In him Bunyan's Pilgrim takes the road again, but now far more defenceless and with no certain destination; he meets new Apollyons, he strives, and—after taking many a fall—only barely prevails. Nor is his prevailing such as his prototype would have recognized as victorious. Yet, in spite of 'doubts, disputes, distractions, fears', he never joined the agnostic band; God was his quest, and deliverance his theme, from beginning to end of his long struggle. It was a struggle, not only with principalities and powers in high places, but with the demons of self-distrust and nervous melancholy within himself. Because of his introversion, his work is not only intense and concentrated but also narrow in scope. He had no free creativeness, no imaginative fecundity; he could only write of what he knew and felt. He told his second wife, in his old age, that he had 'never *created* a character in his life: he had always had somebody before his mind's eye'.[1] Of what is called 'literary ambition' he had none; he hid for years behind his pseudonym; he had a morbid dread of becoming a merely 'literary' character, and disliked all 'literary criticism' that was not criticism of life. 'I wish I had never written stories', he told Dorothy Horace Smith (afterwards Mrs White) in 1909; 'they are somewhat of a degradation. If I had been given you as a wife when I was thirty I would never have let the public hear a syllable from me.'[2] 'How much I might have gained had I taken life as an art I cannot say', he comments in one of his notebooks.[3] He could not take life so; he could only take it, in grim earnest, as a pilgrimage, a conflict, and an endlessly unsatisfied longing. Enjoyment, to him, was more difficult than self-denial. The need to 'take pains to secure pleasure' proved (he thought) his 'sour graceless nature'.

If he could not take life as an art, neither could he take art as a life. He was of that select company whose writing is a by-product, not a first call; like Bunyan, he produced fine prose as it were absent-mindedly, that is, with his mind intent upon the pilgrimage itself. Indeed the excellence of

---

[1] Dorothy V. White, *The Groombridge Diary* (1924), p. 66.
[2] *Ibid.*, p. 176.
[3] *More Pages from a Journal* (1910), p. 258.

his style is achieved not in spite of, but because of, his concentration upon the one thing needful to him—the search
for God. To set down anything not authentic, anything
purely fictitious, seemed to him a self-betrayal, a 'degradation'. This meant that he could not be a 'creative artist' in
the accepted sense; it meant that his own life-experience,
outward and still more inward, and the people and places he
had himself known, must be his only raw-material. But,
given his superiority of mind, it was precisely this Puritan
concern for what is genuine, this fastidious rejection of anything shoddy or tawdry or second-hand, which produced a
literary style so distinguished for transparency, austerity,
reticence and grave beauty. Hale White's father, himself a
man of distinction and a writer, had from earliest years
taught him to value truth and purity of expression: "My
boy," he told him, "if you write anything you consider
particularly fine, strike it out." In one of his father's own
writings, a relevant saying is quoted from Burkitt (a seventeenth century rector of Dedham): "Painted glass is very
beautiful, but plain glass is the most useful as it lets in the
most light." Hale White tells us that he has visited Dedham,
and what he says of its landscape applies also to the effect he
himself produces upon sympathetic readers: 'It is Constable's
country, and in its way is not to be matched in England.
Although there is nothing striking in it, its influence, at least
upon me, is greater than that of celebrated mountains and
waterfalls. What a power there is to subdue and calm in
those low hills. . . .!'[1]

We may think of Hale White, to begin with, as a mal-
content provincial, or to use one of his recurrent images, 'a
wild seagull in a farm-yard of peaceful, clucking, brown-
speckled fowls'.[2] In this, as in many other things, he re-
sembles George Eliot—that Theresa of the Midland flats,
that cygnet among the ducklings of Warwickshire; both
were provincials with an intense need and longing to transcend the limitations of an early environment to which,

---

[1] *Early Life of Mark Rutherford, by Himself* (Oxford, 1913), pp. 31-2.
[2] *Revolution in Tanner's Lane* (1923 ed., p. 86). Cf. 'an Arabian bird . . .
with the ordinary barn-door fowls' (*Deliverance*, do., p. 40).

nevertheless, they were bound by the strongest ties and from which, when they came to write, they derived their imaginative power. Hale White knew Marian Evans in the days of Chapman and the *Westminster Review*; he adored her then from what he felt to be a great distance, and she remained for him, throughout most of his life, an ideal and an aspiration. He reproached himself, in later years, for having allowed the friendship to lapse; this, like his missing the opportunity of seeing Rachel, and of meeting Caroline Fox, was the result of his constitutional diffidence and self-depreciation. 'The curse for me', he says in "Confessions of a Self-Tormentor", 'has not been plucking forbidden fruit, but the refusal of divine fruit offered me by heavenly angels.'[1] He never could believe that anybody—least of all any celebrity—would care to meet him or know him: hence, no doubt, the number of characters in his books whose friendly advances are met with coldness and indifference.

In thus linking Hale White's name with George Eliot's, however, I am thinking much less of his early affection and lasting admiration for one who seemed to him great both in mind and in heart, than of the real intellectual and spiritual affinities between them. With far less copiousness and vitality, with less humour and invention, and with sympathies less widely distributed, Hale White as a novelist may be regarded as a minor George Eliot. The patterns of their inner lives were similar: from narrow, intense provincial piety, through emancipation, to a hard-won and precariously held religion of the heart and conscience. Both had deep roots in their provincial past, both had tenacious memories and the power to re-create the scenes and people of their early lives; both took religion seriously, recognizing the central importance of Church and Chapel in the society they were studying, but alive also to the complex interweaving of religion with the secular caste-system. Hale White returns to his Bedford, as George Eliot to her Warwickshire towns and farms, with the sense that here he belongs, knows his bearings, understands the language and thoughts of the inhabitants—far as he has journeyed meanwhile from that City

[1] *More Pages from a Journal* (1910), p. 120.

of Destruction. Both wrote their novels partly as a kind of expiation or exculpation for their break with the past, as a disguised confession, as an indirect appeal for sympathy, as an attempt to prove to themselves and to others that they were not travelling unprofitably towards the grave. What George Eliot did for rural and small-town Anglicanism in *Scenes of Clerical Life*, Hale White did for Bedford Nonconformity of the mid-nineteenth century. No English novelist had written thus of Dissenting life and thought from within, though others had satirized it from a distance. The Mark Rutherford novels, if they had no other merits (but they have many others), would survive as an indispensable chapter of social history.

It may seem strange to call Bedford, as I have just done, 'the City of Destruction': Bedford, the very core of whose religious life was the 'Bunyan Meeting' itself, in which Hale White was nurtured. But the paradox was intentional, for the rhythm of history had turned that Puritan core to stone, and reduced the life of its members to a cold mechanism. Hale White's life was the pilgrimage of a man of profoundly religious temper who, suffocated by the stale breath of his native conventicle, strikes out into the open to look there for the God he could not find within, and breathes new life from Nature and from the secular breezes that blew across the century: from Spinoza, from Goethe, from Wordsworth and Carlyle.

The classic re-creations of the ethos of Bedford nonconformity are to be found at the opening of *The Autobiography of Mark Rutherford* (1881), in the second part of *The Revolution in Tanner's Lane* (1887), and in *Catherine Furze* (1893). In reading the *Autobiography* (and its sequel *The Deliverance*) it must always be remembered that we are not simply reading the autobiography of Hale White. Not only are some of the main events fictitious or modified, but "Mark Rutherford" himself is a projection from Hale White's personality, not the whole of it. He is Hale White's *alter ego*: that in himself which he had to distance, to see objectively; that which he often judged most severely, and tried to transcend. '"I wish sometimes I could write, as a warning, a real history of my own inner life," he said in later years, "but it would be too dangerous. . . . I wish sometimes that Saul could have written something for us. It would not have been a Psalm.'"[1] It will not do to say that "Mark Rutherford" is Saul to Hale White's David—though sometimes, when one compares the dereliction and squalor of Mark's existence with the outward prosperity of Hale White the well-placed Civil Servant, one may be tempted to think so. In dealing with a character so complex, so self-inwrought, as Hale White's, no such simple analysis will suffice. There was Saul in him to the very last— black moods of despair and horror ('ever the damning, cold hand on all pleasure, forbidding gratitude')—and, conversely, there are touches of David in "Mark Rutherford" (in his sacrificial slum-work, for example), so that sometimes he becomes a wish-fulfilment, a projection not of what Hale White condemned in himself, but of what he aspired to be and to do. He habitually saw both sides of every question, every situation and every character (including his own). But there was a side which he naturally saw, and another which he forced himself to see. And though he is always returning upon himself, fighting against his own desponding thoughts, trying to deal justly with what he has condemned—though, for example, he finds deep truth in the creed he has outgrown —it is on the whole a Saul's-eye view that he gives of the religion of his boyhood and youth. Nor can one doubt the essential truth of his report; it was Puritanism in decline that he knew at Bedford and at New College, a Puritanism petrified and mammonized, clinging to shibboleths without real conviction, perpetuating old forms from which the life had departed. What he came to value was the intellectual rigour of Calvin, the impassioned spirituality of Bunyan, the stern republicanism of nonconformity in its prime: never the religion of Tanner's Lane in the reign of the Rev. John Broad. He may round upon "Mark Rutherford" (and other characters in his novels) for spiritual pride in condemning the people to whom he felt himself becoming superior, yet Tanner's Lane and 'Cowfold' were that from which he must at all costs escape.

[1] *Groombridge Diary*, p. 78.

First for the Sundays, 'a season of unmixed gloom', when no book 'more secular than the Evangelical Magazine' was tolerated, when 'we never had a hot dinner even in the coldest weather' (except for 'a boiled suet pudding which cooked itself while we were at chapel'), and no letter was opened 'unless it was clearly evident that it was not on business'—and even then put aside for Monday reading if a cursory glance showed it to contain no urgent message. Mrs Coleman's Sunday tea-party, with its attendant casuistry, illustrates the quality of this sabbatarianism. Major Cartwright and the Caillauds were expected, so

> 'Mrs Coleman, although it was Sunday, was very busy. She had made hot buttered toast, and she had bought some muffins, but had appeased her conscience by telling the boy that she would not pay for them till Monday. The milk was always obtained on the same terms. She also purchased some water-cresses, but the water-cress man demanded prompt cash settlement, and she was in a strait. At last the desire for the water-cresses prevailed, and she said "How much?"
>
> '"Three half-pence."
>
> '"Now, mind I give you two pence for yourself—mind I give it you. I do not approve of buying and selling on Sunday. We will settle about the other ha'porth another time."
>
> '"All right ma'am; if you like it that way, it's no odds to me"; and Mrs. Coleman went her way upstairs really believing that she had prevented the commission of a crime.'

Although Mrs Coleman symbolizes all that was most repugnant in Hale White's early life and religion—probably embodying too what was least sympathetic in his own mother—he compels himself even here, in a characteristic comment, to see the other side: 'Let those of us cast the stone who can take oath that in their own morality there is no casuistry. Probably ours is worse than hers, because hers was traditional and ours is self-manufactured.'[1]

Inside the crowded Meeting-house, where (it is perhaps surprising to learn) the clarinet, flute, violin and cello still led the singing, as at Hardy's Mellstock, the young Mark

---

[1] *Revolution in Tanner's Lane*, pp. 82-3.

Rutherford suffered alike from the foul atmosphere ('the glass panes streaming with wet inside, and women carried out fainting') and from asphyxiation of mind and spirit:

'Each service consisted of a hymn, reading the Bible, another hymn, a prayer, the sermon, a third hymn, and a short final prayer. The reading of the Bible was unaccompanied with any observations or explanations, and I do not remember that I ever once heard a mistranslation corrected. The first, or long prayer, as it was called, was a horrible hypocrisy, and it was a sore tax on the preacher to get through it. Anything more totally unlike the model recommended to us in the New Testament cannot well be imagined. It generally began with a confession that we were all sinners, but no individual sins were ever confessed, and then ensued a kind of dialogue with God, very much resembling the speeches which in later years I have heard in the House of Commons from the movers and seconders of addresses to the Crown at the opening of Parliament. In all the religion of that day nothing was falser than the long prayer. Direct appeal to God can only be justified when it is passionate. To come maundering into His presence when we have nothing particular to say is an insult, upon which we should never presume if we had a petition to offer to any earthly personage. Nobody ever listened to this performance. . . . The sermon was not much better. . . . The minister invariably began with the fall of man; propounded the scheme of redemption, and ended by depicting in the morning the blessedness of the saints, and in the evening the doom of the lost.'[1]

When he reached the age of about fourteen, he was told it was time he became 'converted'. Hale White does not deny that conversion is a fact of spiritual experience; not only in apostolic times but ever since, under the influence of powerful preaching or indeed of earthly love, men have suddenly put off the old man and put on the new. What he denies is that the routine 'conversions' of Tanner's Lane had any meaning:

'I knew that I had to be "a child of God", and after a time professed myself to be one, but I cannot call to mind that I was anything

[1] *Autobiography* (10th ed.), pp. 6-7.

else than I always had been, save that I was perhaps a little more hypocritical; not in the sense that I professed to others what I knew I did not believe, but in the sense that I professed it to myself. I was obliged to declare myself convinced of sin; convinced of the efficacy of the atonement; convinced that I was forgiven; convinced that the Holy Ghost was shed abroad in my heart; and convinced of a great many other things which were the merest phrases. . . . It was the custom to demand of each candidate a statement of his or her experience. I had no experience to give; and I was excused on the ground that I had been the child of pious parents, and consequently had not undergone that convulsion which those, not favoured like myself, necessarily underwent when they were called.'[1]

The only noticeable result was that he was now expected to attend, and did attend, the extra prayer-meetings held exclusively for the initiates. He quite enjoyed the feel.ng of belonging to the privileged inner circle, but his candour compels him to add

'that the evening meetings afforded us many opportunities for walking home with certain young women, who, I am sorry to say, were a more powerful attraction, not only to me but to others, than the prospect of hearing brother Holderness, the travelling draper, confess crimes which, to say the truth, although they were many according to his own account, were never given in that detail which would have made his confession of some value. He never prayed without telling all of us that his soul was a mass of putrefying sores; but everybody thought the better of him for his self-humiliation. One actual indiscretion, however, brought home to him would have been visited by suspension or expulsion.'

The minister of this congregation (called in *Tanner's Lane* the Rev. John Broad) was a fitting embodiment of its prevailing tone. Unlike his predecessor the Rev. James Harden, who had really 'wrestled even unto blood with the world, the flesh, and the devil in Cowfold for thirty years', and 'would send an arrow sharp and swift through any iniquity, no matter where it might couch', Mr Broad was 'moderate',

<hr>

[1] *Ibid.*, pp. 10-11.

that is to say nebulous, in all his views: neither too Calvinist nor too Arminian, 'not rigid upon Baptism', neutral in politics, and anxious to conciliate all parties—especially those who paid a substantial pew-rent. Since Mr Harden's time the congregation had apparently undergone no change, but in reality its fervid Evangelical piety had sunk to ashes. Mr Broad was 'a big, gross-feeding, heavy person with heavy ox-face and large mouth, who might have been bad enough for anything if nature had ordained that he should have been born in a hovel at Sheepgate or in the Black Country'. Hale White allows that he was not 'an ordinary novel or stage hypocrite' (though he is a Chadband more searchingly probed than Dickens's); he did not doubt his own doctrine, 'yet he could not believe as Harden believed'. He was up-right—if 'a little greedy and hard'—scrupulously respect-able, and 'temperate in his drink'. In his drink, but not 'in his meat': 'supper was his great meal, and he would then con-sume beef, ham, or sausages, hot potatoes, mixed pickles, fruit pies, bread, cheese and celery in quantities which were remarkable even in those days.'[1]

It need hardly be said that the denominational distinctions in Cowfold (or 'Eastthorpe', in *Catherine Furze*) had little theological or spiritual meaning, but corresponded closely with its elaborate class- or caste-system. Thus the doctor and the inn-landlord (of Cowfold) supported the Establishment, though they seldom went to church and 'were charitably excused because of their peculiar calling'. 'The rest of Cow-fold was Dissenting or "went nowhere".' The Wesleyan Chapel (an imported affair, with no roots in the town) was 'supported mainly by the brewer', because though he was 'not in trade' and objected to being classified with those who 'stood behind counters', the Church did not suit him, for there the wealthy Mr and Mrs Muston, and the Seminary for Young Ladies, stood in his way. When Mrs Furze, the ironmonger's wife, proposes the move from the shop to 'The Terrace', she has in mind also a consequential transfer from Chapel to Church: '"there is no denying",' she urges upon her reluctant spouse, '"that the people who go to

---

[1] *Revolution in Tanner's Lane*, pp. 252-4.

church are vastly more genteel, and so are the service and everything about it—the vespers—the bells—somehow there is a respectability in it."[1]

Hale White tells us, in his non-fictional *Early Life* (1913), that his own mother had 'a slight weakness in favour of rank', and was 'a little weak in her preference for people who did not stand behind counters'. It is safe to guess, with a writer like Hale White, that Mrs Furze, Mrs Coleman and other embodiments of the old, unawakened provincial spirit—with its snobbery, its inaccessibility to ideas, and its sectarian rigidity—are modelled from his mother. Hale White was essentially a father's son, and there is no reason to believe that he owed much to his mother except his nervous temperament and his abortive training for the Independent Ministry. The hero of his early life was his father, William White, to whom he looked up, and from the thought of whom he drew strength, to the very last. The portrait of his father—a profile silhouette—was always before him in his study, and as a man of over eighty he could say that this portrait, 'erect, straightforward-looking, firmly standing, one foot a little in advance, helps me and decides me when I look at it'.[2] Amidst so many foreheads villainous low, amidst all the intellectual nullity of 'Cowfold', William White stood out conspicuously as a man of true intelligence, a reader of Milton and Byron and Carlyle, a man whose interests and whose life (in a favourite phrase of his son's) 'touched the universal' at various points—a man, that is, concerned with ideas and not merely with petty particulars of day-to-day existence. He was a Puritan of the older, more heroic cast, one to whom religion involved politics, and radical politics at that. In 1832 he had not only been besieged in the Swan Inn, but had his own windows smashed by the mob for supporting the Reform Bill. Originally a bookseller, he was prominent in all local affairs, a trustee of the Bunyan Meeting and of the Bedford Charity, and an excellent public speaker. Of one of his speeches Lord Charles Russell, who had heard it along with others on the same

---

[1] *Catherine Furze*, p. 23.
[2] *Early Life*, p. 38 (where this portrait is also reproduced).

occasion, said, "His was the finest speech, and Sir David Dundas remarked to me, as Mr White concluded, 'Why that is old Cobbett again *minus* his vulgarity.'"[1] He later (1854) became doorkeeper to the House of Commons, holding this post for twenty-one years. It was through his acquaintance with the Russells that Hale White 'was permitted with him to call on Carlyle, an event amongst the greatest in my life, and all the happier for me because I did not ask to go'.

The mention of Carlyle brings us to the turning-point of our story. William White, by virtue of his powers and attainments, was already the prototype of the Zachariah Colemans and the Allens and Mark Rutherford himself—of the Puritan, that is, who rises above the limitations of his surroundings. But by 1851 he had still more strikingly exhibited this character, anticipating not only his son's development but also a central trend in nineteenth century nonconformity, by leaving the Bunyan Meeting. And according to Hale White (I have quoted this passage elsewhere),[2] it was Carlyle, above all—

'it was the *Heroes and Hero Worship* and the *Sartor Resartus* which drew him away from the meeting-house. There is nothing in these two books directly hostile either to church or dissent, but they laid hold on him as no books had ever held, and the expansion they wrought in him could not possibly tolerate the limitations of orthodoxy.'[3]

Few or none today owe their salvation or emancipation to Carlyle; few or none can find their religion in his pantheism, their church in his Temple of Nature, their Bible in literature (with special reference to Goethe, Jean Paul and Novalis), or their saints in Heroes. Indeed, 'emancipation' of this kind is the very last thing now looked for or regarded as spiritual progress. But one must try, by an effort of imagination, to realize that a hundred years ago Carlye's message did come upon many, especially (but not only) upon Puritans with growing-pains, of whom William White and his son were typical, with the force of a new revelation.

[1] *Ibid.*, p. 34.   [2] *Nineteenth Century Studies*, p. 103.
[3] *Early Life*, p. 38.

11. Within These Walls

At the very time when the father was crossing his Rubicon, the son was facing a comparable ordeal at the theological training-college. In 1848 Hale White, largely because his mother wanted him to be a minister like his cousin (her nephew) T. W. Chignell, had entered Cheshunt College; from thence he proceeded to New College, London, in 1851. It is not necessary to repeat in this context what has been said above (and what is in any case well known) about the corrosive agencies at work, during the 'fifties of the last century, upon the fabric of popular Protestantism, and especially upon its bibliolatry. Hale White may very possibly have caricatured or maligned Dr John Harris, his Principal at both Colleges, but his account of the attitude of College authority to free enquiry by the students is accurate enough, whether we read it in the *Autobiography* or in the *Early Life*. The College, as far as its formal instruction went, resolutely ignored the critical ferment then so actively working in the great world outside. Three students, of whom Hale White was one, were arraigned for heresy on the result of an examination about the Inspiration of Scripture. During the oral, two of them had enquired

> 'about the formation of the canon and the authenticity of the separate books. They were immediately stopped by the Principal in summary style. "I must inform you that this is not an open question within these walls. There is a great body of truth received as orthodoxy by the great majority of Christians, the explanation of which is one thing, but to doubt it another, and the foundation must not be questioned." '[1]

Accordingly the inquisitors confronted the suspects with the following test questions:

> ' "Will you explain the mode in which you conceive the sacred writers to have been influenced?"

[1] *Early Life*, p. 64. For a full account of this episode see Wilfred Stone, *Religion and Art of W. Hale White* (Stanford Univ. Press, 1954), ch. II. This is by far the best extant study of Hale White.

' "Do you believe a statement because it is in the Bible, or merely because it is true?"

' "You are aware that there are two great parties on this question, one of which maintains that the inspiration of the Scriptures differs in kind from that of other books: the other that the difference is only one of degree. To which of these parties do you attach yourself?"

' "Are you conscious of any divergence from the views expounded by the Principal in [his] introductory lecture?" ' [1]

Their answers to these formidable questions were considered ' "incompatible" with the "retention of our position as students" ' (as Hale White remarks, 'idiomatic English was clearly not a strong point with the council'), and, to cut the story short, they were expelled. The case became something of a *cause célèbre*; William White wrote a pamphlet, 'in defence of us', called *To Think or Not to Think* (1852), and received letters about it from F. D. Maurice and Charles Kingsley. Kingsley's letter (published in the *Early Life*, pp. 74 ff.) is characteristically ardent and emphatic; he hopes the young man will not fancy 'that such men as have expelled him are the real supporters of the Canon and inspiration of Scripture, and of orthodoxy in general', predicts ruin for the Church from the fatal compound of 'Calvinist doctrine with Rabbinical theories of magical inspiration', and ends by declaring that the true Faith should welcome 'continual inrushes of new light' from science and philology.

More than forty years later Hale White was writing a letter to a friend about clerical Subscription, and his thoughts went back to the crisis just described. 'If a man', he has been saying,

'to gain his own ends, repeats a phrase, which to the majority of his hearers conveys a sense different from that which he intends, he misleads; if he knows that he misleads, he lies. . . . There is no theological dogma so important as the duty of veracity. . . . Conceive, if you can, the prophet Elijah signing "as a pure convention" the 39 Articles of Baal in order that he might secure a platform from which to preach Jehovah to Baal's worshippers!'

[1] *Ibid.*, pp. 65-6.

He continues:

> 'More than forty years ago the whole course of my life was changed by my refusal to slur over a difference between myself and my teacher on the subject of the inspiration of the Bible. I might easily have told him "You and I mean really the same thing", or used some other current phrase contrived in order to stifle conscience. I might have succeeded in being content with a *mush* of lies and truth, a compound more poisonous than lies unmixed, but I was enabled to resist. I have never regretted the decision then taken. . . . I can see now that if I had yielded I should have been lost for ever.'[1]

It will not be supposed that this squeamishness about biblical inspiration was a maggot suddenly generated in the young man's brain. His intellectual honesty, his refusal to prevaricate, were part of that very Puritan birthright from which he was being outwardly cut off. But there was more in it than this; other influences had been silently at work in him for some years, processes of growth which had stretched his old doctrinal chrysalis to bursting-point. The impulse to make real to himself the dogmas he had received from outside, to reach through what was fixed and dead to some living centre within, had been coming more and more strongly upon him. 'The thoughts which have worked upon me, and perhaps changed me,' he wrote long afterwards,[2] 'have not been those which men usually consider the most important. . . . The discovery that the book of Leviticus was not written by Moses and that there were two Isaiahs has made no difference to me. . . . Many persons could not live without an active belief or disbelief in heaven and hell. Their existence or non-existence has never produced any effect on me correspondent to the magnitude of the question. . . .' What then did change him? Three influences he singles out as all-important: Spinoza, the stars, and Wordsworth. And of these it was Wordsworth who counted for most at the time we are speaking of; indeed, we may say that what Carlyle did for his father, Wordsworth did for him.

---

[1] *Letters to Three Friends* (1924), pp. 162-4.
[2] *Last Pages from a Journal* (1915), p. 88.

III. Wordsworth

In the *Autobiography*, Mark Rutherford picks up the *Lyrical Ballads* while he is at College, and though it conveyed no new doctrine, yet

> 'the change it wrought in me could only be compared with that which is said to have been wrought on Paul himself by the Divine apparition'.[1]

What sort of change? Nothing that can be put neatly into a phrase; what Wordsworth did was to excite in him 'a movement and a growth which went on till, by degrees, all the systems which enveloped me like a body gradually decayed from me and fell away into nothing'. Wordsworth encouraged in him the 'habit of inner reference, and a dislike to occupy myself with anything which did not in some way or other touch the soul, or was not the illustration or embodiment of some spiritual law'. The theology of the Bunyan Meeting, and of New College, had not touched his soul; it had been proffered as a fixed and closed scheme, *natura naturata*, supernaturally certified and expressible only in technical language. Mark Rutherford had 'accepted' it, but it had not been 'born from within him'. He now began to search for the *natura naturans*, the living natural core and original meaning of this theology, and 'it was precisely this reaching after a meaning which constituted heresy. Heresy began, and in fact was altogether present, when I said to myself that mere statement of the atonement as taught in class was impossible for me, and that I must go back to Paul and his century, place myself in his position, and connect the atonement through him with something which I felt.' And Wordsworth—how does he come into all this? I have quoted elsewhere[2] the following passage, which however is so central for this chapter that I must repeat it here:

> 'There is, of course, a definite explanation to be given of one effect produced by the "Lyrical Ballads". God is nowhere formally deposed, and Wordsworth would have been the last man to say that

---

[1] *Autobiography*, pp. 18-21. [2] *Nineteenth Century Studies*, p. 118.

he had lost his faith in the God of his fathers. But his real God is not the God of the Church, but the God of the hills, the abstraction Nature, and to this my reverence was transferred. Instead of an object of worship which was altogether artificial, remote, never coming into genuine contact with me, I had now one which I thought to be real, one in which literally I could live and move and have my being, an actual fact present before my eyes. God was brought from that heaven of the books, and dwelt on the downs in the far-away distances, and in every cloud-shadow which wandered across the valley. Wordsworth unconsciously did for me what every religious reformer has done—he recreated my Supreme Divinity; substituting a new and living spirit for the old deity, once alive, but gradually hardened into an idol.'

In the *Early Life* we have much the same account, except that there Hale White discovers Wordsworth at home, at the age of eighteen. It ends with the remark that 'it was Wordsworth and not German research which caused my expulsion from New College'. The naïve and rather sentimental pantheism of the passage just quoted (sentimental, because we are not to find God on the downs unless we also find him in the depths) was a thing he outgrew: 'When first I read Wordsworth I saw God in Nature. As I grew older I felt a difficulty in saying so much'[1]—there were storm, flood and drought in Nature; there were disease and pain; there were Behemoth and Leviathan. But Wordsworth had added something to the 'wonder and glory of the world', and 'the "something added" has always remained and will remain as long as I live'. The love of natural beauty, which Wordsworth had awakened, not only remained but grew more intense with advancing age; it produced, as he says, a 'secret joy' strong enough to make him 'careless of the world and of its pleasures'. He owed to Nature not only joy, but relief from pain. For Hale White, like many others (Wordsworth among them) who have felt Nature's healing power, was all his life subject to fits of black depression, and to this mind diseased, this rooted sorrow, Nature could minister better than any other physician.

[1] *Last Pages from a Journal,* p. 94.

iv. Apollyon

No account of Hale White would be complete or intelligible without some reference to this 'hypochondria', which attacked him soon after he left College, and never permanently relaxed its grip for the rest of his life—though he learnt by degrees how to deal with it. He was, presumably, of the manic-depressive type, and it would be misleading to ascribe his moods of 'black, moveless gloom' to his religious doubts. He himself came to believe that they were physical in origin, though they constantly masqueraded in intellectual disguises. Mrs D. V. White has summarized his life after the expulsion from New College thus:

'. . . he went for six months to Portsmouth, apparently for no particular purpose; then, for something to do, took a mastership, after two days left the school with "the horrors", went to some friend . . ., got work at Chapman's, and there met George Eliot.'[1]

The *Autobiography* and the *Early Life* give differing accounts of this period; Mark Rutherford enters the ministry, whereas Hale White himself never did (though he 'supplied' the pulpit at a small Unitarian Chapel at Ditchling in 1856-1857). But both books refer to the two-days' horror at the school, and the *Early Life* points to it as the first onset of his lifelong trouble:

'Then there fell upon me what was the beginning of a trouble which has lasted all my life.'[2]

Bunyan, with whom Hale White had so much in common, knew this experience, as any reader of *Grace Abounding* will remember: 'down fell I, as a bird that is shot from the top of a tree, into great guilt and fearful despair. I went moping into the fields, but God knows, with as heavy a heart as mortal man, I think, could bear.' Bunyan's despairs, though they may (like Hale White's) have been neurotic in origin, invariably assumed a theological form; they were due, above all, to doubts of his own salvation, or (as in the quoted example) to capitulation, after agonizing struggles, to the

---

[1] *Groombridge Diary*, pp. 71-2.   [2] *Early Life*, p. 80.

third-degree suggestions of Satan. Hale White, as we have partly seen, was not troubled by such doubts as Bunyan's— doubts about his 'election', about hell-fire, about the authority of the Scriptures. He did not torment himself, as Bunyan did, with the illusion that he had sinned more deeply than Judas Iscariot because, after battling for weeks against the words "Sell Him! Sell Him!" repeated incessantly in his mind by what William James calls 'verbal automatism' (but Bunyan called The Tempter), he had yielded in a moment of fatigue to the suggestion "Let Him go if He will." With Hale White the melancholia was rather a nameless terror, a sense of innermost abandonment, a panic-fear of the Gorgon's Head; but it is clear that this often took definite shape in some obsession or *idée fixe*. In the *Autobiography* Mark Rutherford fancied that his brain was failing: 'for months— many months, this dreadful conviction of coming idiocy or insanity lay upon me like some poisonous reptile with its fangs driven into my very marrow, so that I could not shake it off'. He did not know then, what he learned later, 'that this fixity of form is a frequent symptom of the disease, and that the general weakness manifests itself in a determinate horror, which gradually fades with returning health'.[1] There is some evidence that, when in a state of dereliction or weakness, he could be prostrated also by ideas unconnected with himself, provided that they were of a kind to stand as intellectualizations of his plight. Thus Zachariah Coleman (one of his many partial self-portraits), when recovering from an illness, came upon Ferguson's *Astronomy* and read there that the earth, a subordinate planet in the vast abysses of space, would one day surely fall into the sun. This idea pierced him with its 'fang', and in helpless misery he wished he had never opened the book. Hale White's comment on this proceeds so clearly from his own dearly purchased wisdom that Zachariah's experience may be taken as his own:

'It is an experience, I suppose, not new that in certain diseased conditions some single fear may fasten on the wretched victim so that he is almost beside himself. He is unaware that this fear in

[1] *Early Life*, p. 36.

itself is of no importance, for it is nothing but an index of ill health, which might find expression in a hundred other ways. He is unconscious of his ill health except through his fancy and regards it as an intellectual result. . . . However, [Zachariah] began to get better, and forthwith other matters occupied his mind. His difficulty was not fairly slain, pierced through the midst by some heaven-directed arrow, but it was evaded and forgotten. Health, sweet blood, unimpeded action of the heart, are the divine narcotics which put to sleep these enemies to our peace and enable us to pass happily through life.'[1]

Similarly, what he tells us of Miriam, in *Miriam's Schooling*,[2] is undoubtedly true to his own experience:

'For years, even to the day of her death, the poison of one sentence in The Tale of a Tub remained with her—those memorable words that "happiness is a perpetual possession of being well deceived".'

All this gives us the clue to his remarks on Godwin and Wordsworth in *More Pages from a Journal*. Wordsworth's 'temporary subjugation by *Political Justice*' was like Zachariah Coleman's by Ferguson's *Astronomy*; it was not due to pure intellectual conviction. Hale White brings forward evidence, from Coleridge and from Wordsworth's own poetry, that Wordsworth had in him a 'hypochondriacal graft', and then, transferring his own experience to the poet, he goes on:

'Hypochondriacal misery is apt to take an intellectual shape. The most hopeless metaphysics or theology which we happen to encounter fastens on us, and we mistake for an unbiased conviction the form which the disease assumes. The *Political Justice* found in Wordsworth the aptest soil for germination . . .'

—because of his depressed condition between 1793 and 1795. 'There is no evidence', he adds,

'that Wordsworth attempted any reasoned confutation of *Political Justice*. It was falsified in him by Racedown, by better health, by the society of his beloved sister, and finally by the friendship with Coleridge. . . . This, then, is the moral . . . that certain beliefs, at

[1] *Revolution in Tanner's Lane*, pp. 212-15.   [2] p. 128.

any rate with men of Wordsworth's stamp [Hale White being one], are sickness, and that with the restoration of vitality and the influx of joy they disappear.'[1]

I have dwelt upon this topic because I believe that we shall never properly understand Hale White's work and thought unless we see it as part of his lifelong struggle to defeat, or better, to by-pass and forget this Apollyon. He wrote his books, as he tells us Wordsworth wrote *The Borderers*, partly to rid his bosom of perilous stuff by objectifying it. It is a mistake to think of him as merely another sufferer from the Victorian malady of honest doubt, or loss of faith. He suffered less pain from the loss of the certainties and consolations of religion than he might have done if he had ever been really comforted or strengthened by the theology of Tanner's Lane. On the contrary, we must reckon the deadness, the petrifaction, of Cowfold Dissent as amongst the chief causes of his depression. Here was a man of religious temperament, a man miserable without God, who like Job was forced to break through inherited notions—not in order to curse God and die, but in order to find God Himself. One may perhaps accept the view that his depression was constitutional, yet one can also see that the Tanner's Lane ethos would encourage an unhealthy introspectiveness, an undue preoccupation with the state of one's soul, without at the same time offering any compensating imaginative enrichment through sacramental or ritual beauty. What George Eliot says of Dorothea Brooke is true of Hale White: he had 'a certain spiritual grandeur ill-matched with opportunity'; he had an intellectual nature 'struggling in the bands of a narrow teaching, hemmed in by a social life which seemed nothing but a labyrinth of petty courses'. He longed to escape and be 'a sublime man', he longed for something great to know and to do; he longed for ideal love and friendship, a marriage of true minds. In every direction he was thwarted, and he thus became habituated to a state of defeat. He was checked above all by a sense of inadequacy in himself; his aspirations, he felt, outran his powers. In the *Auto-*

[1] *More Pages from a Journal*, pp. 209-14.

biography he makes Reuben Shapcott condemn the young Mark Rutherford as 'an example of the danger and folly of cultivating thoughts and reading books to which he was not equal, and which tend to make a man lonely'. Innumerable, throughout his books, are the occasions where he or his representatives acknowledge their own failure, inaccuracy, lack of mastery of any subject, lack of charm or readiness in conversation. Conscious of superiority and 'a certain spiritual grandeur', he was still more conscious of an inability to make this superiority felt by others, to make himself loved and admired. Why was this? There must be something wrong, something repellent, in himself. Probably, then, his very efforts to break loose from provincialism were simply signs of spiritual pride? These too must be checked? Hemmed in thus on all sides, at once condemning and self-condemned, it is little wonder that he sank periodically into despair.

Contributing to this condition—but also a source of his literary power—was an extreme, call it if you will a 'morbid', sensitiveness to impressions from without, particularly to discouraging impressions. There was in him a certain passiveness or inertness, a lack of resiliency and joy, whereby instead of triumphing over circumstance he was prone to sink beneath it, to be paralysed or withered by the disheartening thing. No one has ever depicted forlornness or sinkings of the heart with greater effect, and the effect is the more searing for the restraint of Hale White's statements. Significantly, some of the most chilling of these scenes of dereliction are taken from the life of provincial Dissenting congregations. There is Water Lane, 'in the eastern counties', where Mark Rutherford has his first ministry, where the cause was 'so woefully emaciated' that there were 'not above fifty persons in a building which would hold seven hundred', and where the leading deacon was the unspeakable Mr Snale the draper. Mark Rutherford reads *The Vicar of Wakefield* aloud at a Dorcas meeting, and is taken to task afterwards by Mr Snale,

' "Because you know, Mr Rutherford," he said, with his smirk, "the company is mixed; there are young leedies present, and *perhaps*,

Mr Rutherford, a book with a more requisite tone might be more suitable on such an occasion." '

Mark Rutherford tries George Fox's *Journal*, but 'Mr Snale objected to this too':

'It was "hardly of a character adapted for social intercourse", he thought; and furthermore, "although Mr Fox might be a very good man, and a converted character, yet he did not, you know, Mr Rutherford, belong to us".'[1]

Mark preached his first sermon on 'a dull day in November', but there was as yet no dullness in him. Fired by youthful insight, he tried to present Christianity as an answer to spiritual needs and questionings; as a living thing with relevance to daily experience and not a mere system of formulae. When the service was over he went down into the vestry:

'Nobody came near me but my landlord, the chapel-keeper, who said it was raining, and immediately went away to put out the lights and shut up the building. I had no umbrella, and there was nothing to be done but to walk out in the wet. When I got home I found that my supper, consisting of bread and cheese with a pint of beer, was on the table, but apparently it had not been thought necessary to light the fire again at that time of night.'

Or there is the later occasion, when, as a stage in his 'emancipation', Mark Rutherford accepts the ministry in a small Unitarian chapel at D[itchling]. Here 'a few descendants of the eighteenth century heretics' still testified 'against three Gods in one and the deity of Jesus Christ', but although the congregation had this 'freethought lineage' he had never met a more 'petrified set' in his life. 'They were perfectly orthodox, except that they denied a few orthodox doctrines. . . . Sympathy with the great problems then beginning to agitate men, they had none.' With touch after refrigerating touch, Hale White lowers the temperature until he thicks our blood with cold. On the first Sunday he 'went straight

---

[1] *Autobiography*, pp. 31-2.

to the chapel, and loitered about the graveyard till a woman came and opened a door at the back'.

'I explained who I was, and sat down in a Windsor chair against a small kitchen table in the vestry. It was cold, but there was no fire, nor were any preparations made for one. On the mantel-shelf were a bottle of water and a glass, but as the water had evidently been there for some time, it was not very tempting. I waited in silence for about twenty minutes, and my friend the dealer then came in, and having shaken hands and remarked that it was chilly, asked me for the hymns. These I gave him and went into the pulpit. I found myself in a plain-looking building designed to hold about two hundred people. There was a gallery opposite me, and the floor was occupied with high, dark, brown pews, one or two immediately on my right and left being surrounded with faded green curtains. I counted my hearers, and discovered that there were exactly seventeen, including two very old labourers, who sat on a form near the door. The gallery was quite empty, except a little organ or seraphine, I think it was called, which was played by a young woman.'

Benumbed and unnerved, he spoke for about half an hour on 'the real meaning of the death of Christ', as he understood it. After the service all the seventeen departed, save for one 'thin elderly gentleman' who came into the vestry, bowed slightly, and said "Mr Rutherford, will you come with me, if you please?" The ensuing dinner at this gentleman's house consisted of 'neck of mutton (cold), potatoes, cabbage, a suet pudding, and some of the strangest-looking ale I ever saw— about the colour of lemon juice, but what it was really like I do not know, as I did not drink beer. I was somewhat surprised at being asked whether I would take potatoes *or* cabbage, but thinking it was the custom of the country not to indulge in both at once, and remembering that I was on probation, I said "cabbage".' When the things had been cleared away his host, 'having remarked that it was beginning to rain', sat down near the basket-stove and 'fell into a slumber'. After the afternoon service the same gentleman came forward, and presented him with nineteen shillings. 'The fee was a guinea, but from that two shillings were abated for my entertainment.'

In both these incidents we can see how the nightmare death-in-life of mid-nineteenth century Puritanism oppressed and nearly broke his spirit. There is, of course, a strain of self-pity in all this: "here am I", he says in effect—"a sensitive person of superior gifts, a man of spiritual insight too, and is *this* all that is done for me?" He still expected the world, and individuals, to come and meet him, or at least to respond warmly to his advances. He had not yet learnt, as he did later, that 'thou must give, else never canst receive'. In the *Autobiography* he defends Mark Rutherford against the charge of reserve or failure in communicativeness; it was not this at all, he claims: it was just the opposite—an excessive desire to express his 'real self', thwarted by the discovery that his remarks 'produced blank silence in the majority of those who listened to me'. He was always in dead earnest, had no use for small talk, and consequently found what is called social intercourse, which consists of verbal 'fencing and trifling', a game he could not master. It does not seem to have occurred to the young Mark Rutherford (or to the young Hale White?) that he may have carried with him, and inflicted upon others, the low temperatures he everywhere complained of. Later he learnt to value the simple chatter of 'ordinary' people, and discovered that one must not be always making bids for intimacy or intellectual sympathy.

I will give one more example of Hale White's 'realism', this time a scene where the dereliction is not his own, but that of London itself—though London viewed, it is true, through eyes which impart to it a visionary dreariness comparable with Wordsworth's in some of his London passages, or Vaughan Williams's in the London Symphony.

'London on a dark Sunday afternoon, more especially about Goodge Street, is depressing. The inhabitants drag themselves hither and thither in languor and uncertainty. Small mobs linger at the doors of the gin palaces. Costermongers wander aimlessly, calling "walnuts" with a cry so melancholy that it sounds as the wail of the hopelessly lost may be imagined to sound when their anguish has been deadened by the monotony of a million years.

'About two or three o'clock decent working men in their best clothes emerge from the houses in such streets as Nassau Street. It is part of their duty to go out after dinner on Sunday with the wife and children. The husband pushes the perambulator out of the dingy passage, and gazes doubtfully this way and that way, not knowing whither to go, and evidently longing for the Monday, when his work, however disagreeable it may be, will be his plain duty. The wife follows carrying a child, and a boy and girl in un-accustomed apparel walk by her side. They come out into Mortimer Street. There are no shops open; the sky over their heads is mud, the earth is mud under their feet, the muddy houses stretch in long rows, black, gaunt, uniform. The little party reach Hyde Park, also wrapped in impenetrable mud-grey. The man's face brightens for a moment as he says "It is time to go back", and so they return, without the interchange of a word, unless perhaps they happen to see an omnibus horse fall down on the greasy stones.'[1]

Hale White's Puritan upbringing, together with his natur-ally desponding temperament, made of him a person not easily 'surprised by joy'. He needed, as we have seen, to 'take pains to secure pleasure'. No doubt he had been 'con-ditioned', once his boyhood—with its pagan joys and glad animal movements—was over, to check pleasure-seeking and spontaneous impulse as sinful. Thus his emotions, de-prived of natural outlet, turned inwards, and he found a sort of inverted pleasure in self-laceration or self-pity, and in such visions of outward squalor as the above. It must not be supposed, however, that he surrendered to Apollyon; on the contrary, he had in him enough of Bunyan's flint and steel to fight his way through the Valley of the Shadow of Death, and to gain in the end, inch by inch and with many a set-back, a vantage-point on the Delectable Mountains which others, more happily endowed, had easily reached long before. We have seen how Wordsworth helped; in a moment I shall speak of his other supports and means of grace. But since my main purpose is to sketch the development of his religious thought, I must say a word in passing about "Edward Gibbon Mardon" (of the *Autobiography*) and "M'Kay" (of *The Deliverance*).

[1] *Deliverance*, pp. 17-18.

v. Edward Gibbon Mardon

Mr Wilfred Stone has not discovered any 'original' for
Mardon, and if he has not, there is probably none to be
found. He regards Mardon as a 'symbol of the negative
forces' at work in Mark Rutherford during the Water Lane
period, and as the mouthpiece of the self-questionings which
beset Hale White during this twilight period of religious
faith.[1] Mardon is indeed a type of the devout 'unbeliever' of
the nineteenth century, and may be thought to include some
traits of men like Francis Newman, Frederic Harrison,
Leslie Stephen, W. R. Greg, T. H. Huxley and the rest. In
him Mark Rutherford at last finds someone to whom he can
unlock his heart. But Mardon is uncompromisingly logical;
he will not allow Mark to take refuge in the kindly mists of
Hegelian or Straussian metaphysics. In reply to Mardon's
'higher criticism' of the Bible, Mark had urged that it did
not matter whether Christ had ever lived or not; the 'Christ-
idea' was eternally 'true' whether or no it was 'ever incarnated in a being bearing His name'.

> ' "Pardon me," said Mardon, "but it does very much matter.
> It is all the matter whether we are dealing with a dream or with
> reality." '[2]

To Mardon Christ was a myth, and therefore not a basis for
faith; Mark Rutherford, who had been trying to have faith
in the myth, was thus rudely shaken out of his temporary
resting-place. Mardon's talk, exciting as it was, 'darkened
my days and nights'; he felt that Mardon left something
vital out of account, but, unable to resist his logic, he shrank
from him.

I quoted above (p. 200) Hale White's assertion, made in
old age, that he had not been worried by biblical criticism,
nor about the existence or non-existence of Heaven and Hell.
One might suppose from this that he had escaped the usual
pangs attending loss of faith, yet in the *Autobiography* he

[1] *Religion and Art of W. H. W.*, p. 46.
[2] *Autobiography*, p. 51.

tells us, in the context of Mardon's talks, that 'the struggle to retain as much as I could of my creed was tremendous'. 'The dissolution of Jesus into mythologic vapour', he goes on, 'was nothing less than the death of a friend dearer to me then than any other friend whom I knew.' But the worst stroke of all, he says, 'was that which fell upon the doctrine of a life beyond the grave'. He had long supposed, in theory, that he despised the idea of regulating conduct by such hopes and fears, but when Mardon's pitiless logic showed up the absurdities and contradictions of the belief, he realized how much he had really been depending upon it, and flinched at the thought of 'blank darkness before me at the end of a few years'. What are we to make of this? It may be that when Hale White wrote the quoted remark in his Journal, years later, the struggles of his youth had grown dim, or had become insignificant in the wider perspective of his long pilgrimage. Another race had been, and other palms were won. Or we may ask, knowing that "Mark Rutherford" is not simply Hale White, whether in the novel he was not dramatizing a typical experience rather than recounting his own. I think the former is the more likely explanation; Hale White's habit is to stick closely to the inner facts, however he may alter the outward details of his own life. Similarly, the reasons he gives for Mark's abandonment of the ministry must correspond to a stage in his own thought: what was there left for him to preach? The Atonement had become a 'summing up as it were of what sublime men have to do for their race'; immortality, as usually pictured, had become inconceivable; God was no longer a 'person', but a personification of 'immutable laws'—and what tendency had these laws? They produced misery as well as joy; the mystery of pain as well as the glory of sunrise. As for morality, it was no use telling people to be good; 'reformations in morals' have never come about in that way, but 'have always been the result of an enthusiasm for some City of God, or some supereminent person'. To amplify Bible stories and characters, neglecting the supernatural; or to use the old phrases with new meanings unknown to his hearers, had become for him an intolerable prevarication.

vi. M'Kay

There was nothing left but action of some sort, and one might think from *The Deliverance* that Hale White, like Mark Rutherford, had followed "Robert Elsmere's" example and turned from preaching to slumming. Mr Stone can find no evidence that he did this, though certain articles of his in the provincial press show that he knew the squalor of the Drury Lane slums and approved of Cowper-Temple's coffee-shop venture. Mr Stone conjectures that Hale White wished he had, in fact, set his own hand to rescue-work of this kind; he certainly thought it the best, and perhaps the only way of spreading whatever gospel might remain. 'There are few gospels now-a-days which we can all believe, but assuredly this of Mr Cowper-Temple's is one, and as much as in me lies I mean to preach it.'[1] Whether or no M'Kay (as Mr Stone thinks possible) is studied from Cowper-Temple, he at least represents something like the Christian socialism of men like Maurice, Kingsley and Ludlow, or more broadly perhaps the social conscience of those who felt that no spiritual appeal could 'do anything in the back streets of great cities so long as they are the cess-pools which they are now'. M'Kay's idea was to save a few souls, amidst the rank corruption and degradation of Drury Lane, by opening there a room where people could escape occasionally from their misery, and enter 'a different region'. M'Kay 'did not convert Drury Lane, but he saved two or three'—by giving them new hope, new interests, and sometimes by helping them to find more suitable employment. These were people (and the detailed case-histories Hale White gives read like authentic stories) who, if they had gone to church or chapel, 'would have heard discourses on the usual set topics, none of which would have concerned them. Their trouble was not the forgiveness of sins, the fallacies of Arianism, the personality of the Holy Ghost, or the doctrine of the Eucharist. They all *wanted* something distinctly.' 'The very centre of

---

[1] Hale White in the *Birmingham Daily Post*, December 28, 1878 (quoted by W. Stone, *op. cit.*, p. 137).

the existence of the ordinary chapel-goer and church-goer', says Mark Rutherford, 'needs to be shifted from self to what is outside self, and yet is truly self, and the sole truth of self.' So he and M'Kay tried above all to interest their flock 'in what is universal and impersonal, feeling that in that direction lies healing'.[1]

Hale White said, near the end of his life, that 'he had never *changed* anybody'.[2] Making all allowances for his habit of self-depreciation, this is probably not far from the truth. It may be doubted whether he ever had much enthusiasm for the saving of souls; he was fully enough engaged in trying to save his own. It is therefore safest, I think, to read the Drury Lane sections of *The Deliverance* as an allegory of his efforts to adjust his faith to the facts of social evil and individual suffering. It is significant that here we have his statement of what can be salvaged from the wreck of orthodoxy. Above all there was the idea of Reconciliation, 'the reconciliation of man with God', and the certainty that in mere scepticism or negation there could be no resting-place. 'This is the reason', he characteristically says, 'why all great religions should be treated with respect, and in a sense preserved. It is nothing less than a wicked waste of accumulated human strivings to sneer them out of existence. They will be found, every one of them, to have incarnated certain vital doctrines which it has cost centuries of toil and devotion properly to appreciate.' What we must do, and what he did after the needful preliminary escape from Tanner's Lane, was to 'rediscover and restore' these truths. We must not 'halt in indifference or hostility', but go on and fight for firm ground, making it our own ground and not someone else's. He found the inmost truth of Christianity in 'the depth of its distinction between right and wrong'. In saying this he may seem to be over-stressing the moral aspect of religion in the usual Victorian style, but for him the distinction ran so deep as to become almost metaphysical. Take the following passage, which is central enough to deserve full quotation:

'Herein [Christianity] is of priceless value. Philosophy proclaims

[1] *Deliverance*, p. 88 (and see chs. II, V and VI generally).
[2] *Groombridge Diary*, p. 114.

the unity of our nature. To philosophy every passion is as natural as every act of saintlike negation, and one of the usual effects of thinking or philosophizing is to bring together all that is apparently contrary in man, and to show how it proceeds really from one centre. But Christianity had not to propound a theory of man; it had to redeem the world. It laid awful stress on the duality in us, and the stress laid on that duality is the world's salvation. The words right and wrong are not felt now as they were felt by Paul. They shade off into each other. Nevertheless, if mankind is not to be lost, the ancient antagonism must be maintained. The shallowest of mortals is able now to laugh at the notion of a personal devil. No doubt there is no such thing existent; but the horror at evil which could find no other expression than in the creation of a devil is no subject for laughter, and if it do not in some shape or other survive, the race itself will not survive. No religion, so far as I know, has dwelt like Christianity with such profound earnestness on the bisection of man—on the distinction within him, vital to the last degree, between the higher and the lower, heaven and hell. What utter folly is it because of an antique vesture to condemn as effete what the vesture clothes! Its doctrine and its sacred story are fixtures in concrete form of precious thoughts purchased by blood and tears.'[1]

There is no explaining away pain or death; we can only say, 'there is another side', there is some compensation. If, on the one hand, there is 'rain slowly rotting the harvest', and 'children sickening in cellars', there are also, on the other hand, 'an evening in June, the delight of men and women in one another, in music, and in the exercise of thought'. In facing the prospect of death, we must remember that it is the *dogmatism* of doubt which 'pulls us down'; the open grave seems final, but what has really happened we do not know, and here agnosticism (in the strictest sense) is better and more rational than blank unbelief. The new theology must shift the stress from *saving* one's soul to *losing* one's soul in what is not oneself. It is said that 'the attempt to replace the care for self in us by a care for the universal is ridiculous. Man cannot rise to that height. I do not believe

[1] *Deliverance*, pp. 90-1.

it. I believe we can rise to it. Every ordinary unselfish act is a proof of the capacity to rise to it. . . .' Lastly, there is Nature, and especially the starry heavens above. 'No man can look up to the stars at night and reflect upon what lies behind them without feeling that the tyranny of the senses is loosened, and the tyranny, too, of the conclusions of his logic.' Infinite space is a 'visible warning not to make our minds the measure of the universe'.

vii. The Stars

This brings us to the second of the three great positives, or means of grace, in Hale White's experience: The Stars. I have spoken of Wordsworth (the first), and it is not easy to separate these two; both led him away from self in the direction of the impersonal, wherein lies healing. Indeed all his deepest needs were of the same general kind, and therefore whatever helped him tended to operate upon him in the same general direction. The different elements making up his complex need were so interfused that each could stand as a symbol of the rest; and the same is true of his 'helps'. First came the need to transcend Cowfold and Tanner's Lane; the sense of aspiration ill-matched by opportunity; the longing to 'lift himself out of his little narrow town or village circle of acquaintances', or the 'dull, daily round of mechanical routine'.[1] There was next the need to check the pride and self-pity which sprang from this very longing. There was the homelessness following upon loss of early faith, and the need for sources of strength and consolation other than those proffered in vain by orthodoxy. There was the hypochondria, at once the symptom of all these maladjustments and their final outcome and symbol. To all this should be added the longing for perfect human companionship, which his first marriage seems to have left unsatisfied. The theme of incompatibility in marriage sounds so persistently throughout Hale White's writings that it must, in view of his habitual adherence to fact, refer to (or at least symbolize) something important in his experience. To this I shall return later,

[1] *Autobiography*, p. 48.

though Mr Stone has written of it so understandingly that little remains to be said. One other recurrent symbol of evil must be mentioned: London itself, a veritable City of Destruction and a malignant spectre threatening his peace. The awful vision of London at night, which brought on his first attack of nervous prostration, and his many evocations of its gloom, squalor and poisonous air, sufficiently display this. Two passages from his Journals show how it persisted throughout his life:

> 'What are the facts? Not those in Homer, Shakespeare, or even the Bible. The facts for most of us are a dark street, crowds, hurry, commonplaceness, loneliness, and, worse than all, a terrible doubt which can hardly be named as to the meaning and purpose of the world.'[1]

Here it will be noticed how the dark street is associated with the dark question, both suggesting the metaphysical *frisson* and symbolizing it. The 'terrible doubt' either did not arise, or could be put aside, in the fields, by the sea, or looking at the night sky. In the little fable called "A Home-Made Religion" he tells how a country woman, Susan Templeton, had made a background for the New Testament out of the fields, the sun and the ripening corn of her home landscape, seeing Jesus and his disciples walking through the Midland cornfields. She went to London, and Capernaum became the shadow of a dream: 'London contradicted the gospels, and belief had fled.' The sermon of a fashionable town preacher, demonstrating the necessary existence of God, left her still more bewildered. She went back to the farm, lay in her own bed and 'listened to the weir before she fell asleep. Without internal argument, Capernaum and Jesus were restored to her, and she was at peace.'[2] The other passage is from Hale White's "Diary on the Quantocks":

> 'Went over to East Quantock's [*sic*] Head and came back across the hill. It was a dark day; the sky was overcast, and the moors were very lonely. The thought of London and other big cities over

---

[1] *Last Pages from a Journal*, pp. 289-90.
[2] *Pages from a Journal*, pp. 320 ff.

the horizon somewhat marred the solitude. Nevertheless there are
the deserts of Arabia and Africa, the regions of the North and
South Poles, the Ocean, and, encompassing the globe itself, silent,
infinite space.'[1]

The thought of a wider world beyond Cowfold had exhil-
arated him from boyhood days. Cowfold, lying some miles
west of the Great North Road, slept undisturbed in provincial stagnation, but if you walked to where the muddy
side-road joined the main road, what an imaginative expansion was there! At that point stood a sign-post with three
pointers: the first and second respectively bearing, in large
letters, "TO LONDON" and "TO YORK", and the third in small
italics "*To Cowfold*".

> 'How strange it was to emerge from the end of the lane and to
> see those wonderful words, "TO LONDON", "TO YORK"! What an
> opening into infinity! Boys of a slightly imaginative turn of mind
> . . . would, on a holiday, trudge the three miles eastward merely to
> get to the post and enjoy the romance of those mysterious fingers.
> No wonder; for the excitement begotten by the long stretch of the
> road—London at one end, York at the other—,by the sight of the
> *Star, Rover, Eclipse* or *Times* racing along at twelve miles an hour,
> and by the inscriptions on them, was worth a whole afternoon's
> cricket or wandering in the fields. Cowfold itself supplied no such
> stimulus.'[2]

Sign-posts stood at intervals along the road of his pilgrimage, all pointing away from Cowfold and self, 'opening
into infinity'; these became his holy symbols of deliverance:
Wordsworth, Spinoza, Nature in general and the Stars in
particular; certain numinous places—the Quantocks, Cornwall, the North Downs, the sea. In the *Autobiography*, one of
the most persistent of Mark Rutherford's nervous depres-
sions (lasting from November to June) was lifted thus:

> 'I had been there [at Ilfracombe] about a week, when on one
> memorable morning, on the top of one of those Devonshire hills,
> I became aware of a kind of flush in the brain and a momentary

[1] *More Pages from a Journal*, p. 191.
[2] *Revolution in Tanner's Lane*, pp. 230-2.

relief such as I had not known since that November night. I seemed, far away on the horizon, to see just a rim of olive light low down under the edge of the leaden cloud that hung over my head, a prophecy of the restoration of the sun, or at least a witness that somewhere it shone.'

Such moments of sudden relief, or sudden vision—generally accompanied by a sense of escape from self into the impersonal, and therefore a sense of absolution and remission —occur throughout his writings, and give rise to some of his best imaginative effects. After that dreadful service at Ditchling, Mark Rutherford walked home in the rain, 'miserable and desponding':

'But just before I reached home the clouds rolled off with the south-west wind into detached, fleecy masses separated by liquid blue gulfs, in which were sowed the stars, and the effect upon me was what that sight, thank God, always has been—a sense of the infinite, extinguishing all mean cares.'[1]

While he was at Water Lane his walks almost always led him along the river to where it became tidal, and as often as possible to within sight of the sea itself:

'the sea was a corrective to the littleness all around me. With the ships on it sailing to the other end of the earth it seemed to connect me with the great world outside the parochialism of the society in which I lived.'[2]

The way of escape from Cowfold had pointed to London, but London proved a Slough of Despond from which escape was seldom possible. It must be made, if at all, through the starry heavens above or the moral law within. The first way was the more congenial, but it is part of Hale White's greatness that he understood the importance of doing without such help, and living from inward resources alone. When Mark Rutherford first came to London, he felt (like "Susan Stapleton") that 'hope, faith and God seemed impossible amidst the smoke of the streets', and he wondered 'how men could be worth anything if they could never see the face of

---

[1] *Autobiography*, p. 95. [2] *Ibid.*, p. 34.

nature'. For this he blames his early training on *Lyrical Ballads*—and thence, with a characteristic return upon himself, proceeds to immolate one of his own most constant sources of joy. Like everything else in his life, it had all been a mistake; a Londoner cannot live by a landscape-religion:

> 'I cannot help saying, with all my love for the literature of my own day, that it has an evil side to it which none know except the millions of sensitive persons who are condemned to exist in great towns. It might be imagined from much of this literature that true humanity and a belief in God are the offspring of the hills or the ocean; and by implication, if not expressly, the vast multitudes who hardly ever see the hills or the ocean must be without a religion.'[1]

It was necessary, then, to learn how to find the essentials for living 'even though I should never see anything more than was to be seen in journeying through the High Street, Camden Town, the Seven Dials, and Whitehall'. It was a hard lesson:

> 'many and many a time, as I walked along that dreary New Road or Old St Pancras Road, have I striven to compel myself not to look at the image of Hampstead Heath or Regent's Park, as yet six days in front of me, but to get what I could out of what was then with me'.

One day it flashed into him 'like a sudden burst of the sun's rays', that he had no *right* to happiness. It was a sort of conversion, like Carlyle's in the rue St Thomas de l'Enfer, and 'straightway it seemed as if the centre of a whole system of dissatisfaction were removed'. Just so Zachariah Coleman, pacing the dismal Manchester pavements in despair, feeling that his wife was 'not the helpmeet he had a right to expect' and questioning the justice of Providence, suddenly rebukes himself for having held all his life the doctrine of God's predestinating will, and yet rebelling directly 'God touched him'. He submits ('it is the gospel according to Job'), and at once finds that, having thus seen himself as part of a universal order, he no longer feels oppressed by the Manchester gloom.

[1] *Deliverance*, p. 5.

All this is bravely argued, but these mountings of the mind were rare and short-lived, and the 'infinite need' persisted. Glimpses of the sky in early morning or at night—the only 'openings into infinity' left to a Londoner—were treasured up and waited for, and a whole day's holiday by the sea was like translation to another planet. The Caillauds' workroom, in an attic off Fleet Street, overlooked 'an innumerable multitude of red chimney-pots pouring forth stinking smoke which, for the six winter months, generally darkened the air during the whole day':

> 'But occasionally Nature resumed her rights, and it was possible to feel that sky, stars, sun and moon still existed, and were not blotted out by the obscurations of what is called civilized life. There came, occasionally, wild nights in October or November, with a gale from the south-west, and then, when almost everybody had gone to bed and the fires were out, the clouds, illuminated by the moon, rushed across the heavens, and the Great Bear hung over the dismal waste of smutty tiles with the same solemnity with which it hangs over the mountain, the sea, or the desert.'[1]

One of Hale White's most characteristic star-passages (it deserves to be quoted in full) is the account of Zachariah Coleman's night walk to Lancaster, after a terrible scene with his wife, to visit Caillaud in the condemned cell:

> 'Amidst all his troubles he could not help being struck with the solemn, silent procession overhead. It was perfectly clear—so clear that the heavens were not a surface, but a depth, and the stars of a lesser magnitude were so numerous and brilliant that they obscured the forms of the greater constellations. Presently the first hint of day appeared in the east. We must remember that this was the year 1817, before, so it is commonly supposed, men knew what it was properly to admire a cloud or a rock. Zachariah was not, therefore, on a level with the most ordinary subscriber to a modern circulating library. Nevertheless he could not help noticing—we will say he did no more—the wonderful, the sacredly beautiful drama which noiselessly displayed itself before him. Over in the east the intense deep blue of the sky softened a little. Then the trees in that quarter

---

[1] *Revolution in Tanner's Lane*, p. 65.

began to contrast themselves against the background and reveal their distinguishing shapes. Swiftly, and yet with such even velocity that in no one minute did there seem to be any progress compared with the minute preceding, the darkness was thinned, and resolved itself overhead into pure sapphire, shaded into yellow below and in front of him, while in the west it was still almost black. The grassy floor of the meadows now showed its colour, grey green, with the dew lying on it, and in the glimmer under the hedge might be discerned a hare or two stirring. Star by star disappeared, until none were left, save Venus, shining like a lamp till the very moment almost when the sun's disc touched the horizon. Half a dozen larks mounted and poured forth that ecstasy which no bird but the lark can translate. More amazing than the loveliness of scene, sound and scent around him was the sense of irresistible movement. He stopped to watch it, for it grew so rapid that he could almost detect definite pulsations. Throb followed throb every second with increasing force, and in a moment more a burning speck of gold was visible, and behold it was day! He slowly turned his eyes and walked onwards.'[1]

In *Miriam's Schooling*, two of Hale White's recurring themes, the stars and incompatibility in marriage, are interwoven, the starry heavens becoming the means whereby Miriam and her husband (Didymus Farrow) are reconciled. Miriam, finding after her marriage that Farrow is rough and coarse and quite unable to share her literary interests, realizes with horror that she is beginning to hate him. She takes to walking out disconsolately alone, and one day meets the vicar of a neighbouring country parish whose hobby is astronomy. This Mr Armstrong, who kept a telescope on the top of his church tower ("Do you think our Saviour would have sanctioned the erection of a profane instrument over the house of prayer?" —asked a scandalized farmer's wife), invites Miriam to come with her husband some clear night to look at the stars through it:

'Miriam looked first. Jupiter was in the field. She could not suppress a momentary exclamation of astonished ecstasy at the spectacle. . . . What affected her most was to see Jupiter's solemn,

[1] *Ibid.*, pp. 222-4.

still movement, and she gazed and gazed, utterly absorbed, until at last he had disappeared. The stars had passed thus before her eyes ever since she had been born, but what was so familiar had never before been emphasized or put in a frame, and consequently had never produced its due effect.'[1]

Its effect on Miriam was the same as its effect on Mr Armstrong—and on Hale White himself—it was medicine for her mind; it pacified her and contented her with her lot. But what was more, it revealed unsuspected powers in her husband, for he understood Mr Armstrong's astronomical explanations and she did not. Patiently, and with the aid of ingenious home-made contrivances, Didymus not only enables her to understand the celestial motions, but at the same time displays his own intelligence—so different from her own, and, in its mathematical grasp, so superior. Her renewed respect for him is brought to a head when, with infinite care and precision, he constructs an orrery for Mr Armstrong. Miriam had thus gained, at one stroke, not only a new source of calming and chastening emotion, but also new insight into her husband's nature. Hale White knew—none so well as he—that such high moods are not lasting; he does not spare Miriam the inevitable reaction, the relapse into disgust at her husband's boorish ways and lack of interest in poetry. But she has had her 'schooling', and their final reconciliation is ushered in by another of Hale White's natural symbols: the South-West Wind. For this great natural force, linking, like the stars, each petty parish with things remote and impersonal, and bearing with it warmth and moisture from beyond the Mexique bay, Hale White felt, like Meredith, a sentiment of religious devotion. Miriam, after another fit of exasperation, listens to the rain falling at night:

> 'She dropped off to sleep, and at four she rose and went to the window and opened it wide. In streamed the fresh south-west morning air, pure, delicious, scented with all that was sweet from fields and woods, and *the bearer inland even as far as Cowfold of Atlantic vitality, dissipating fogs, disinfecting poisons—the Life-Giver.*'[2]

[1] *Miriam's Schooling*, p. 140.   [2] *Ibid.*, p. 151 (my italics).

Dawn follows, and 'the dead storm contributed its own share to the growing beauty', the night's rain-cloud being now flushed with scarlet.

Like Pascal, and like all who have deeply pondered such matters, Hale White knew that we cannot base religion upon Nature alone—that no creed which is to serve for living can be 'a simple impression from the seal of external nature',[1] nor be derivable from what we see of natural laws. Yet, like a true son of his century who had felt the spell of Wordsworth, he always retained, together with great sensibility to natural beauty, a sense of kinship with the wisdom and spirit of the universe, and especially with those manifestations of it which could bring admonishment or restoration. True, part of the very lesson of Nature was that God's ways are not our ways, nor His thoughts our thoughts ('so great a difference is there', as Bacon had said, 'betwixt the spirit of man and the spirit of the Universe'). The Universe contained Leviathan as well as the Pleiades; there were thunderclouds as well as sunrise over a summer sea; there were droughts and floods and the blighting north-east winds, as well as the benign south-west, the 'Life-Giver'. Yet, in comparison with the 'idle and dead ecclesiastical reiteration of what had long since ceased to be true', the lesson of Job, *'to look abroad over the world'*, seemed to be the injunction of God himself to Hale White, as it was long ago to the man of Uz. 'Job demands of his opponents that they should come out into the open universe. If they will but lift their eyes across the horizon which hitherto has hemmed them in, what enlargement will not thereby be given to them?' It is out of the whirlwind that God answers Job: "Where wast thou when I laid the foundations of the earth? . . . when the morning stars sang together, and all the sons of God shouted for joy?" And, says Hale White, 'what more have we to say now than God said from the whirlwind over 2500 years ago?' There was no revelation, no promise of immortality, no solution of the riddle of the painful earth; merely, 'an injunction to open the eyes and look abroad over the universe. . . . God reminds us of His wisdom, of the mystery of things, and that man is

[1] *Last Pages from a Journal,* p. 284.

not the measure of His creation.' All we are taught, besides the lesson of reverent submission to transcendent power, is that God's wisdom 'when it is brought down to man, is morality'. This does not mean that 'nature' is moral; it means that, for man, morality is the wisdom which, at an infinite remove, places us in line with the transcendent wisdom of the Creator. It is significant that Hale White should have found in the book of Job a tract for the times; he saw his own agony in Job's, and like Job, found release in the thought of Orion and the Mazzaroth.[1] With this he fused the lesson of Wordsworth to the nineteenth century, and especially to sick and doubting souls like his own, that in Nature, which lifted one clean out of morbid introspection, could be found 'for this uneasy heart of ours, A never-failing principle of joy, And purest passion'.

So deeply, and increasingly in later years, did Hale White draw on this source of joy, that it will be good to have before us some illustrations, particularly from his Journals. Not only do these notes reveal a side of him which is less familiar to many, but they display a sensibility akin to Dorothy Wordsworth's—though more sicklied o'er than hers with the pale cast of thought. The most characteristic of them show a response to whatever leads off into the illimitable, or brings an influx of new life. Take this from "The End of October":

'It is the first south-westerly gale of the autumn. Its violence is increasing every minute, although the rain has ceased for awhile. For weeks sky and sea have been beautiful, but they have been tame. Now for some unknown reason there is a complete change, and all the strength of nature is awake. It is refreshing to be once more brought face to face with her tremendous power, and to be reminded of the mystery of its going and coming. . . . The air has a freshness and odour about it to which we have long been strangers. It has been dry, but now it is deliciously wet and clean. The wind during the summer changed lightly through all the points of the compass, but it has never brought any scent save that of the land,

[1] For these references, see *Notes on the Book of Job*, given (in the Unwin ed. of 1923) at the end of *The Deliverance*, pp. 131 ff.

nothing from a distance. *Now it is charged with messages from the ocean.'*[1]

Or again:

'The south-west wind is roaring round the house, bringing up from the sea a storm of rain, splashing against the windows and streaming down them. How much better to be a breath of that south-west wind than to be a pitiful *personality* like myself, crouching over a fire.'[2]

'Presently the wind rose again, and a rain-squall followed. It passed, and the stars began to come out, and Orion showed himself above the eastern woods. He seemed as if he were marching against the moon-lit scud which drove against him. How urgent all the business of this afternoon and evening has been, and yet what it meant who could say? I was like a poor man's child who, looking out from the cottage window, beholds with amazement a great army traversing the plain before him with banners and music and knows nothing of its errand.'[3]

"Under Beachy Head: December"

'At the top of the hill the north-westerly wind blows fresh, but here under the cliffs the sun strikes warm as in June. There is not a cloud in the sky, and behind me broken, chalk pinnacles intensely white rise into the clear blue, which is bluer by their contrast. In front lies the ealm, light-sapphire ocean with a glittering sun-path on it broadening towards the horizon. . . . I look southward: there is nothing between me and the lands of heat but the water. It unites me with them.

'It is wonderful that winter should suddenly abdicate and summer resume her throne. On a morning like this there is no death, the sin of the world is swallowed up; theological and metaphysical problems cease to have any meaning.'[4]

Sometimes, especially at a sundown when the sky clears from the west after rain, he is 'hushed and reassured'. Or, he feels the power of stillness and solitude:

'A November day near the end of the month—the country is

---

[1] *Pages from a Journal*, pp. 22-3 (my italics).
[2] *Last Pages from a Journal*, p. 288.
[3] *More Pages from a Journal*, p. 150.   [4] *Ibid.*, pp.169-70.

left to those who live in it. The scattered visitors who took lodgings in the summer in the villages have all departed, and the recollection that they have been here makes the solitude more complete. . . . The wind, what there is of it, is from the south-west, soft, sweet and damp; the sky is almost covered with bluish-grey clouds, which here and there give way and permit a dim, watery gleam to float slowly over the distant pastures. . . . It is a delightful time.' No demand is made for ecstatic admiration; everything is at rest, nature has nothing to do but sleep and wait.'[1]

And again, from the Quantock diary:

'Whitsunday morning: sat at the open window between five and six: the hills opposite lay in the light of the eastern sun. Bicknoller church and the little old village were beneath me. Perfect quietude, save for the bells of Stogumber church ringing a peal two miles away. Earth has nothing to give compared with this peace. The air was so still that delicious mingled scents floated up from the garden and fields below. It was one of those days on which every sense is satisfied, and no mortal imperfection appears. Took the *Excursion* out of doors after breakfast, and read *The Ruined Cottage*.'

The piece he quotes from Wordsworth, and his comment thereon, are too significant to be passed by. He goes on:

'Much of the religion by which Wordsworth lives is very indefinite. Look at the close of this poem:—

"I well remember that those very plumes,
Those weeds, and the high spear-grass on that wall
By mist and silent rain-drops silver'd o'er,
As once I pass'd, did to my heart convey
So still an image of tranquillity,
So calm and still, and look'd so beautiful
Amid the uneasy thoughts which fill'd my mind,
That what we feel of sorrow and despair
From ruin and from change, and all the grief
The passing shows of Being leave behind,
Appear'd an idle dream, that could not live
Where meditation was. I turn'd away,
And walk'd along my road in happiness."

[1] *Pages from a Journal*, pp. 25-7.

228

Because this religion is indefinite it is not therefore the less supporting.'[1]

This kind of meditative trance, in which the mind, first stilled by images of tranquillity, is then rapt from itself and fuses with the images, losing all habitual sense of distinction between self and not-self, subject and object, is seen in the following extract, which will serve also as a bridge to Spinoza. Hale White has been saying that in earlier life he had held a kind of general pantheism—God in nature, the same God in him—but that this belief had been 'taken over from books' as an intellectual proposition. One morning, however,

'when I was in the wood something happened which was nothing less than a transformation of myself and the world, although I "believed" nothing new. I was looking at a great, spreading, bursting oak. The first tinge from the greenish-yellow buds was just visible. It seemed to be no longer a tree away from me and apart from me. The enclosing barriers of consciousness were removed and the text came into my mind, *Thou in me and I in thee.* The distinction of self and not-self was an illusion. I could feel the rising sap; in me also sprang the fountain of life uprushing from its roots, and the joy of its outbreak at the extremity of each twig right up to the summit was my own: that which kept me apart was nothing. I do not argue; I cannot explain; it will be easy to prove me absurd, but nothing can shake me. *Thou in me and I in thee.* Death! what is death? There is no death: *in thee* it is impossible, absurd.'[2]

VIII. Spinoza

Spinoza's influence upon Hale White has been so acutely analysed by Mr Wilfred Stone[3] that a few words here will suffice. Hale White was only one of many who, from the late eighteenth century onwards, found in Spinoza a compensation, intellectual or emotional or both, for the loss of traditional beliefs (Mr Stone mentions, for example, Shelley, Coleridge, Goethe, Maurice, Froude, Lewes, Arnold and

---

[1] *More Pages from a Journal,* pp. 196-7.
[2] *Ibid.,* pp. 181-3.
[3] *Op. cit.,* ch. VII (pp. 101 ff.).

George Eliot). It is another of the links between Hale White and George Eliot that they both translated Spinoza's *Ethics*, though George Eliot's translation (finished in 1856) was never published, while Hale White's (1883) was 'the first reliable translation to be published in English'.[1]

Spinoza did for Hale White what the vision in the Old St Pancras Road did for Mark Rutherford, or Zachariah Coleman's on the Manchester pavements did for him, or God's utterance from the whirlwind for Job—he removed 'the centre of a whole system of dissatisfaction' by plunging the 'poor, petty self' in the vast ocean of being. Spinoza, like the stars, was medicine for Hale White's self-absorption and self-pity, giving repose to his tormented soul by what Goethe called his 'all-composing calmness'. By his conception of God as an infinite being of whom the only attributes manifested to us are thought and extension, he not only sidetracked many of the dreary difficulties of orthodox theology, but abolished the vexatious opposition between thought and matter. The realization that this antithesis is a fiction came upon Hale White as an immense relief from his self-centredness; it meant that his mind was 'a part of the infinite intellect of God', that he was not 'a mere transient, outside interpreter of the universe', but had 'a relationship with infinity', which would emancipate him. Spinoza could relieve that sense of the commonplaceness of life, and of himself, which lay heavy upon Hale White's spirit; through Spinoza he could feel that 'being part of the whole, the grandeur and office of the whole are ours'. It had been one of his great discoveries that in the direction of the universal and impersonal lies healing, and Spinoza, with his impersonal God, his serene intellectual detachment, his technique for conquering the passions by clear and adequate thinking, and his substitution (in Mr Stone's phrase) of 'a psychological for a cosmological hereafter', produced in Hale White that *acquiescentia mentis* 'which enables us to live', and which for the most part he found so difficult of attainment. 'We are anxious about what we call "personality", but in truth there

---

[1] *Ibid.*, p. 101. Hale White's translation appeared in three later revised editions: 1894, 1899 and 1910, with elaborate prefaces.

is nothing in it of any worth, and the less we care for it the more "blessed" we are.'[1]

ix. At Enmity With Joy

At the head of this chapter I quoted Hale White's remark that 'a childlike faith in the old creed is no longer possible, but it is equally impossible to surrender it'. This, I think, is the key that unlocks the heart of his mystery. Others of like upbringing in his age could surrender it, and find fulfilment in science, in various 'causes' —social or political, in the joy of artistic creation, or in sheer epicureanism. For him, none of these alternatives was open; there was that in him which blocked all such avenues of escape. As he says of his own Mr Cardew (the clergyman in *Catherine Furze*), 'he lived an entirely interior life', 'prone to self-absorption', and 'the happy, artistic, Shakespearian temper, mirroring the world like a lake, was altogether foreign to him'. Thus he could never, like Edmund Gosse or Stevenson, find emancipation in gusto, high-spirits or the bohemianism of the literary smart-sets. Tied for ever to respectability by early home-influence, and to seriousness by Tanner's Lane, he passed his life in a kind of limbo, 'never by passion quite possess'd, and never quite benumb'd by the world's sway'.

In the *Early Life* he tells us, as George Eliot has also done, that 'at first, after the abandonment of orthodoxy', he thought 'nothing in the old religion worth retaining'; but 'this temper did not last long'.

> 'It would be a mistake to suppose that the creed in which I had been brought up was or could be for ever cast away like an old garment. The beliefs of childhood and youth cannot be thus dismissed. I know that in after years I found that in a way they revived under new forms. . . .'[2]

What new forms? His main answer is that 'many mistakes may be pardoned in Puritanism in view of the earnestness

---

[1] This and previously quoted phrases are from "Spinoza", *Pages from a Journal*, pp. 32-58.
[2] *Early Life*, pp. 77-8.

with which it insists on the distinction between right and wrong'. He found that 'in modern religion the path is flowery', and this for him was a sure sign of decadence. Rather than the modern religion-without-tears, with its 'sloppy mess of words', let us have Bunyan or Calvin, whose beliefs, however scandalous to the 'enlightened', were at least founded upon ineluctable *facts*—the facts of sin, justification by faith, repentance, reconciliation with God, grace and redemption. The stern predestinating God of Calvinism was, he found, far truer to experience than the magnified Lord Shaftesbury of modern liberal theology. The God who demanded the sacrifice of Isaac and of Jephthah's daughter, and who spoke to Job from the whirlwind, turned out to be indeed the God of this dark, inscrutable world, and this was the God to whom his deepest allegiance was given—even when his intellect or his nerves found comfort in the Supreme Being of Spinoza. Zachariah Coleman, in the depths of his despair, found escape through reflecting: ' "Thus hath He decreed; it is foolish to struggle against His ordinances; we can but submit." ' ' "A poor gospel", says his critic', Mark Rutherford adds; 'yes—it may be; but it is the gospel according to Job, and any other is a mere mirage. . . . Poor!—yes; but it is genuine; and this at least must be said for Puritanism, that of all the theologies and philosophies it is the most honest in its recognition of the facts; the most real, if we penetrate to the heart of it, in the remedy which it offers.'[1] Experience had confronted Hale White with a God who must be conceived as Will rather than as Love, and in his own submission there was more of Stoicism than of Christianity.

One of the most enduring of his inheritances from Puritanism was an inveterate habit of self-criticism. The natural man is at enmity with God: this teaching had sunk far beneath his conscious mind, so that it had become an instinct with him to suspect and check all spontaneous movements towards pleasure, all escapes through light-heartedness, laughter or the society of 'ordinary' people. We learn that the atmosphere he created in his Carshalton home was joy-

[1] *Revolution in Tanner's Lane*, p. 127.

less, and that his children sought relaxation outside the family shadow. Life must not be taken as a game, or as an art, but as an agony; and if others could not take it so, this was yet another proof that they misunderstood both him and life itself. His remorseless self-condemnation thus led him towards enmity with joy in others also. But this was far from being the whole story. His self-criticism was so profound that it passed, by a strange dialectic, into condemnation of himself for judging others. Whatever else might be doubtful, one thing was or became certain, that he himself, in any judgment or attitude that came naturally to him, must be wrong. Thus Hale White suffered the intolerable strain of fighting life on two fronts at the same time; he resisted Nature as a Puritan intellectual, and then condemned himself for doing so. This is what makes him so baffling and elusive; he is for ever returning upon himself and finding deeper wisdom on the far side of his own point of view. We have just seen this dialectic at work, on the grand scale, in his championship of the very Puritanism he had mentally rejected. But it appears also at many other points. For example, one of the main irritants of his early life, one of the chief causes of his longing for wider horizons and a more liberal culture, had been the narrow provincialism, the un-awakened minds, mean cares and earthbound conversation of his Bedford associates. And yet, like Bunyan checking a blasphemous thought, he checks his own natural distaste as a motion of unregenerate pride. The elders of the Bunyan Meeting were tradesmen or farmers, and they were ignorant 'to a degree which would shock the most superficial young person of the present day'. They certainly shocked the superficial person who was the young Hale White. Yet this is what he afterwards forced himself to see concerning them:

'The farmer could not discuss Coleridge's metres or the validity of the maxim, "Art for Art's sake", but he understood a good deal about the men around him, about his fields, about the face of the sky, and he had found it out all by himself, a fact of more importance than we suppose. He understood also that he must be honest, and everything about him, house, clothes, was a reality and not a sham.

One of these elders I knew well. He was perfectly straightforward, God-fearing also, and therefore wise. Yet he once said to my father, "I ain't got no patience with men who talk potry (poetry) in the pulpit. If you hear that, how can you wonder at your children wanting to go to theātres and cathredrals?"[1]

This might be discounted as the tolerance of old age, but already in *The Revolution in Tanner's Lane* Hale White is harping on this theme. The conversation of Cowfold, he tells us there,[2] was 'personal, trivial, and even scandalous', and it knew nothing of abstractions such as 'the nature of ethical obligation'. But 'it was very keen indeed in apportioning blame to its neighbours who had sinned, and in deciding how far they had gone wrong'. Then follows the characteristic return upon himself:

> 'The young scholar fresh from his study is impatient at what he considers the unprofitable gossip about the people round the corner; but when he gets older he sees that often it is much better than his books, and that distinctions are expressed by a washerwoman, if the objects to be distinguished eat and drink and sleep, which he would find it difficult to make with his symbols.'

And in the Preface to the second edition of the *Autobiography* we have this even more significant comment (ascribed to Reuben Shapcott):

> 'Many a man goes into his study, shuts himself up with his poetry or his psychology, comes out, half understanding what he has read, is miserable because he cannot find anybody with whom he can talk about it, and misses altogether the far more genuine joy which he could have obtained from a game with his children, or listening to what his wife had to tell him about her neighbours. . . . Many persons with refined minds are apt to depreciate happiness, especially if it is of "a low type". Broadly speaking, it is the one thing worth having, and low or high, if it does no mischief, is better than the most spiritual misery.'

'Many a man', in Hale White's terminology, means himself,

---

[1] *Early Life*, pp. 20-1.
[2] pp. 240-1.

and the doctrine that happiness is 'the one thing worth having', which 'many'—or rather nearly all—men take for granted, was with him a costly discovery. 'Spiritual misery' was his native element, and joy was what had to be painfully sought and contended for. First his Puritan sense of election set him apart from the Cowfold farmers and washerwomen, from his own wife and children, and then his Puritan sense of reprobation sent him back to them in humility. Even in the humility there was spiritual pride: "I, the superior person," he says in effect, "am superior enough to see through my own superiority and condemn it." Always the present predicament is the one to be transcended or overcome: in Cowfold, he stands gazing at the signpost 'To London and York', or turns for escape to Wordsworth, Carlyle and Byron; emancipated, he harks back to the beliefs and people of his childhood, or, from the spiritual misery of his study, turns for relief (in theory rather than in practice, perhaps) to the domestic simplicities. In all this he was not singular; it was characteristic of Puritans of his generation, and a symptom of the impoverishment of their spiritual condition, to expect and welcome truth from the other side. One was probably wrong about most things—this feeling, which sprang originally, perhaps, from the Puritan conviction of sin, had come to represent a loss of confidence in the Puritan philosophy of life. Thus nonconformist-liberal readers of the *Daily News*, in the later decades of Hale White's lifetime, absorbed with delight the weekly articles of G. K. Chesterton praising the very things they were supposed to detest most: war, beer and Catholicism.

To this self-reproving thither-sightedness of Hale White may be ascribed his exaltation of the simple, shrewd, good-hearted types in his novels, such as Mrs Carter in *The Revolution in Tanner's Lane* ('like the south-west wind and sunlight after long north-easterly gloom and frost'), Nurse Barton in the same, the admirable Mrs Taylor in *The Deliverance*, Mrs Joll (*Miriam's Schooling*), or Mrs Caffyn (*Clara Hopgood*). Or, in other key, Phoebe Crowhurst, the poor consumptive housemaid to whom Catherine Furze ministers in her last illness. Catherine's meditations, after

Phoebe's death, embody some of Hale White's maturer insights:

> 'She [Phoebe] had faced sickness and death without a murmur; she had no theory of duty, no philosophy, no religion, as it is usually called, save a few dim traditional beliefs, and she was the daughter of common peasants; but she had attained just the one thing essential which religion and philosophy ought to help us to obtain, and if they do not help us to obtain it, they are nothing. She lived not for herself, nor in herself, and it was not even justice to herself which she demanded. . . . She [Catherine] knew herself to be Phoebe's superior intellectually, and that much had been presented to her which was altogether over Phoebe's horizon. But in all her purposes, and in all her activity, she seemed to have had self for a centre, and she felt that she would gladly give up every single advantage she possessed if she could but depose that self and enthrone some other divinity in its place. Oh the bliss of waking up in the morning with the thoughts turned outwards instead of inwards!'[1]

x. When Hearts Are Ill-Affined

There is another important class of persons in the Mark Rutherford novels through whose story Hale White judges himself: the uncongenial or under-valued spouse (generally the wife, though it is the husband in *Miriam's Schooling*), whose nature nevertheless contains stores of selfless devotion, and even intelligence, only to be unlocked by a loving insight which at first is lacking. The classic example is Mrs Cardew in *Catherine Furze*, whose devotion to her husband and whose real powers are contemned by him because she cannot comment aptly on his sermons or say clever things about Milton. But the theme of incompatibility runs persistently throughout the novels and short stories: there is Mrs M'Kay in *The Deliverance*, who despite her love for M'Kay irritates him by echoing all his opinions, and to whom therefore (to her bitter distress) he speaks only of household details; there is (as we have seen) Didymus Farrow, who so much offends the fastidious Miriam; there

---

[1] *Catherine Furze*, pp. 326-7.

is the wife in that strange fantasy "A Dream of Two Dimensions",[1] who, because in that shadow-land she has only two dimensions to her husband's three, becomes the unhappy object of his spleen and cruelty; there is the husband in the story "The Sweetness of a Man's Friend",[2] who is exasperated by his wife's irrelevant remarks about Shelley's *Alastor*, and breaks out: '"O Margaret, I do wish I could find a little more sympathy in you. What a joy it would be for me if you cared for the things for which I care, those which really concern me."' In all these cases (except the "Dream") the discontented partner awakens in time, through fear of loss or through someone else's chance comments, to the other's true worth, and there is repentance and reconciliation. In each of these examples the husband's (or wife's) disgruntlement is exposed as the result of self-absorption, self-pity and blindness to all superiority save his own. There is, however, another group of ill-affined couples from whose misery there is no escape through deepened love or understanding. In depicting these Hale White's sympathies, far from being divided, are wholly on one side. Every reader of Mark Rutherford will think at once of Zachariah Coleman, whose wife Jane, despite a few feeble efforts at impartiality, is represented as almost wholly detestable, cold, conventional, stupid and unloving. There is no criticism of Zachariah when, infuriated by her selfishness and incomprehension, he breaks out:

> 'Whose fault is it that I do not talk to you? When did I ever get any help from you? What do you understand about what concerns me, and when have you ever tried to understand anything? Your home is no home to me. My life is blasted, and it might have been different.'

Jane Coleman, indeed, is almost a spectre—an emanation from all that was deadliest in the old religion, an embodiment, too, of Mark Rutherford's hypochondriac obsessions, clinging to him with monstrous fangs. But there are many other repetitions of this or a similar pattern: Hexton in the story of Miss Arbour (*Autobiography*), the misery of Esther with

[1] *Last Pages from a Journal*, pp. 138 ff.   [2] *Ibid.*, pp. 37 ff.

237

her husband (in the story "Esther"),[1] of Tom Carpenter with his first wife ("The Love of Woman"),[2] or the unhappy first choice of Dr Midleton, and of Mrs Fairfax, in the story "Mrs Fairfax".[3] The case of George Allen and Priscilla in *The Revolution* is almost, but not quite, in this class; not quite, because Priscilla, though she is silly and superficial and cannot understand the principles of Free Trade, is at least affectionate and pathetic. It is not suggested, however, that George could have discovered unsuspected riches in her; he, like Zachariah, had marched blindly into an avoidable trap.

It is difficult to believe that a writer so autobiographical as Hale White would have been drawn so repeatedly to treat this subject of married incompatibility, and to treat it with such evident anguish, and in a strain of self-vindication or— more frequently—of self-reproach, unless it had corresponded to something central in his own experience. Mr Wilfred Stone, who has devoted great care to the topic and ascertained all that can be known about it, thinks that on the whole Hale White's 'fascinated preoccupation with the theme reflects his own experience of married life'.[4] But, as Mr Stone himself gives us evidence for concluding, it is no simple reflection, and to avoid misjudgment we have to distinguish very carefully. It is certain that Harriet Arthur (the first Mrs White) was no Jane Coleman; on the contrary, she was loved and reverenced as a saint by her children, and she was William White's (her father-in-law's) 'dear Harriet'. We know from one of her sons that her attitude to her husband was 'one of devotion, almost of adoration; she was absorbed in him'. Was she then perhaps a Mrs M'Kay, too much his echo? a Mrs Cardew, striving unsuccessfully to enter his (superior) intellectual world? Miss C. M. Maclean, in her recent biography,[5] shares none of Mr Stone's misgivings; she takes, instead, what might be called the 'correct' or 'official' view: Mrs White was a beautiful soul, Hale White

---

[1] *More Pages from a Journal*, pp. 31 ff.
[2] *Last Pages from a Journal*, pp. 95 ff.
[3] *Pages from a Journal*, pp. 218 ff.
[4] See Mr Stone's subtle and searching analysis in ch. XI of his book (pp. 184 ff.).
[5] *Mark Rutherford, a Biography of William Hale White* (1955).

was devoted to her and inconsolable at her loss. The clue to the mystery is to be found in this sentence by Sir William Hale-White, their eldest son: "My father cannot be understood by those who are unaware of his wife's illness."[1] About five years after their happy marriage, Harriet was attacked by 'disseminated sclerosis', a terrible and incurable disease which, through gradually-worsening stages of paralysis, turned her existence into a martyrdom of thirty years. "Both he and she", says Sir William, "bore this thirty year long tragedy without wincing, devoted in their affection for one another." When at last the end came (June 1, 1891), Hale White wrote to his old friend Mrs Colenutt:

'. . . you can hardly imagine what it is to be deprived of an outlet for what you feel most intimately. Much as children are loved, it is impossible to impart to them all one's hopes or fears. My poor wife daily heard from me what nobody now can hear, offered a sympathy which nobody else can give. The world, aware of so small a portion of what was in her shy, unpretending soul, would have been astonished perhaps that she could be of such service to me, but she was for me and not for the world. The lesson of her heroic patience and perfect unselfishness was obvious to everybody, and that daily teaching has also departed.'[2]

With these words before us we might well pass on in respectful silence, and probe no further. But Zachariah's agonized cry re-echoes in one's mind: 'My life is blasted, and it might have been different.' Not through any fault or defect in Harriet, but through unkind Fate, Hale White's life had also been blasted; and we know that, deep down in his unregenerate ego, this is how he took it. He resented it like Job; he had not deserved this at God's hands; he pitied himself more than he pitied his wife; he was even jealous of the sympathy which others lavished on her rather than on him. In all this he was no worse than other men; where he differs from most is in the depth and remorselessness of his self-knowledge and self-criticism. If he had written nothing, we should only know of his life (if in that case we knew anything) what we know of most men's: the decorous surface,

[1] Stone, *loc. cit.*   [2] *Letters to Three Friends*, p. 50.

239

the self-schooling, the daily and lifelong victory of the better self over the natural man. As it is, we have in the novels the projection of his resentments, his egotism, his sense of injustice, and his depression. We have also, however, the record of his struggle against these Apollyons, of his hard-won victory and his painful ascent of those Delectable Mountains where love casts out both fear and self. It is impossible to miss the self-judgment in his comment on Phoebe Crowhurst's last illness, when, after telling us how perfect were her father and mother, brother and sister, in their tenderness and self-forgetfulness, he adds:

> 'It was not with them as with a man known to the writer of this history. His wife, whom he professed to love, was dying of consumption. "I do not deny she suffers", he said, "but nobody thinks of *me*."'[1]

Had Hale White any other just grievance on the score of intellectual disparity? We hardly know, but we can surmise that this 'shy, unpretending soul' was no George Eliot or Pauline Caillaud; she liked Cowper, but not 'Tennyson's *Maud* and so on'; she 'did not understand that kind of poetry'.[2] The hint is sufficient.

xi. Holding Fast With Claws

Why so much biographical detail in a book purporting to deal with ideas and beliefs rather than with people? It is because with Mark Rutherford the man and the beliefs are inseparable. In his lifelong toil of rebuilding a workable new faith from the ruins of the old, he had no other cement with which to bind its fragments than what his own experience, inward and outward, could supply. In this he is representative of a half-century which, if it did not abandon faith entirely, had to do just this; and it is because in his life and thought the process can be seen with exceptional clearness that I think him deserving of an important place in these Studies.

It is difficult to summarize his final faith; it was indefinite,

---

[1] *Catherine Furze*, p. 318.   [2] *Groombridge Diary*, p. 93.

and full of contradictions. But though indefinite it was, like the faith he ascribed to Wordsworth, none the less supporting. The strength of a religion, he believed, was proportionate to its 'applicability to life'. This is not to say that he reduced religion to subjective feelings; on the contrary, he insisted that it must be objective, and he saw that it was the strength of Rome to assert this. It did mean, however, that all the affirmations of faith, to be valid for him, must be proved upon the pulses, felt to have meaning in the context of daily living. Treated in this way, many of the beliefs of Christianity turned out to be true after all, though not in the sense assumed by the orthodox. The Atonement, for example, became 'a sublime summing up as it were of what sublime men have to do for their race; an exemplification, rather than a contradiction, of Nature herself, as we know her in our own experience'.[1] Or again, speaking of the Christian doctrines of a future life and of Christ's return to judge the quick and the dead, he says:

> 'surely if we are to have any reasons for being virtuous, this is as good as any other. It is just as respectable to believe that we ought to abstain from iniquity because Christ is at hand, and we expect to meet Him, as to abstain from it because by our abstention we shall be healthier or more prosperous.'

Paul dreamt of Christ's speedy return—'a baseless dream, and the enlightened may call it ridiculous'. But was it? No; 'putting aside its temporary mode of expression, it is the hope and the prophecy of all noble hearts, a sign of their inability to concur in the present condition of things'.[2] These examples are taken from the account of Ellen Butts's faith; she had, he says, 'laid hold upon heaven'—which, being interpreted, meant that a new spirit had been breathed into her from the New Testament. She had learnt from thence that she must show charity not only to those 'whom she loved by nature', but 'to those with whom she was not in sympathy, and who even wronged her'; and that, hoping for no return for her love, she must be merciful as her Father in heaven is merciful. Hale White remarks that the publicans,

---

[1] *Autobiography*, p. 22.   [2] *Deliverance*, pp. 59 ff.

whom Jesus credited with loving those who loved them, must have been better Christians than the 'natural' men of today who find it hard to love anybody but themselves; while the duty of loving our *enemies* is quite beyond all men now except 'a few of the elect in whom Christ still survives'. This doctrine of disinterested love, he goes on,

> 'is really the expression of the *idea* in morality, and incalculable is the blessing that one great religious teacher should have been bold enough to teach the idea, and not any limitation of it. He always taught it, the inward born, the heavenly law towards which everything strives. He always trusted it; He did not deal in exceptions; He relied on it to the uttermost, never despairing. This has always seemed to me to be the real meaning of the word faith. It is permanent confidence in the idea, a confidence never to be broken down by apparent failure. . . .'

'Faith, the belief which saves', he wrote in later life, 'is not to be preserved without a struggle. It is not a conclusion which comes automatically from evidence presented.' What then is it? Hale White did not know the terminology of Kierkegaard or the modern religious existentialists, but he had attained their insight. 'A hundred times a day suggestions are made within us to abandon this or that result we have achieved with much effort'—and what are we then to do? Not balance arguments, but *'hold fast with claws'*.[1]

Genuine religion is not 'constructed out of notions'; it is the practice of the indwelling of God: 'How simple, how exclusive of theology!'[2] And for us this means the indwelling of Christ; not 'the official, symbolic, ecclesiastical Christ' but 'the real Galilean', the Christ who 'is I, more than I am myself'. 'Even the parsons', he says, 'do not and cannot believe that there was as much God in Jesus Christ as I believe there was.' Of this indwelling he had seen an example in Caleb Morris, the Welsh preacher of his early London days, without whom (as he said in old age), he might have been merely 'Church', or else 'broken away from creeds altogether'. Of Morris he wrote that he had

---

[1] *Last Pages from a Journal*, p. 302 (my italics).
[2] *Letters to Three Friends*, p. 222.

'never met a man in whom Christianity, *or rather Christ*, was so vitally inherent. With him Christianity was not assent to certain propositions, nor external obedience to its precepts. It was an indwelling of the Christ of the Gospels, shaping thought, speech and life.'[1]

'Mere perception of the advantages (whether in this world or the next) of doing that which is right is insufficient to make us do it. There must be something more, impulse, obligation, call it what you will, of which no further explanation can be given.' This 'something more' was, specifically, the indwelling of God; 'Thou in me and I in Thee'. That is why Hale White would have none of the formal arguments for the existence of God; 'the proof lies', he says, 'in hints and dreams which are not expressible by human language'. The conception of 'an Infinite which actually exists' may be a paradox to the understanding, but (as Coleridge would have agreed) it is 'more influential than any truth which the understanding can define'. In spiritual experience the great thing is not to be disobedient to the heavenly vision, however dimly or uncertainly it may come to us. 'The faintest vision of God is more determinative of life than a gross earthly certainty.' Religion is not 'an intellectual subtlety', it is a question of discipleship to Christ; unless we are disciples, salvation is a mere 'outside transaction'.

One might have supposed in the light of all this that Hale White would be in sympathy with modernists like Jowett who were trying to restate the truths of religion in a manner not scandalous to the modern mind. Yet we find him advising any candidate for Holy Orders, who may be hesitating when asked to affirm what is 'no longer a reality for him', to 'expel all conjectures as to what Maurice, Kingsley or, far worse, what Jowett would have advised. Jowett, by the way, is to me the representative of modern Infidelity'.[2] Elsewhere he calls Jowett's 'so-called thinking' a 'sloppy mess of words'. The explanation probably is that Jowett, like the other Broad Churchmen, was suspect from the very fact of his staying

---

[1] *Last Pages from a Journal*, p. 247 (my italics).
[2] *Letters to Three Friends*, pp. 163-4.

within the Church while holding views incompatible with its official creed. Jowett thus seemed to him to live in what he calls the strange 'element of ecclesiastical lying', and to purvey 'a mush of lies and truth, a compound more poisonous than lies unmixed'. In thinking of Jowett as a trimmer or prevaricator he did him injustice; what made him unjust, however, was the feeling that Jowett had not fought for faith as he himself had done; that Jowett, instead of painfully winning for himself more of truth than other men, had contented himself with believing less. 'I have much more respect for the Pope.'[1] It marks, I think, Hale White's separation from what might be called official 'liberalism' or modernism, that when (as occasionally happens) he uses one of its current phrases he appears not to be speaking in his own voice. When, for example, George Allen read in the *Imitation of Christ* that "He to whom the Eternal Word speaketh is delivered from a world of unnecessary troubles," his heart was dilated; 'it was the birth in him,' says Mark Rutherford, 'of what philosophers call *the idea*, that Incarnation which has ever been our Redemption'.[2] Or again, at the end of *Clara Hopgood*, he makes Mazzini say (apparently with his own approval) that the Crucifixion was sublime, 'but let us reverence also the Eternal Christ, who is for ever being crucified for our salvation'.[3] These are the stock profundities of Hegel or Strauss; if they had come from Jowett, he would have dismissed them as "Bubbles that glitter as they rise and break On vain Philosophy's aye-babbling spring". We hear his authentic voice more surely when he tells us that belief in the harsh theology of Calvin was 'more meritorious than the weak protests of so-called enlightenment', and Calvinism itself preferable to modern 'flowery' Christianity. Or again, when he writes that

> 'Consolation and light will often come, not by seeking for them directly, but by just putting ourselves straight. Intellectual trouble may disappear by simply doing our duty.'[4]

[1] *Ibid.*, p. 258.
[2] *Revolution in Tanner's Lane*, pp. 341-2.
[3] *Clara Hopgood*, p. 298.
[4] *Last Pages from a Journal*, p. 301.

Here at least he was at one with Jowett, and it is interesting to find that he kept a letter he had received from Jowett, which contained the following remark:

‘ “I believe that in our day those who have speculative difficulties about Christianity must try to get rid of them by a Christian life.” ’[1]

Endlessly brooding on the problem of pain and evil, and the co-existence of beauty and pestilence in Nature, his final wisdom was *not to think about it*; not, of course, to ignore the sufferer, but to ‘be silent . . . and busy ourselves rather with what is productive of quiet content and joy. Every moment wasted on insoluble problems is so much taken from time which might be spent in the absorption of sunlight.’[2] We are to avoid the ‘dark wood of metaphysics and theology. Be satisfied with the Love of God, a different thing altogether from the science of God and theology.’[3] Gloom exists, but so do the stars; our duty, especially if we are ‘constitutionally sad’, is ‘to affirm the stars rather than the gloom’.

‘Patience; patience; a little more climbing and in a moment when you least expect it they [clouds of fog] will lie beneath you.’[4]

It is easy to be melancholy about this tragic and unintelligible world; the true heroism lies in ‘resolving the commonest difficulty’. ‘Annihilation of this swarm of petty invading cares by adoration!’;[5] ‘begin each day with reference to a Higher Power’.[6]

In his last years he had a ‘strong *wish* to be able to belong to some Church’.[7] ‘What right had anyone to “stand aloof” from others?’[8] Yet Mrs D. V. White spoke truly when she remarked that ‘we must certainly say of him, as he said of Wordsworth . . ., that “any sect inclined to adopt” him “will find him a dangerous ally” ’.[9] It was a pity, for, as I hope this chapter may have shown, the adoption of so devout a spirit would have brought gain to ‘any sect’. It was the weakness of the Churches in that age (and not that age alone)

[1] *Groombridge Diary*, pp. 405-6. [2] *Letters to Three Friends*, pp. 80-1.
[3] *Groombridge Diary*, p. 147. [4] *Pages from a Journal*, p. 344.
[5] *Last Pages from a Journal*, p. 290. [6] *Groombridge Diary*, p. 365.
[7] *Ibid.*, p. 139. [8] *Ibid.*, p. 183. [9] *Ibid.*, p. 451.

that such men had to remain outside them. One of Hale White's saddest entries, near the end of his Journal, was: 'Not a soul has said a word to me for years about God.'

XII. Sunset and Evening Star

Often throughout his life, Hale White had drawn consolation from those sundowns when, after hours of gloom and rain, the sun looks out for a few brilliant moments before sinking. It was one of his sacred symbols of reassurance—'a forgiveness', as he said. It might have been a heavenly promise too, for near the close of his overcast life the clouds were rolled back, and he was granted a sundown of great and most unexpected bliss. His love for Dorothy Vernon Horace Smith, her love for him, and their all-too-short spell of marriage and perfect companionship, satisfied the 'infinite need' of his life, and crowned it with a glory well-nigh miraculous. 'I flew to you', he told her; and what was more marvellous in a woman some forty-five years his junior, she flew to him. What might have been the result if she had been his lifelong helpmeet we can only guess; almost certainly, as he himself said, there would have been no Mark Rutherford novels. What is quite certain is that by her infinite patience, tact, high spirits and humour, and by her victorious love—a love, too, which abounded in *knowledge*—she accomplished more for his deliverance in a few short years than all the sages could, and more than his own lifelong toil had done. It was a love without illusion or sentimentality, a pure invisible flame. She saw him just as he was, his egotism, his jealous possessiveness, and his relapses into gloom—which, like the trapdoor into Hell at the very Gates of Heaven—still recurred to mar their joy. But she also saw his nobility, his courage, his veracity and his self-conquests, and she loved him not only for these but for all that he was. To her love were also revealed sides of him which were unknown to himself, and would not be guessed from his writings: his charm in conversation, and his power to draw the best from everyone, making 'ugly, uninteresting people look beautiful and wise'.

I will end with a quotation from *The Groombridge Diary*,[1] which, without comment of mine, will show how this sunset glow wrought upon him a transformation nearer, perhaps, to true 'conversion' than anything he had known—nearer, certainly, than the one he had feigned at the Bunyan Meeting:

'It is strange that he sees now a strain in his nature which I am convinced he never saw before; a wretchedness in himself which seems as if it *must* vent itself in making wretchedness for others; not with any cruel intention, but just from sheer misery; an instinctive desire to damp enthusiasm or joy. The odd thing is that this instinct lies so closely and comfortably side by side with an instinct for those very qualities which he damps; he loves joy and enthusiasm as well as hates them spitefully. I said "You sometimes feel wretched." He said "Yes"; he was making up the fire. I said: "And you feel as if you must make other people wretched." "Yes," he said bitterly, "it's damnable", and he gave the fire a savage poke. *We laughed a great deal* [my italics]. . . . It has been a merciful thing that some instinct . . ., of a diametrically opposite kind, should have from the first withstood his instinct. I have clung passionately, obstinately, to exuberant joy and health and happiness all through these three years; and I suppose the whole time, though I did not realize it (except bit by bit, slowly, unconsciously, and as it were with resolutely shut eyes), the whole time he was instinctively at war with me trying to wreck his happiness and my own. As by degrees his nature has straightened out—*here and there it was very much curled up, fold within fold* [my italics again]—this instinct has become plainer to himself. . . . He has implored me in a sort of terror once or twice of late never to yield to this instinct, never to allow myself to be damped, however strong his mood is upon him. I do not think I should yield now, for joy daily grows in me, and misery in him is daily dying. . . . I doubt if two people ever loved one another so furiously and victoriously.'

The love of Dorothy was the nearest he had known to the love of God, and as he went down to the River it was given to him to hear the trumpets sounding from the other side.

---

[1] pp. 393-4.

CHAPTER VI

JOHN MORLEY
(1838-1923)

1. Liberalism

LYTTON STRACHEY was a little disappointed
with Viscount Morley's *Recollections*, which appeared
towards the end of the First World War (in 1917).
Though he recognized the great interest and historical value
of Volume II, in which Morley's statesmanship as Secretary
of State for India was impressively displayed, he found the
first volume 'curiously tame'. Perhaps it was because that
volume, dealing with Morley's early life and his career as a
man of letters, seemed 'impregnated with the Victorian
spirit'. 'An air of singular solemnity hovers over it, and its
moral tone is of the highest.' 'Only a Victorian,' says
Strachey, 'having made his reputation by writing the lives of
Diderot, Rousseau and Voltaire, would, on his return from
a visit to Paris, have thrown, in horror, two French novels
out of the railway-carriage window.' He complains that in
the Victorian Age even the atheists (of whom Morley was
one) were religious, and 'the religious atmosphere fills his
book'.

If it is true that Morley was 'impregnated with the Victorian spirit', and if he knew what it meant to disbelieve
religiously, then he seems to deserve a chapter in the present
book, which is largely concerned with those very things.
But, further, he deserves to be recognized and revalued by
any historian or student of Victorian literature and ideas. As
editor of the *Fortnightly Review* during fifteen of its most
exciting years (1867-82), as editor of the *English Men of
Letters* Series, as reviewer, essayist, biographer and historian,
he was one of the most influential critics of his time, sharing
the literary and intellectual dictatorship only, perhaps, with
Leslie Stephen and Matthew Arnold. In the 'history of
ideas' (or in his own phrase, of 'opinion') his studies of

Burke, De Maistre, Voltaire, Rousseau, Diderot and many others show him as an eminent pioneer, and his *On Compromise*, though it lacks the gracefulness of *Culture and Anarchy*, can be classed with it as a responsible critique on the times. And although questions on Morley are never found in university examinations on Victorian literary criticism, his essays on Macaulay, Carlyle, Byron, Browning and Wordsworth (to mention no more) are quite as worthy of inclusion in the canon as some of Arnold's—his Milton or his Shelley, for example. Of Morley's more strictly political and historical writings—his lives of Cobden and of Gladstone, of Cromwell and of Pitt—I do not propose to speak, nor am I directly concerned with his public career as Liberal statesman—'the last survivor of the heroic age', as Asquith called him. Not directly, because Home Rule and Indian Reform, and the policies of Gladstone, Lord Salisbury and Sir Henry Campbell-Bannerman, are outside the scope of this book. But in all thinking or writing about Morley it must never for a moment be forgotten that the editor and critic was afterwards Gladstone's Irish Secretary and Campbell-Bannerman's Indian Secretary, that literature with him was always secondary to 'social action', and that for him Liberalism was no mere party affair, but the very stuff of his being: at once religion, philosophy, inspiration and *raison d'être*. Morley was one of the very few English statesmen— and surely, we must believe, one of the very last—who was also an eminent scholar and man of letters. And all his early writings, which we are now about to consider, were mental rehearsals for his later actions on the world's stage.

About fifty years ago (1909) Algernon Cecil, rather surprisingly for that date, proclaimed that Liberalism was near its end, and that in twenty years from then we should have reverted, 'doubtless with many and formidable changes, to an earlier type'.[1] Whether Cecil was thinking of Liberalism as a political party, or as a political philosophy, or as both, there was true prescience in his remark. Of the Liberal Old Guard, Morley was, indeed, one of the last survivors, and as a political philosophy Liberalism has now to be content with

[1] *Six Oxford Thinkers* (1909), p. 255.

supplying saving principles to both the main parties of the day. But as I have suggested, Liberalism for Morley was far more than a party programme; it was a stream of tendency, a philosophy of history, a call to action, an ethic and a religion. It meant to him what every intelligent man should try to think, and every good man try to do, in the hundred years following the French Revolution. In the last analysis, Morley's Liberalism was Christianity minus the creeds, and that is the chief reason why I include him in the present volume. 'To have been deprived of the faith of the old dispensation', he said, 'is the first condition of strenuous endeavour after the new',[1] and in this strenuous endeavour towards what he deemed to be right and true, an endeavour maintained with stoical awareness that to him at least only a Pisgah-sight of the promised land (if that) would ever be granted, Morley's Liberalism and his religion consisted. This, the clue to his inmost mind, may be seen in all his writings, but a few examples will suffice. In *On Compromise* he thus summarizes the philosophy of Liberalism:

'That the conditions of the social union are not a mystery, only to be touched by miracle, but the results of explicable causes, and susceptible of constant modification: that the thoughts of wise and patriotic men should be perpetually turned towards the improvement of these conditions in every direction: that contented acquiescence in the ordering that has come down to us from the past is selfish and anti-social, because amid the ceaseless change that is inevitable in a growing organism, the institutions of the past demand progressive re-adaptations: that such improvements are most likely to be secured in the greatest abundance by limiting the sphere of authority, extending that of free individuality, and steadily striving after the bestowal, so far as the nature of things will ever permit it, of equality of opportunity: that while there is dignity in ancestry a modern society is only safe in proportion as it summons capacity to its public counsels and enterprises: that such a society to endure must progress: that progress on its political side means more than anything else the substitution of Justice as a governing idea, instead of Privilege, and that the best guarantee for justice in public

[1] *On Compromise*, p. 75 (ed. of 1888).

dealings is the participation in their own government of the people most likely to suffer from injustice.'[1]

In his essay on Carlyle[2] he expresses his ideal much more briefly and generally:

'the transformation of the West from a state of war, of many degrees of social subordination, of religious privilege, of aristocratic administration, into a state of peaceful industry, of equal international rights, of social equality, of free and equal tolerance of creeds.'

And more briefly still: 'Respect for the dignity and worth of the individual is its root.'[3]

Algernon Cecil sighed over Morley's dogged belief in Progress: 'the most credulous adherent of threadbare superstition never pledged himself so unreservedly to the truth of his crumbling dogmas as Lord Morley to this faith in Progress'. But Morley never held the belief in its truly superstitious form, namely that progress is automatic and proceeds independently of human effort. The belief appears not ignoble when stated by one of Morley's greatest heroes, J. S. Mill, in words that Morley loved to quote:

'All the grand sources of human suffering are in a great degree, many of them almost entirely, conquerable by human care and effort; and though their removal is grievously slow—though a long succession of generations will perish in the breach before the conquest is completed, and this world becomes all that, if will and knowledge were not wanting, it might easily be made—yet every mind sufficiently intelligent and generous to bear a part, however small and unconspicuous, in the endeavour, will draw a noble enjoyment from the contest itself, which he would not for any bribe in the form of selfish indulgence consent to be without.'[4]

Morley's was such a mind.

11. Upbringing and Oxford Days

It is no surprise, indeed one would expect, to find that Morley, like Leslie Stephen, Frederic Harrison, George

[1] *Ibid.*, pp. 125-6. [2] *Critical Miscellanies*, vol. i, p. 194 (1888 ed.).
[3] *Recollections*, vol. i, p. 21.
[4] Quoted by Morley from *Utilitarianism*, *Crit. Misc.*, vol. iii, p. 87.

Eliot and nearly all the company of the agnostic angels, had a religious upbringing. His father, Jonathan Morley, was the son of a Wesleyan cloth and cotton manufacturer in Yorkshire, and was himself a Wesleyan until he set up as a surgeon at Blackburn, when he became an Anglican. His mother, a Northumbrian, was 'all her life an ardent Wesleyan.'[1] Sabbatical observance and general discipline at home were strict, but one suspects that some tares were sown in John's mind, along with much good seed, by Dr Jonathan. Though a Churchman, he was negligent of Church ordinances, and critical of the clergy: 'impatient', his son tells us, 'as if of some personal affront, of either Puseyites on the one hand, or German infidels on the other'. He had taught himself Latin and French, and John Morley 'long possessed the pocket Virgil, Racine, Byron, that he used to carry with him as he walked to the houses of handloom weavers on the hillside round'. John was sent to school at Hoole's Dissenting Academy, which 'abounded in the unadulterated milk of the Independent word'. Here he attended the Independent Chapel twice every Sunday, and had to commit to memory each day five or six verses of Scripture 'and on Sundays to repeat the whole'. No doubt this accounts for the biblical allusions which occur so frequently throughout Morley's writings, and the strenuous Puritan tone imparted to his mind there remained with him for life. From thence he went for a short time to University College School in London, the only Public School which then, and for nearly a century afterwards, prided itself upon its non-religious (or irreligious) basis, and lastly to Cheltenham College. It was at Cheltenham that he wrote a sixth-form poem which, in the judgment of the Headmaster, gave promise of his being likely some day to write 'very fair prose'. He won a scholarship at Lincoln College, Oxford, in 1856, and for many terms 'was lodged in Wesley's rooms, sometimes ruminating how it was that all the thoughts and habits of my youthful Methodism were so rapidly vanishing'.

The Oxford of the later 'fifties, when 'the star of Newman had set, and the sun of Mill was high', abounded, as we have

[1] F. W. Hirst, *Early Life and Letters of John Morley* (1927), vol. i, p. 7.

already seen from Frederic Harrison's experience, in corrosive influences, and it is the fact that in Wesley's rooms Morley lost his faith.[1] At the moment of his entry at Lincoln, Mark Pattison had just withdrawn in 'black, unphilosophic mortification from all college work', so Morley missed the benefit of an influence which, he thinks, might have made 'all the difference in a thousand ways'. We do not know as much as we could wish about Morley's Oxford life, but we know that, like Harrison and others, he was exposed to many contrary winds of doctrine. He listened to Stanley on ecclesiastical history; he seldom missed Bishop Wilberforce's sermons at St Mary's ('he excelled any man I ever heard, ecclesiastic or secular, in the taking gift of unction'); he attended Mansel's Bampton Lectures, which he calls the 'official answer' to the points at issue between Mill and Hamilton. He was influenced by the 'liberal champion', Goldwin Smith, and enjoyed the 'captivating comradeship' of J. Cotter Morison, who introduced him to Carlyle's works. But on the whole we have to be content with the rather unsatisfying generalization in the *Recollections*, that 'the force of miracle and myth and intervening Will in the interpretation of the world began to give way before the reign of law'. Morley had been intended for Holy Orders, but 'life at Oxford had shaken the foundations'. There was a painful quarrel with his exasperated father, and Morley, after taking a mere pass degree, went down (1859) to face poverty and drudgery in London.

Probably the most decisive intellectual influence in Morley's Oxford days had been that of Mill. 'For twenty years', he wrote in his obituary essay on Mill (May 1873), 'no one at all open to serious intellectual impressions has left Oxford without having undergone the influence of Mr Mill's teaching.'[2] But what was Mill's influence on Morley? Not merely the influence of the author of the *System of Logic*, of *Utilitarianism*, of *Liberty*; not merely that of the arch-enemy of theology and the intuitionist philosophy. It was also that of Mill the author of the essay on Coleridge, the Mill who

[1] See F. W. Knickerbocker, *Free Minds: J. M. and his Friends* (Harvard, 1943), p. 36. [2] *Crit. Misc.*, vol. iii, p. 39.

had felt the power of Carlyle, and of all that could be said against the classic Benthamism of his father; the Mill who persisted in loving Wordsworth in spite of his radical friends. This strange and fascinating ambivalence of Mill—one of the surest signs of his greatness, if not of his consistency—is memorably noted by Morley in his review of Cross's *Life of George Eliot*,[1] where he is showing how she, too, while welcoming all new light, never became unmindful of older wisdom. Mill, he says, defended Wordsworth on the ground that he 'was helping to keep alive in human nature elements which utilitarians and innovators would need when their present and particular work was done'. Morley continues:

> 'His famous pair of essays on Bentham and Coleridge were published (for the first time, so far as our generation was concerned) in the same year as *Adam Bede*,[2] and I can vividly remember how the "Coleridge" first awoke in many of us, who were then youths at Oxford, that sense of truth having many mansions and that desire and power of sympathy with the past, with the positive bases of the social fabric, and with the value of Permanence in States, which form the reputable side of all conservatisms.'

The light of this awakening never went out; it shines throughout all Morley's writing and thinking, and points him to his best insights as an interpreter of history and of his own times.

Not at Oxford, but in London soon afterwards, Morley's Comtist friends confirmed what he had learnt from Mill. The Oxford Comtists had flourished two academic generations before Morley, and George Eliot once told him she saw no reason why the Religion of Humanity should not have taken root in England if Congreve had been more of an apostle. Morley himself was at one time not far from joining the new positivist 'Church', which seemed to promise the emotional satisfaction and spiritual impulse of the old without offending the intellect. He was held back, however, by a certain instinctive suspicion of new 'sects', and by the like

[1] *Ibid.*, p. 131.
[2] 1859. Mill's essays had originally appeared in the *Westminster Review*, 1838 and 1840.

suspicions in others whom he respected, such as Mill, Huxley, Spencer and Tyndall. Nevertheless Comte's reading of history, and above all his summons to cease destroying, and begin constructing a new world on the old foundations —a positive synthesis between revolution and reaction—all this sank deep into Morley's mind, and 'seemed to him a development of Mill's best wisdom'. Henceforth, throughout his life, Morley strove in this spirit with the aftermaths of the French Revolution. That Revolution had temporarily failed, because it had attempted too much and too soon. The aim of the wise Liberal, who had learnt his lesson from Mill and Comte, must be to bring to slow realization its essential and best idea, without disregarding, as it had done, the ineluctable facts of human nature and of history. From amongst the London Comtists with whom Morley now associated (a circle which included G. H. Lewes and George Eliot), he singles out Pierre Laffitte, the friend (and literary executor) of Comte himself, as the man who 'did more than anyone else to furnish the key and the direction of my French studies'. Laffitte had the wisdom 'not to labour the pontifical side of Comte's system', but to lay emphasis upon his conception of history as an 'ordered course'. Frederic Harrison, too, 'incomparable as controversialist, powerful in historical sense and knowledge', became at this time what he remained for fifty years, Morley's intimate friend. From these influences Morley learnt once again, and still more deeply than he had learnt it from Mill's *Coleridge*, that to build the new you must understand the old; that all powerful reactions witness to some truth which revolutions have forgotten; that forces, ideas and institutions now effete or obstructive have once played a necessary rôle in history, and cannot be superseded without fulfilling, in some other and higher way, the needs they had formerly met. Morley himself tells us that it was 'in this school' that he 'began to absorb the lesson that I tried to apply all through—to do justice to truths presented and services rendered by men in various schools, with whom in important and even in vital respects I could not in the least bring myself to agree'.

All this helps to explain the seeming paradox that the first important writings of this staunch liberal and progressive were studies of the leaders of reaction, Burke and De Maistre. The French Revolution never ceased to be, for him, the starting-point of all that was best and worthiest in the modern world, but to further its ideals effectively we must try to understand why it failed, and why progress has since been so painfully slow. To understand this we must reckon with all that its wisest and weightiest enemies have to say. As he puts it in the essay on De Maistre:

> 'unless the modern Liberal admits the strength inherent in the cause of his enemies, it is impossible for him to explain to himself the slow advance and occasional repulse of the host in which he has enlisted, and the tardy progress that Liberalism has made in that stupendous reconstruction, which the Revolution has forced the modern political thinker to meditate upon, and the modern statesman to further and control'.[1]

III. Early Writings

1. Burke was from the beginning, and always remained, a 'high idol' of Morley's. He owed more to him 'for practical principles in the strategy and tactics of public life' than to any of the other guides of his youth. His first book was on Burke (1867), and he wrote the "English Men of Letters" volume on him twelve years later. In agreement for once with Macaulay, he regarded Burke as 'the greatest man since Milton'. Until 1790 Burke had steadily advocated popular principles; he supported the progressive side in the Constitutional struggle; he was in the right about Ireland, and India, and America; he was in the politics of the eighteenth century what Wesley was in its religion, the inspirer of high principle and ennobling passion. And when the French Revolution came, 'he changed his front, but he never changed his ground'.[2] Long before Comte, he exposed the fundamental error of revolutionary politicians, the idea that 'society was at their disposal, independent of its past develop-

---

[1] 1868. *Crit. Misc.*, vol. ii, 1898 ed., p. 306.
[2] *Burke* (1867), p. 53.

ment, devoid of inherent impulses and easily capable of being morally regenerated by the mere modification of legislative rules'.[1] 'The nature of man is intricate,' he quotes with deep approval from Burke's *Reflections*, 'the objects of society are of the greatest possible complexity; and therefore no simple disposition or direction of power can be suitable, either to man's nature, or to the quality of his affairs'. Burke's was the noblest type of conservatism, because it was based upon a profound insight into history and human nature. 'We are afraid', he had said, 'to put men to live and trade each on his own private stock of reason, because we suspect that this stock in each man is small, and that the individuals would do better to avail themselves of the general bank and capital of nations and of ages. Many of our men of speculation, instead of exploding general prejudices, employ their sagacity to discover the latent wisdom which prevails in them.' Morley, the rationalist, learnt from Burke that the 'naked reason is in itself a less effective means of influencing action, than when it exists as one part of a fabric of ancient and endeared association'.[2] In the great revolutionary issue Burke took the 'wrong' side, but he took it in the right spirit. Tom Paine, for example, was more 'correct' in his views, but who could compare him with Burke for wisdom and enduring usefulness? And so, while recognizing moral grandeur in the revolutionary impetus, Morley could yet see in the writing of its arch-enemy, 'a wiser, deeper, broader and more permanent view of the elements of social stability'. Finally, 'to foresee the Empire in 1790 was a feat of sagacity to which probably no man in Europe except [Burke] was then competent'.[3]

2. In tackling De Maistre next after Burke, Morley showed in the most striking possible way how well he had learnt the lesson to know one's enemies. Burke had opposed the Revolution, but he had understood it and foreseen its outcome. De Maistre, on the other hand, was a Catholic and an aristocrat who, though he lived on till 1821, 'never dreamt

[1] *Burke* ("English Men of Letters", 1879), p. 158.
[2] *Ibid.*, p. 174.   [3] *Burke* (1867), p. 265.

257

that his cause was lost', and 'mocked and defied the Revolution to the end'. His ruling idea was *'absolument tuer l'esprit du dix-huitième siècle'*. According to him, the philosophy of that century will one day be seen as 'one of the most shameful epochs of the human mind'. 'Contempt for Locke is the beginning of knowledge.' Remarks like these remind one of the scarcely less violent fulminations of Coleridge (after 1801) against Locke and the 'philosophy of death', of which the fruit was Jacobinism. And indeed Morley suggests to us that if Coleridge had been a Catholic his reaction against the godless century might have been almost identical with that of De Maistre. This prophet of reaction impressed Morley, as he had impressed Comte, by the rigorous consistency and the ability with which he propounded his Catholic interpretation of history. The Papacy had been, at the beginning of Christendom, the centre of cohesion; it had disciplined and organized the chaos of the dark ages, and had continued, under divine guidance, to be the unifying and saving principle of Western civilization until challenged by the godless Revolution. Now, in the new dark age following the Revolution, the Papacy must reassume its former task, for there is no alternative to spiritual unity except disintegration and dictatorships. Of all this Morley gives a perfectly fair and non-ironic summary; he feels the cogency—and indeed, given De Maistre's premises, the unanswerable force—of the argument. He notes, however, that De Maistre speaks of the Church 'not theologically nor spiritually, but politically and socially'. 'In the eighteenth century men were accustomed to ask of Christianity, as Protestants always ask of so much of Catholicism as they have dropped, whether or no it is true.' But now, after the Revolution, the question became how strong it was, and how far it might be able to contribute to the reconstruction of society. This approach, it may be noted in passing, is familiar to us in our own time, when Christianity (sometimes, but not always, specifically the Roman Catholic Church) is often spoken of as a 'bulwark against', or the 'only alternative to', Communism. Morley's reply to De Maistre proceeds on orthodox Comtean lines. What De Maistre did not see was that the forces which had

once brought order into European chaos were now themselves in decay, and that the new forces of order were precisely those eighteenth century ideas of freedom, justice and
equality which De Maistre abominated. 'De Maistre's mind',
he says (using Comte's historical formula), 'was of the highest
type of those who fill the air with the arbitrary assumptions
of theology, and the abstractions of the metaphysical stage
of thought.' Those can best appraise him who perceive how
anachronistic he is. In his concluding passage Morley drops
his pose of balanced objectivity, and delivers a knock-out
blow at the Catholic pretensions. 'Dogmas which cannot by
any compromise be incorporated with the daily increasing
mass of knowledge'; 'forms of the theological hypothesis
which all the preponderating influences of contemporary
thought concur . . . in discrediting'; a history which for five
centuries has shown the Church to be the 'sworn enemy of
mental freedom and growth'—how, in the light of all this,
can the Church regenerate the modern world? Its claims, as
set forth by De Maistre, are 'pitiable and impotent'.

Lessing said that Christianity had been tried and failed,
but that the 'religion of Christ' remained to be tried. On this
Morley remarks, magnanimously and in the spirit of Comte,
that 'Christianity' (meaning the historic organization called
The Church) had *not* failed, until recent times. But—'the
religion of Christ'? Will this perhaps, he asks, 'in changed
forms and with new supplements', be the 'chief inspirer of
that *social and human sentiment* which seems to be the only
spiritual bond capable of uniting men together again in a
common and effective faith'?[1] Perhaps; but at any rate 'it is
certain that the Christianity of the future will have to be so
different from the Christianity of the past, as to demand or
deserve another name'.

iv. French Studies

In the middle of the nineteenth century, as has been said,[2]
it looked as if the eighteenth century were dead—killed by

---

[1] *Crit. Misc.*, vol. ii, p. 336 (my italics).
[2] Cf. Knickerbocker, *op. cit.*, pp. 129-30.

Burke, by the Germano-Coleridgean reaction, by the Catholic reaction, by Romanticism, by the Oxford Movement, and finally buried by Carlyle. Morley, like Leslie Stephen at much the same time, set himself to bring it back to life. But not, of course, in its original form. The reaction lay in between, and Morley, as we have seen, was not the man to underrate its strength and its significance. He turned to the eighteenth century, not with the uncommitted curiosity of historical research, but in order to discover why his own faith, taking its rise there, had proved abortive, and how it could best be reconstructed, in the light of experience, to meet nineteenth century needs. His *Voltaire*, *Rousseau* and *Diderot* are therefore really tracts for the times; here, he is saying, are the bricks with which we have to build: can we, with the aid of Burkean and Comtean cement, construct the future with them? Morley was much influenced, in the early 'seventies, by Matthew Arnold's doctrine about the disinterestedness of the critical spirit, and the need for a free play of mind on all stock subjects and notions. There could be no more effective way of attaining this detachment than by criticizing one's own century obliquely through discussions of its predecessor. In this manner, as Morley himself says in a review of Pater's *Renaissance*, 'a man can take part in the discussion and propagation of ideas, while yet standing in some sort aloof from the agitation of the present'.[1]

I. VOLTAIRE

He began (1872) with Voltaire, 'the very eye of eighteenth century illumination'.

'We may think of Voltairism', he says, 'somewhat as we think of Catholicism or the Renaissance or Calvinism. It was one of the cardinal liberations of the growing race, one of the emphatic manifestations of some portion of the minds of men, which an immediately foregoing system and creed had either ignored or outraged.'[2]

Morley's doctrine of 'the man and the moment' developed as

[1] *Fortnightly Review*, April 1873.   [2] *Voltaire* (1919 ed.), pp. 1-2.

he grew older. Later he came to lay more stress upon social and economic conditions as primary causes of historical change. But even in the *Voltaire*, where he ascribes so much to one man—no less in fact than the transformation of the West—he admits that the man becomes effective only when 'aided by the sweep of deep-lying collective forces'. The appearance of the man at the critical moment seems to be as much a matter of 'chance', as incapable of 'explanation', as the appearance of successful variations in natural selection. Given the conditions, however, the 'right man' will be irresistible. Thus in England, where Protestantism had diluted Church pretensions, and where Whig and bourgeois prosperity had given us toleration, the ideas of Locke and of the Deists produced little disturbance. In France, where the feudal and ecclesiastical system survived intact though riddled with decay, the same ideas, introduced by Voltaire, acted like dynamite. In England, the Protestant spirit, and perhaps especially its Erastian embodiment and the 'reasonableness' of its later theology, prevented any violence or abruptness in the change from 'theological' to 'positive'; it even seemed capable of preventing that change from ever becoming quite complete. It was for that very reason that Comte disliked Protestantism in general, and England in particular, so much; they upset the neatness of his historical scheme.[1] Morley, whose Comtism was mitigated by his nationality, thought Protestantism had done good by allowing orthodoxy to die without too much fuss—though, also, with unconscionable slowness.

In France the intolerance and bigotry of the Church, its 'lynx-eyed' vigilance and its persecuting fury, made it 'a point of honour with most of those who valued liberty to hurl themselves upon the religious system'.[2] It was Voltaire's 'Hegira' to England in 1726, however, which determined the course of his life and the direction of his attack. 'He left France a poet; he returned to it a sage.' He was amazed and excited to find, across the Channel, a land of liberty and philosophy, where a man could go to heaven his own way, where

[1] Cf. ch. VII of my *Nineteenth Century Studies* (1949), especially pp. 192-3.
[2] *Voltaire*, p. 220.

261

men of letters held government posts instead of having their works proscribed and burnt, where peasants ate white bread and wore shoes, and where the nobility thought it no disgrace to engage in commerce. But above all, England was the land of Newton and of Locke, of Toland, Collins, Woolston, Shaftesbury and Bolingbroke. He devoured their works, and afterwards scattered their ideas like sparks through the dry tinder of the *ancien régime*. Above all by translating Newton, and extolling Locke as the best of philosophers, he undermined the prestige of Descartes, the philosophic foundation-stone of orthodoxy. It was from the English Deists that he took most of the ammunition for his raids against 'that amalgam of metaphysical subtleties, degrading legends, false miracles, and narrow depraving conceptions of divine government'—the amalgam of all this with unjust privilege and pitiless cruelty, which Voltaire labelled 'l'infâme'.

In consequence of his campaign against 'the infamous thing', Voltaire was long execrated by believers, not only in France, as a blasphemer and arch-fiend. Dr Johnson, speaking of Rousseau, said that he would sooner sign a sentence for his transportation 'than that of any felon who had gone from the Old Bailey these many years, and that the difference between him and Voltaire was so slight, that "it would be difficult to settle the proportion of iniquity between them."'[1] De Maistre said that 'to admire Voltaire is the sign of a corrupt soul', that if anybody is drawn to his works, 'then be sure God does not love such an one'.[2] It is to be feared, in that case, that Jowett of Balliol (besides Morley and some others) was amongst the unloved, for he had the temerity to whisper that Voltaire had done more good than all the Fathers of the Church put together.[3] Morley agreed with Jowett; he thought, though without Jowett's entire satisfaction, that Voltaire had given Christianity a new lease of life, not only by forcing the French priesthood to set its house in order, but by compelling Christian apologists ever since to shift their position and take up more tenable ground. The apologists could not, of course, all be expected to ac-

[1] *Voltaire*, p. 5. [2] *Crit. Misc.*, vol. ii, p. 288.
[3] *Recollections*, vol. i, p. 97.

knowledge their debt as magnanimously as Jowett did. 'De Maistre', says Morley, 'compares Reason putting away Revelation to a child who should beat its nurse.' The same figure would serve just as well to describe *the thanklessness of Belief to the Disbelief which has purged and exalted it*.[1] All the same, Morley agreed with Frederic Harrison in thinking that the liberal Christianity of his own time, 'purged and exalted' though it might be in comparison with eighteenth century Catholicism, was yet a phase of soft, autumnal decay. He preferred Voltaire's direct attacks on religion to the equivocations of the nineteenth century, when 'people wear the shield and device of a faith', the better to reduce it to a 'vague futility'. What did Voltaire really do? Taking up the pose of a man who has never heard of Jews or Christians, and who, unhappily trusting to unaided reason, reads their records for the first time, he asked whether these records could really be true, whether Christian doctrine could be divinely inspired, and the Church a holy institution. He answered—like the king of Brobdingnag after hearing Gulliver's account of the real state of things in Europe— that, as far as he could see, the records were 'saturated with fable and absurdity, the doctrine imperfect at its best, and a dark and tyrannical superstition at its worst', and the Church 'the arch-curse and infamy'.

The subject of this chapter is Morley, not Voltaire, but I cannot better illustrate what, in the opinion of Morley and his liberal friends, official Christianity stood for even in his own time, than by quoting a long passage in which, using the ventriloquial method so beloved of himself and of Leslie Stephen, he criticizes it obliquely through a summary of Voltaire's objections:

> 'It is superfluous to detail the treatment to which he subjected such mysteries of the faith as the inheritance of the curse of sin by all following generations from the first fall of man; the appearance from time to time, among an obscure oriental tribe, of prophets who foretold the coming of a divine deliverer, who should wash away that fatal stain by sacrificial expiation; the choice of this

[1] *Voltaire*, p. 32 (my italics).

263

specially cruel, treacherous, stubborn, and rebellious tribe to be the favoured people of a deity of spotless mercy and truth; the advent of the deliverer in circumstances of extraordinary meanness and obscurity among a generation that greeted his pretensions with incredulity, and finally caused him to be put to death with infamy, in spite of his appeal to the prophets and to the many signs and wonders which he wrought among them; the rising of this deliverer from the dead; the ascription to him in the course of the next three or four centuries of claims which he never made in person, and of propositions which he never advanced while he walked on the earth, yet which must now be accepted by every one who would after death escape a pitiless torment without end; the truly miraculous preservation amid a fiery swarm of heresies, intricate, minute, subtle, barely intelligible, but very soul-destroying, of that little fragile thread of pure belief which can alone guide each spirit in the divinely appointed path. Exposed to the light, which they were never meant to endure, of ordinary principles of evidence founded on ordinary experience, the immortal legends, the prophecies, the miracles, the mysteries, on which the spiritual faith of Europe had hung for so many generations, seemed to shrivel up in unlovely dissolution. The authenticity of the texts on which the salvation of man depends, the contradictions and inconsistencies of the documents, the incompatibility between many acts and motives expressly approved by the holiest persons, and the justice and mercy which are supposed to sit enthroned on high in their bosoms, the forced constructions of prophecies and their stultifying futility of fulfilment, the extraordinary frivolousness of some of the occasions on which the divine power of thaumaturgy was deliberately and solemnly exerted,—these were among the points at which the messenger of Satan at Ferney was permitted sorely to buffet the church.'[1]

I have quoted this passage at such length because it bears directly upon the central theme of the present book, Victorian agnosticism and religious liberalism. To understand that movement it is necessary not only to grasp mentally, but to feel upon the pulses, exactly what it was that these unbelievers were disbelieving. In the guise of an account of

[1] *Ibid.*, pp. 257-8.

Voltaire, Morley is here telling us that, in his view, contemporary English orthodoxy is still committed to the old
positions. It may be said that he was wrong, and that from
the time of Coleridge and Thomas Arnold down to F. D.
Maurice, A. P. Stanley, Jowett and the rest, Christians of
enlarged outlook had been proving that the Church was *not*
so committed. It lies at the very heart of twentieth century
apologetics to claim that it is not. My present purpose,
however, is simply to point out that so many grave and
honest doubters of the last century, Morley included, would
not have lost their faith, and left the Church of their upbringing, if they had not had good grounds for thinking that
its essential beliefs were still what they had always been. It
is part of my present purpose, also, to suggest that it would
be a salutary exercise for many average Christians of today,
who feel sure that Christianity has once more become safe
and intellectually defensible, to explain, in detail and with
precision, exactly how far Morley's summary seems to them
a travesty of their faith.

Morley had, as we have seen, no sympathy with mere
negation for negation's sake. Voltaire's creed, he admits, remained negative on the whole, but it was a 'negation of
darkness'—of all that, in his day, was responsible for 'the
slow strangling of French civilization'. His attack on the
infamous thing was 'no oubreak of reckless speculative intelligence, but a righteous social protest against a system
socially pestilent'. Morley characteristically points out, moreover, that what Voltaire attacked was 'Christianity', not the
'religion of Christ'; he never attacked the Sermon on the
Mount, or 'the generous humanity which is there enjoined
with a force that so strangely touches the heart'. In his
English Letters Voltaire did not attack the Quakers, that
strange sect 'which conceived the idea that Christianity has
after all something to do with the type and example of
Christ'. Far from mocking the Quakers, he used them as the
standard whereby to satirize the aberrations of pseudo-
Christianity. There was more of Christianity in his gallant
and self-abnegating championship of Calas, Sirven and La
Barre than there was in the ecclesiastical persecutors who, in

the name of Christ, condemned them to torture and death, or than there was in Louis XV when, fresh from the orgies of the Trianon, he ostentatiously knelt in the mud to worship the passing Host.

Morley claimed no more for Voltairism than that, for certain specific evils, it was the right remedy applied at the right moment. He never pretended that it was, or could ever become, a religion of itself. Nor was he blind—and this is of particular importance and interest—to Voltaire's deeper inadequacies, above all to that crippling defect of his historical imagination which prevented him (and his century in general) from ever seeing anything but darkness and imposture behind the 'Catholic legend'. One of his favourite gambits, for example, was to show that various 'beliefs, incidents and personages of Jewish and Christian history' had 'counterparts in some pagan fables or systems'. It was an approach with which we have become not less, but far more familiar since Voltaire's time. But what was Voltaire's inference? That all alike were false, all 'equally the artificial creations of impostors preying on the credulity of men'. The modern historian of comparative religion, as Morley truly says, 'would hold them all equally genuine, equally free from the taint of imposture in priest or people, and equally *faithful representations of the mental states which produced and accepted them*'.[1] Morley adds, however, what Frazer would have endorsed, that the modern interpretation, though greatly superior to the old in historical insight, is just as damaging to the claim of any one of the 'fables' to be uniquely true and sacred.

When men have parted from a religion, Morley observes, it is impossible for them to do it full justice until they are sufficiently detached to view it as a natural, historical force. Voltaire was too busy disproving the supernatural credentials of Catholicism ever to treat it objectively as a beneficent, secular agency in Western civilization. But Morley's profoundest (and probably most oft-quoted) criticism of Voltaire is that he *'missed the peculiar emotion of holiness'*—'holiness, deepest of all the words that defy definition'.[2] Morley's

---

[1] *Ibid.*, p. 260 (my italics).　　　　[2] *Ibid.*, pp. 241-2 (my italics).

recurrent emphasis, throughout his writings, on holiness as the inmost concept of religion, shows that he knew more than some agnostics about its essence. Perhaps this explains what was said of him by a friend, that 'they call him agnostic, but he lived Christianity'.[1] And Algernon Cecil's remark, that 'his counsels have, indeed, been greater than his creed from start to finish'.[2]

When the deistical dragon's teeth sown by Voltaire had sprung up into an armed band of dogmatic atheists, it was said of him *'Voltaire est bigot, il est déiste'*. For Voltaire's substitute-religion, a deism of the kind still acceptable to those of his followers, especially the materially privileged, who find Revelation unacceptable, Morley has little or no use. For one thing, it was historically baseless. Voltaire was innocent enough to substitute, for the theological Eden, an imaginary golden age when all men simply worshipped the Supreme Being. He fancied that monotheism of this kind had preceded polytheism, and supposed that the pure and simple faith of the primitive deists had only been corrupted by the wiles of scheming priests. Even Hume knew better than this, as Voltaire might have learnt if he had read the *Natural History of Religion*. But Voltairian deism could in any case never be a creed for daily living, though he was able to make effective use, for polemical purposes, of his vaguely conceived Supreme Being, the embodiment of 'spotless purity, entire justice, inexhaustible mercy', against men 'who in the sacred name of this idea were the great practitioners of intolerance and wrong'. Voltaire's fair-weather religion was not proof against the Lisbon earthquake, and Morley hints that in his agonized arraignment of the gods for this catastrophe, and in his compassion for the innocent victims, there was more of true religion than in all his earlier optimism. Morley goes further still, and confesses that even those (including himself) to whom 'Catholicism has become as extinct a thing as Mahometanism', can still find more edification in 'the great masters and teachers of the old faith', in a Bossuet or a Pascal, than in 'the fiery precursor of the new'; they speak to our condition from their deeper experience of

[1] Knickerbocker, *op. cit.*, p. 68.   [2] Cecil, *op. cit.*, p. 269.

the 'ghostly things' that are 'ever laying siege to the soul'. By a strange inversion of his usual tactic, he even mounts the orthodox pulpit, and with Christian unction admonishes the deist thus:

'Are you going to convert the new barbarians of our western world with this fair word of emptiness? Will you sweeten the lives of suffering men, and take its heaviness from that droning piteous chronicle of wrong and cruelty and despair, which everlastingly saddens the compassionating air like moaning of a midnight sea; will you animate the stout heart with new fire, and the firm of hand with fresh joy of battle, by the thought of a being without intelligible attributes, a mere abstract creation of metaphysic, whose mercy is not as our mercy, nor his justice as our justice, nor his fatherhood as the fatherhood of men? It was not by a cold, a cheerless, a radically depraving conception such as this, that the church became the refuge of humanity in the dark times of old, but by the representation, to men sitting in bondage and confusion, of godlike natures moving among them under figure of the most eternally touching of human relations, a tender mother ever interceding for them, and an elder brother laying down his life that their burdens might be loosened.'[1]

Whence this impassioned strain? It is not often that Morley writes thus, and it seems strange that one of his most empurpled passages should be a defence of Christianity against the deist. Perhaps this is the infidel's nostalgia for the faith, finding harmless vent in a triumph over a different kind of infidelity? If Morley had become a pastor of the Positivist Church, he would, one feels, have been its most powerful evangelist.

2. ROUSSEAU

"And that self-torturing sophist, wild Rousseau"—? Here was a subject which taxed to the uttermost Morley's powers of doing justice to men with whom he disagreed. For here was the arch-heretic, the blasphemer against the grand article of Morley's creed—the belief in Progress; the morbid

[1] *Voltaire*, p. 280.

dreamer who, stepping right out of society, swept science and patient endeavour passionately aside, and discounted in advance the efforts of future liberals to shape an industrialized world nearer to the heart's desire. Yet on the whole Morley does succeed; his judgments are not unduly warped either by his dislike for many aspects of Rousseau's life and character, or by his repudiation of much of his teaching. In writing of Rousseau he is distracted continually between his recognition of Rousseau's immense power and his misgiving lest Rousseau's dreamy anti-intellectualism may not, in the long run, have done more harm than good. In his *Recollections*, however, he decides that in presenting Rousseau he had done something 'to quicken, justify, and expand into active energy the social pity and fraternal sympathy that must ever be the warm emotions best worth living for'. He quotes with high approval this passage from George Eliot:

> '. . . it would signify nothing to me if a very wise person were to stun me with proofs that Rousseau's views of life, religion, and government were miserably erroneous. . . . I might admit all this, and it would be not the less true that Rousseau's genius had sent that electric thrill through my intellectual and moral frame which has awakened me to new perceptions. . . .'

'It would have been well for me', Morley remarks, 'if I could have known these high truth-speaking words before I began my book. . . . Today the examination of Rousseau as a constitution-monger is being conducted among us with sedulous interest, but his unspeakable effect was really due not at all to juristic novelties, but to feeling.'[1] 'Electric thrill', 'unspeakable effect': these are, in spite of Morley's deference to George Eliot, very adequately conveyed in his book. He sees Rousseau as the heart of the great movement of which Voltaire and the Encyclopaedists were the head, the source of that passionate impulse which 'changed the blank practice of the elder philosophers into a deadly affair of ball and shell'.[2] If Rousseau was warmth without light, Voltaire and Holbach were light without warmth. It may be just, and

[1] *Recollections*, vol. i, p. 99.
[2] *Rousseau*, vol. i (1923 ed.) p. 68.

Morley feels it to be so, to say that 'while the truly scientific and progressive spirits were occupied in laborious preparation for adding to human knowledge and systematizing it [Morley means the Encyclopaedists, and especially Diderot], Rousseau walked with his head in the clouds . . . invoking a Supreme Being to match with fine scenery and sunny gardens'.[1] But, as Morley himself says, 'souls weary of the fierce mockeries' of Voltaire, and of the Helvetius–Holbach view of man, 'turned with ardour to listen to this harmonious spiritual voice', speaking to them of man in his 'natural' state, denouncing the 'gregarious trifling of life in the social groove', and proclaiming with prophetic rage the dream of a society simplified, purged of corruptions and inequalities —a blend perhaps of 'Plutarchian antique and imaginary pastoral', but nevertheless 'natural' in the deeper sense of providing the conditions in which alone man could realize his best self.

Rousseau produced his 'electric thrill', his 'unspeakable effect', precisely because his mode of apprehension was clean contrary to that of the enlightened *philosophes*; it was emotional and intuitive, not intellectual, and therefore supplied just what the age most lacked and needed: passion and yearning. It might be said that his whole teaching was a mere rationalization of his own deep-seated *malaises*, his morbid introversion, his sexual conflict, his social ineptitude, his inadequate sense of reality. To all this Morley pays full attention, or attention as full as the conventions of his time allowed. 'Nothing had come to me by conception, all by sensation. . . . I feel all, and see nothing.' Rousseau's was a gospel of 'being' rather than of 'knowing and acting'. Morley, in spite of his deep repugnance for Rousseau's sensual broodings and self-absorption, had the insight to realize, and make us realize, that it was precisely Rousseau's detachment from the world of outward affairs and speculations—a detachment hurtful and in the end fatal to his own peace and sanity—that enabled him to see that world, as no one fully engaged in it could see it, as a hideous and fantastic distortion of Nature's holy plan. Rousseau's vision on the

[1] *Ibid.*, pp. 77-8.

road to Vincennes, like Paul's on the road to Damascus, had set him for ever in conflict with the principalities and powers, the rulers of the darkness of this world. He was not disobedient to the vision, but the practical details of salvation had to be worked out later, not without fear and trembling, by men of another stamp.

'The prime merit of Rousseau,' says Morley, 'in comparing him with the brilliant chief of the rationalistic school, is his reverence . . . for some of those cravings of the human mind after the divine and incommensurable, which may indeed often be content with solutions proved by long time and slow experience to be inadequate, but which are closely bound up with the highest elements of nobleness of soul. . . . In a word, he was religious.'[1] And religious in the style of the Vicaire Savoyard, that is to say, in a manner which 'did not offend the rational feeling of the time, as the Catholic dogmas offended it'. The brilliant circle of atheists and materialists and necessitarians who met at the "Café de l'Europe", Holbach's country seat at Grandval, were disappointed and surprised to find that religion did not simply disappear now that they had disproved it all. Morley had learnt to know better; Christianity, of course, needs to be superseded, but the 'replacing faith' must 'retain all the elements of moral beauty that once gave light to the old belief that has disappeared'.[2] Now Rousseau did help to 'keep alive in a more or less worthy shape those parts of the slowly expiring system which men have the best reasons for cherishing', that is to say, 'moods of holiness, awe, reverence and silent worship of an Unseen not made with hands'. The unfortunate thing, the thing that chills Morley's approval every time he remembers it, is that Rousseau, by restoring God, Providence and Immortality, made it easy for churchmen later on to 'come back, and once more unpack and restore to their old places the temporarily discredited paraphernalia of dogma and mystery'. However, he credits Rousseau with having 'kept the religious emotions alive in association with a tolerant, pure, lofty, and living set of articles of faith, instead of feeding them on the dead super-

[1] *Ibid.*, p. 298.   [2] *Ibid.*, vol. ii, p. 302.

stitions that were at the moment the only practical alternative'. The deism of the Vicaire, like all deisms, must be
mainly a fine-weather religion, but at least it was not of the
thin, cold type; it was the product, not of reason, but of
'emotional expansion'. If Morley had thought of the comparison, he might have said that it bore the same sort of
relation to Voltaire's as Wordsworth's 'something far more
deeply interfused' does to the Universal Being of Pope or
Thomson. But even this will not do in the last resort, and
Morley ends his *Rousseau*, as he had begun, with an outburst
of pure Comtean ardour. 'Those instincts of holiness', which
it was Rousseau's merit to have preserved, and 'without
which the world would be to so many of its highest spirits
the most dreary of exiles, will perhaps come to associate
themselves less with unseen divinities than with the long
brotherhood of humanity seen and unseen'.

Although *On Compromise* came next after *Rousseau* in
chronological order, it will be convenient to round off
the French trilogy by speaking first of *Diderot* (1878).
This can be done briefly, since many of the themes have
already been heard.

3. DIDEROT

Diderot (1713-1784) was a man after Morley's own heart.
A deeper thinker than Voltaire, a clearer spirit than Rousseau, he was the most universal genius of the French philosophic party, and—as general editor of the *Encyclopaedia*
—its most tremendous worker. In him, and in the *Encyclopaedia* itself, Morley sees the first clear outlines of the new,
'positive' social and intellectual synthesis, disengaging
itself at last from the mists of 'old sacred lore', with 'men
of letters' replacing Jesuits as spiritual directors. This
synthesis had the 'social idea' and the 'scientific idea'; it
only lacked the 'historical idea' to bring it on to the level
of the nineteenth century. Its central moral was Rousseau's,
but with the ideas of social and scientific *progress* super-
added—'that human nature is good, that the world is
capable of being made a desirable abiding-place, and that

the evil of the world is the fruit of bad education and bad institutions'.

It is only now, in the later 1870's, when the last vapours of Carlylean transcendentalism are clearing away, that we begin to see how much of the programme of nineteenth century liberalism was already foreshadowed by Diderot and his colleagues. 'Forty years ago, when Carlyle wrote, it might really seem to a prejudiced observer as if the encyclopaedic tree had borne no fruit.' But now,

'we see that the movement initiated by the Encyclopaedia is again in full progress. Materialistic solutions in the science of man, humanitarian ends in legislation, naturalism in art, active faith in the improvableness of institutions,—all these are once more the marks of speculation and the guiding ideas of practical energy . . . . Europe sees again the old enemies face to face; the Church, and a Social Philosophy slowly labouring to build her foundations in positive science. It cannot be other than interesting to examine the aims, the instruments, and the degree of success of those who a century ago saw most comprehensively how profound and far-reaching a metamorphosis awaited the thought of the western world.'[1]

In this, Morley's largest and most sustained contribution to the history of ideas, he devotes much thought to the problem he had raised in the *Voltaire*, namely, whether 'ideas' can be said to 'cause' history. The Church appeared to think so when it persecuted heretics; the eighteenth century theologians appeared to think so when they persecuted De Prades for championing Locke against Descartes. Morley appears to think that, from their own standpoint, the theologians were right; it really is the conclusions men reach on such questions as whether matter can think, or whether ideas are innate, 'that determine the quality of the civil sentiment and the significance of political organization'.[2] Yet he adds, in consonance with more recent methods in the historiography of ideas, that ideas only begin to work, and determine events, when the material and social conditions are propitious. 'The immediate force of speculative literature hangs

[1] *Diderot* (1878), vol. i, pp. 8-9.   [2] *Ibid.*, p. 172.

on practical opportuneness.' Thus deism, for example, carried, in eighteenth century France, a revolutionary surcharge which it lacked in England, because in France the Catholic Church was identified with the forces of repression. 'We should never', he says, 'occupy ourselves in tracing the thread of a set of opinions, without trying to recognize the movement of living men and concrete circumstances that accompanied and caused the progress of thought.'[1] Here Morley seems to have taken sides with the historical materialists, for whom it is 'circumstances' that cause opinions, not vice versa. The truth is that he, like most other historians of his time, had no consistent doctrine on this matter. All he is sure of is that circumstances accompany, and co-operate with, the developments of opinion, and that opinions, however truly they may in logic be said to 'underly' events, do in fact and in history need the right circumstances to make them operative. Thus Francis Bacon, from whom Diderot took his inspiration, really did influence history, because Europe, when he proclaimed the coming of the Kingdom of Man, was in fact ready to enter into that kingdom. De Maistre was therefore right when he made an 'onslaught upon Bacon the centre of his movement against revolutionary principles'. Roger Bacon, who proclaimed similar principles several centuries too soon, was merely sent to prison as a sorcerer. Can any necessary connexion be traced between the teachings of Bacon and Locke on the one hand, and the spirit of social reform on the other? They had led men to renounce unverified hypotheses in favour of observation, to replace supernatural explanations by explanations from experience. They had fostered a disposition to regard forces outside the phenomenal order as beyond our knowledge, and a corresponding inclination to confine our attention to forces which are within our control. The sensationalist psychology led to an emphasis on environment and education, since the mind, 'originally' a white sheet of paper, is patient of any sort of impression. In this way Morley shows that the Bacon–Locke tradition logically led in the direction of reform. But did it in any sense 'cause' it? All that he can say is that when,

---

[1] *Ibid.*, pp. 43-4.

in Diderot's time, conditions were ripe for change, he and his fellow-workers naturally turned for support to that philosophy which best rationalized their aims.

'It would be obviously unfair to say', he remarks, 'that reasoned interest in social improvement is incompatible with a spiritualist doctrine, but we are justified in saying that, as a matter of fact, energetic faith in possibilities of social progress has been first reached through the philosophy of sensation and experience.'[1]

In the sphere of religious thought the *Encyclopaedia* joined forces with Voltaire, but Diderot had a constructive idea of his own. In Morley's own time a lot was said about keeping science and religion separate from each other, and the separation was generally urged for the purpose of 'saving theology'. Diderot also advocated such a separation, but it was in order to safeguard 'philosophy'. His idea was to dissolve theology, not by refuting it, but by transferring interest elsewhere; not to meet it in head-on collision, but to by-pass it. It was the technique recommended by Locke for dealing with the dissenters: if you attack them, they will stiffen their resistance; ignore them, and they will shrivel. So with Diderot; his method was to fix men's gaze on the new world of profit and delight which science was opening up before them; enraptured by this prospect, they would find theology withering away of its own accord. Meanwhile Diderot was content to hold the sufficiency of 'natural religion'. Shaftesbury, whom Diderot greatly admired (and whose *Enquiry Concerning Virtue and Merit* he translated into French), had 'identified religion with all that is beautiful and harmonious in the universal scheme', surrounding the new faith with (what Morley calls) 'a pure and lofty poetry'. Whatever Morley or we may think of Shaftesbury's religion, it was new daylight for those who associated religion with the Bull Unigenitus and the fiendish torturing of La Barre.

I will conclude this section by further reference to a thought which occurred in the *Voltaire*, but which is, in my opinion, important enough, and relevant enough to our own times, to bear repetition. It concerns the debt of Christianity

[1] *Ibid.*, p. 178. ('Spiritualist', of course, as opposed to 'materialist'.)

to the freethinkers, a debt upon which Morley frequently insists. In the *Encyclopaedia* article on Geneva, the writer (D'Alembert) praised the Genevan pastors for being kind and tolerant Socinians who disbelieved in hell, and who thought we should not take literally anything in the Bible which seemed to 'wound humanity and reason'. The Genevan Church was furious, but then, says Morley, 'the church had not yet, we must remember, borrowed the principles of humanity and tolerance from atheists'.[1] Let us never forget that 'it was not the comparatively purified Christian doctrine of our own time with which the Encyclopaedists did battle, but . . . a strange union of Byzantine decrepitude, with the energetic ferocity of the Holy Office'. And what was it that purified the doctrine? The very agency which produced the improved Catholicism of Chateaubriand and of Lamennais —the *Encyclapaedia*! The same thing is happening in our own time, says Morley:

> 'The Christian churches are assimilating as rapidly as their formulae will permit the new light and the more generous moral ideas and the higher spirituality of teachers who have abandoned all Churches, and who are systematically denounced as enemies of the souls of men.'[2]

Morley is nothing if not doggedly fair. He adds, characteristically:

> 'Yet I should be sorry to be unjust. It is to be said that even in [those] bad days when religion meant cruelty and cabal, the one or two men who boldly withstood face to face the King and the Pompadour for the vileness of their lives, were priests of the Church.'

v. *On Compromise*

If any one of Morley's works were to be chosen to represent him, it should be, I think *On Compromise* (1874). It is his central pronouncement, and one of the central documents of the Victorian age, ranking with such works as Mill's *Liberty* (from which it largely derives) and Arnold's *Culture and Anarchy*. It is also a pure distillation of the spirit of the

---

[1] *Ibid.*, pp. 151-2.   [2] *Ibid.*, p. 126.

Fortnightly Review, of which Morley became editor, succeeding G. H. Lewes, in 1867. That Review aimed, as Morley says, at 'the diffusion and encouragement of rationalistic standards in things spiritual and temporal alike'. Its unity 'was in fact the spirit of liberalism in its most many-sided sense'. Many-sided indeed, for it numbered amongst its contributors at this time Arnold, Swinburne, Meredith, D. G. Rossetti, Bagehot, Huxley, Pater, Lewes, Harrison, Dicey, Leslie Stephen, Tyndall, W. K. Clifford, Trollope, Mark Pattison and F. W. H. Myers—to mention only some of the best known. In the 'seventies the *Fortnightly* was on tiptoe with expectation and desire. This was the classic decade of Victorian rationalism, culminating in 1877, when, as Morley tells us, nearly every number of the Review contained some attack on theology or some article of belief. The atmosphere pulsed with the excitement of applying the principles of Evolution to all things in heaven and on earth —to religious doctrines, to society and to human character. 'It was the day of battle and the hour for plain speaking'; the time of which it could be said that 'the clergy no longer have the pulpit to themselves'. Huxley was then at the height of his struggle against 'false and adulterated metaphysics', and Morley, looking back on this heroic time forty years later, remarks that Huxley's valiancy is only less needed now 'because the climate has changed, and changed in the direction that makes mankind the Providence of men'. At the very time when Morley was writing *Compromise*, Mill's posthumous essays on religion (1874) were dismaying his disciples. 'It seemed a duty to keep the agnostic lamps well trimmed.'[1]

These considerations help to explain not only the impulse which led Morley to strike his blow for 'truth', honesty and plain-speaking, but also the strenuous and belligerent tone of the book. No Arnoldian banter lightens its gravity; life was earnest indeed for this Ironside of rationalism.

The right to freedom of thought, he begins, is now conceded by 'every school of thought that has the smallest chance of commanding the future'. How far ought respect

[1] *Recollections*, vol. i, p. 105. (On all this, see ch. VI in general.)

for prejudice, for the feelings of others, or any practical consideration, to outweigh respect for truth? A 'measure of accommodation', or compromise, is admitted in practice by all except the fanatic, who injures his own cause 'by refusing timely and harmless concession'. But Morley proposes to consider within what limits this is allowable, and to consider it in relation to the three main provinces to which it is relevant: Thought, or the formation of opinion; Speech, or the expression and publication of opinion; and Action, or the attempt to realize opinion in practical form.

Surveying the contemporary English scene, he finds, as Mill had found, and as Arnold more recently had complained, that the general mental climate has 'ceased to be invigorating' (except, he rightly adds, in the domain of physical science). There is a 'profound distrust of general principles'. 'What stirs the hope or moves the aspiration of our Englishman? Surely nothing either in the heavens above or on the earth beneath'—except (and here, as elsewhere, Morley echoes Arnold) doing a roaring trade. 'What political cause, her own or another's, is England befriending today?' None, and this is the more deplorable because there is no nation 'the substantial elements of whose power are so majestic and imperial'. Forty years ago, it was otherwise: we were then ardent for good causes such as Parliamentary Reform and the abolition of slavery; we could sympathize with the aspirations of Poland, of Hungary, of Italy. But now, humdrum facts and expediencies take precedence over ideas. Our press was narrowly opportunist in its attitude to the American Civil War, and now, to crown all, it even reduces scientific truth to the level of political expediency— *The Times* having blamed Darwin for publishing *The Descent of Man* 'while the sky of Paris was red with the incendiary flames of the Commune'.

What are the causes of this sad decline, this lowering of tone, this failure to see things as in themselves they really are? There is, of course, our absorption, already mentioned, in acquiring immense wealth: 'nothing like a roaring trade for engendering latitudinarians'. And here, doubtless remembering Dr Jonathan Morley of Blackburn, he remarks, in an aside, that it is not a firm 'persuasion of the greater scripturalness of episcopacy that turns the second generation of dissenting manufacturers in our busy Lancashire into churchmen'. But there are other causes: we have been scared by France since 1848, scared of Socialism; and the French disregard of the good kinds of compromise has confirmed us in our rooted love for it, good or bad. Some of us, forgetting that *'morality is the nature of things'*,[1] have even admired Napoleon III for some transitory successes, vainly imagining, perhaps, that because the inevitable nemesis lingered, evil might for once, for a time, be good.

Very significantly, Morley includes, among the causes, the 'historic method' itself, which in general he approved as the grand solvent of religious prejudice. In applying the notion of historical evolution to moral and social questions, we have come to regard opinions as 'phenomena to be explained', and not as matters of truth or falsehood. The eighteenth century, as he had pointed out in the *Voltaire*, asked of an opinion or belief 'Is it true?' Nowadays we ask, 'How did men come to take it as true?' We are more interested in tracing the history of an idea than in judging its goodness or badness. It is a well-known fact that a belief which has been historically explained, whose origins and growth have been traced, tends to lose its authority over the mind. When we know how it arose and how it came to be credited, we need no longer believe it ourselves. 'Howbeit we know this man, whence he is'—the inference drawn by the men of Jerusalem from this knowledge is familiar to us. I need hardly repeat, what is also familiar to us—and what is above all the theme of this present book—that this application of the historical method to religion (as to everything else) was the great discovery of the nineteenth century, and the most potent of all the influences then at work to soften and loosen the rigidity of the old orthodoxy. Then Morley ought to have approved of it wholeheartedly? He not only ought, but in large measure he did. He approved of it not only as a solvent of 'superstition', but (being a nineteenth and not an eighteenth century man) as a benign solvent, one

---

[1] *Compromise* (1888 ed.), p. 26 (my italics).

which did its work with sympathetic understanding, not with satiric violence. Speaking in *Recollections* of the triumph in his time of the 'principle of relativity in historical judgment', he says:

'The great intellectual conversion of this era, as Renan not any too widely put it, transformed the science of language into the history of languages; transformed the science of literature and philosophies into their histories; the science of the human mind into its history, not merely an analysis of the wheel-work and propelling forces of the individual soul. In other words, the marked progress of criticism and interpretation of life has been the substitution of *becoming* for *being*, the relative for the absolute, dynamic movement for dogmatic immobility. Pattison's essay on English deism in the eighteenth century, first printed in a volume long since dead and buried [*Essays and Reviews*], was an early attempt in this country to investigate the history of self-development in successive phases of religious opinion, without reference to the truth of either the Thirty-Nine Articles or any other fixed formulae. It was only one of the many services rendered to thought and letters by the same learned and ingenious man—the author, among many other wise things, of the deep saying, so well worth reading and reading over again, that what is important for us to know of any age, our own included, is not its peculiar opinions, but the complex elements of that moral feeling and character in which, *as in their congenial soil, opinions grow.*'[1]

What Morley did *not* approve of was the flaccid and spineless Laodiceanism to which this 'relativity' might lead. For him it did matter very much indeed which side one took in the great struggle between 'truth' and error, and it horrified him to realize that his own sort of 'truth' might, on the same principle, be explained away as yet another 'think-so'. 'Difference of opinion may possibly mean everything', he says, and he adds that Pope Paul III knew what he was about when he told the Council of Trent 'that Belief is the foundation of life, that good conduct only grows out of a right creed, and that errors of opinion may be more dangerous even than Sin'.

Morley's main target, throughout most of *On Compromise*,

[1] *Recollections*, vol. i, pp. 71-2 (my italics).

is the Established Church, which, 'while thought stirs and knowledge extends', remains 'fast moored by ancient formularies'. The Church mutilates the minds of its ordinands, binding them at the age of three-and-twenty 'never again to use their minds freely so long as they live', turning them into hypocrites, and making of the clergy a veritable 'army of obstruction to new ideas'.

Morley turns next to consider the alleged Utility of Error; whether, for instance, a 'religious belief may be "morally useful without being intellectually sustainable." ' (The use of this phrase, which is quoted—without acknowledgment—from the second of Mill's *Three Essays*, shows that Mill's posthumous work was in Morley's mind as he wrote.) Can error ever be useful? 'hell a useful fiction for the lower classes', for example? Or if we dislike this police view, shall we learn from Renan (he might have added Matthew Arnold) how 'the instructed' should regard the Church after they have ceased to believe in its doctrines? To concentrate, that is, upon its 'charm'; the beauty of its sentiment; the value, and the 'truth to feeling', of the awe and reverence it preserves? Morley allows weight to Renan, but he cannot abide the notion of leaving 'error' undisturbed. Throughout this and all his books, he shows as much certainty about what is 'truth' on the one hand, and what 'error', 'false belief', 'worn-out institution', 'narrow superstition', 'gross symbols' and so forth on the other, as Newman did about Catholic dogmas. His main reasons for rejecting the 'dual system'— i.e. hell for the lower classes, and 'charm' for 'the instructed' —are, first, that if you associate false beliefs with right morality you expose the morality to the ruin which awaits the beliefs. Secondly, for all right morality and good habits there are 'real' reasons always to be found; reasons 'in the nature of things', not mere superstitions. Thirdly, the little good which 'superstition' may do is outweighed by the harm, for it is itself the cause of that irrationality of the masses for which it is supposed to be the necessary remedy. Morley admits once again that the religious sentiment, in spite of 'false dogmas and delusive liturgies', has conferred 'enormous benefits on civilization'. We must not repeat the mistake made by the 'zealous unhistorical school of the last century,' that of condemning our foregoers as impostors. Error must indeed be extirpated with great tact and care, but that does not excuse us for perpetuating 'a complete system of religious opinion which *men of culture have avowedly put away*'.[1]

Our national bias towards the practically expedient and feasible, then, has stifled manly freedom of enquiry and fearlessness in forming opinions. And this is a serious matter, for—and Morley here swings back to the ideal rather than the sociological view—it is only opinion that can effect great changes. We should take pains to form right views, even on matters incapable of speedy realization, because 'what we think has a prodigiously close connection with what we are'. If you are a Conservative, be one on the noblest conservative principles: be one along with Burke! If you are a Liberal, be a Liberal with Mill and Morley! But above all avoid floating along complacently in a mist of latitudinarianism, holding no strong convictions at all. Two great questions underly all our discussions: Is there a God? and Is the soul immortal? Yet men do not seem to *agonize* as they should over these questions, or feel the duty of conclusiveness about them. Morley does not often write like a governess, a policeman, or a regimental sergeant-major, but he suggests all three when he bullies his unfortunate generation (surely a generation more prone to 'agonize' than any other in history) with his "Come along now! Make up your minds smartly about God! Hands up those in favour! Against? Don't know?" What worried him most, however, was that so many people *spoke* affirmation, *acted* denial, and *thought* agnosticism. In religion, too, emotional comfort is placed first and truth second; truth, which should come first, is waived for the sake of 'keeping undisturbed certain luxurious spiritual sensibilities'. The Savoyard Vicar, now as of old, remains the type of those who acquiesce 'in indefinite ideas for the sake of comforted emotions', making havoc with 'plain and honest interpretation, in order to preserve a soft serenity of soul undisturbed'.

In the formation of opinion, truth alone claims allegiance,

---

[1] *Compromise*, p. 79 (my italics).

but in expressing our views publicly we have to consider other people. In the matter of religious conformity a degree of 'economy of truth' is usually considered praiseworthy, which in any other field would be condemned. Does duty to truth sometimes 'require us to inflict keen distress on those to whom we are bound by the tenderest and most consecrated ties?' This is a question which no one will refuse to consider, unless he is 'drunk with the thin, sour wine of a crude and absolute logic'. Before embarking on the hints towards a new casuistry, of which much of the remainder consists, Morley has a few comforting reminders to offer. This is now the nineteenth century, not the eighteenth, and both the attack upon orthodoxy and its defence are being conducted on different lines. The victory of Voltaire and the Encyclopaedists has purged orthodoxy of some of the 'coarse and realistic forms of belief', and apologists now speak rather of 'elastic' modes of interpretation, 'non-natural' senses of words, and the like. Similarly, on the attacking side, 'no one of any sense or knowledge now thinks the Christian religion had its origin in deliberate imposture'. In fact, as we have already abundantly seen, the modern freethinker does not attack it at all; he *explains* it. 'And what is more, he explains it by referring its growth to the better, and not to the worse part of human nature.' Thus a nineteenth century freethinker can treat the creed with understanding and respect; 'he can openly mark his dissent from it, without exacerbating the orthodox sentiment by galling pleasantries or bitter animadversion upon details'. We have learnt, or we ought by now to have learnt, the proper strategy for dealing with orthodoxy, that is to say, not to begin at the wrong end by attacking deductions or particular points as impossible, but to build up, patiently and sedulously, 'a state of mind in which their impossibility would become spontaneously visible'. It is pleasant, in one's idler moments, to conceive of imaginary conversations between an orthodox Victorian parent and an unbelieving child—say between Robert Evans and Marian, or Thomas Stevenson and R. L. S.—conducted on these enlightened and up-to-date principles. The reverse situation, in our own day quite common, in which a believing child confronts an agnostic parent, was one that Morley could dismiss as utterly visionary.

Having thus comforted the orthodox parent by assuring him that he is not likely nowadays to be pained by 'gross and irreverent attacks', he adds the further consolation that 'the notion that heresy is the result of wilful depravity is fast dying out'. Thus a father need no longer fear that his doubting son is a profligate. 'In ninety-nine cases out of a hundred, he no longer supposes that infidels, of his own family or acquaintance at any rate, will consume for eternal ages in lakes of burning marl.'

Morley knew that man cannot live without a religion of some kind; he could not live without one himself. But, like the near-Comtist that he was, he wanted and expected a 'new' religion, one which should extract the permanent elements of the old faith to make 'the purified material of the new'. He did not, however, expect to see this realized in his own time. Meanwhile, in the 'bleak noonday', after 'the first great glow and passion of the just and necessary revolt of reason against superstition', it is permissible to dwell fondly 'upon some of the ideas of the old religion of the West':

> 'Nothing is more natural than that those who cannot rest content with intellectual analysis, *while awaiting the advent of the Saint Paul of the humanitarian faith of the future,* should gather up provisionally such fragmentary illustrations of this new faith as are to be found in the records of the old.'[1]

The modern denier should be like Christian to Jew, Gospel to Law: he should develop, transform, and fulfil the old, not destroy it. 'It is hard', says Morley, 'to imagine a time when we shall be indifferent to *that sovereign legend of Pity.*'[2] But we shall have to incorporate it, somehow, in 'some wider gospel of Justice and Progress'.

Yet, when all concessions and allowances have been made, Morley returns to the thought that it is no use putting new wine into old bottles. There remains a 'terrible controversy' between the clingers and those of us 'who have made up our minds to face the worst'. And this suggests another basic

[1] *Ibid.,* p. 153 (my italics).   [2] *Ibid.,* p. 156 (my italics).

human relationship in which 'compromise' may seem necessary: that between husband and wife. Morley is intensely
Victorian on this subject; it constantly happens, he says, that
the man rejects what the woman clings to. Women are 'at
present', he observes sententiously, 'far less likely than men
to possess a sound intelligence and a habit of correct judgment'. Perhaps Morley's own experience confirmed this, for
he had himself, we learn, married a 'charming girl' who
made him an excellent wife but who took no interest in
politics, in ideas or in books. What the good unbelieving
husband of the believing wife should do, is to avoid all
unseemly wrangling in the home, and hold his own in a
manly way, as in secular affairs. 'If there are women who
petulantly or sourly insist on more than this kind of harmony,
it is probable that their system of divinity is little better than
a special manifestation of shrewishness.' Milton would have
approved of Morley's assertion of masculine superiority, but
he would have been not a little astonished to find a new
Adam-and-Eve concordat based upon 'he for doubt only,
she for God alone'.

And what of children? the children of such a home as this,
for instance? Their upbringing must in its early stages, alas,
be left to the woman, but see to it that she does not teach
them 'wicked and depraving doctrines'. How exactly this
sort of supervision could be carried out by the conscientious
atheist-father he does not explain; here he could not speak
from experience, for he had no children of his own. Where
the parents happily agree in 'dissenting from orthodoxy'
(for even in this imperfect world such bliss is not unknown),
then there can be no excuse for teaching children 'a number
of propositions' which you believe to be false. Bring up your
children not to be self-conscious about finding themselves
different from those around them! (Did Morley, one
wonders, really know what this means, or can mean, for
children? Perhaps he would have said, "Well, send the boys
to University College School! It doesn't matter about the
girls.") When they ask you if the Creation story is true, or
whether the miracles really happened, tell them the truth as
it seems to you. Teach them the Bible, but teach it as 'a noble

and most majestic monument of literature'. 'That a man who regards it solely as supreme literature, should impress it upon the young as the supernaturally inspired word of God and the accurate record of objective occurrences, is a piece of the plainest and most shocking dishonesty.'

And the clergyman who loses his faith, the Robert Elsmere, what of him? It is, of course, very sad when a man's living depends on his 'abstaining from using his mind'. But faithful dealing with conscience and his fellow-men is the supreme value, and matters far more than any supposed 'good influence' he could exert by conformity to a 'cause'. The section ends with a passage of eloquent rhetoric in which 'huge mass of brute prejudice', 'baseless prejudice' and other such emotive phrases are balanced against 'human improvement', 'spread of light', 'honest and fearless men', 'clear and steadfast eye', 'firm step and erect front'.

Finally, there is the Realization of Opinion by practical measures. We have by now become thoroughly accustomed, largely through the influence of Mr Herbert Spencer, to thinking of society as an evolving organism. But this evolutionary theory does not mean that modifications happen without human effort and volition. '*Progress is not automatic.*'[1] We must persist in 'pertinacious attack upon institutions that have outlived their time, interests that have lost their justification'. The progressive tendency only becomes a reality when it works through men or groups of men who are *possessed* by it. If such men remain silent, then 'worn-out beliefs and waste institutions' linger on to enfeeble society. The time may not have come for full realization; in that case the 'compromise' of wise delay is applicable. But for the announcement of the fruitful idea the time is always ripe. Perhaps—very likely—the upholders of an old institution are zealous and good men? Then the innovators must be at least as good and zealous. Grant that the Churches are doing good work, what then?

'. . . if you are convinced that the dogma is not true; that a steadily increasing number of persons are becoming aware that it is not

[1] *Ibid.*, p. 210 (my italics).

true; that its efficacy as a basis of spiritual life is being lowered in the same degree as its credibility; that both dogma and church must be slowly replaced by higher forms of faith, if not by more effective organizations—'

then your duty is clear. Perhaps; but would that it were equally 'clear' what the 'higher forms of faith' exactly are, how they are to be authenticated, and what kind of 'organizations' would prove more 'effective'! Jowett, and Christian modernists generally (including Bultmann) would agree with most of what Morley says; they would agree that the theology then current involved 'depraved notions of the supreme impersonation of good', that it 'restricts and narrows the intelligence, misdirects the imagination, and has become powerless to guide conduct'. But they would maintain that the purging of doctrine, the 'demythologizing', can be best conducted without breaking the continuity, and that the old organization, with its established cultus and its continuous witness to spiritual reality, is still its best receptacle and transmitter.

vi. Morley as Literary Critic

Lytton Strachey said that to the Victorian critic 'literature was always an excuse for talking about something else'. And certainly, if we take Morley, or Leslie Stephen, or Arnold, as representative Victorian critics, they appear amateurish when compared with some leading schools of criticism in our own time, in which close analysis of the printed page, or of imagery, or of ambiguity, has become a primary concern, and has been conducted with such unexampled skill and subtlety. Literary critics have always, however, found it difficult to avoid talking occasionally about 'something else', and this is because the subject-matter of literature happens to be life, and its evaluation therefore cannot proceed without reference, however concealed or implicit, to the critic's own scale of values, to his ultimate ethical and religious position, his sense of what, in the end, is most worthy of choice. There are still, it is true, *soi-disant* critics who are not really interested in literature as such at all, whose concern is with the 'sociological soil' from which it grew rather than with the flower itself. Such writers, the 'history of ideas' school, sometimes treat poets as though their poetry were simply or mainly an exposition of their own (or more often someone else's) 'theories' and 'key-concepts'. It was in reaction from this historical school, which deals with things about literature rather than with the thing itself, that the 'new criticism' took its rise. A possible danger attending this reaction, though one that is avoided by its ablest exponents, is that of severing literature so completely from 'life' as to suggest not only that it can be evaluated in a sort of historical vacuum, but that the analysis of the printed page, and the exhibition of the critic's own complex sensibility, are the most important things in life itself.

We shall never understand the Victorian critics, of whom I am now taking Morley as representative, unless we realize that they avowedly and unashamedly subordinated 'literature' to 'life'. In his literary criticism Morley is, even more decidedly than Dr Trevelyan in our time, the layman and not the ordained priest; one to whom literature is a delightful and enthralling side-line, a means to the fuller enjoyment, or perhaps even more to the stoical endurance, of living. In this Morley was not peculiar; his view was shared by Dr Johnson, Wordsworth, Matthew Arnold, and indeed by the greater number of critics until recent times—not to mention most of the creative writers themselves, and the mass of readers at all times.

In Morley this fundamental evaluation often appears more clearly between the lines, or in asides, than in his direct criticism. Speaking, in the delightful chapter IV of his *Recollections*, of his early friendship with Meredith, he says that 'it would be hard to imagine finer personal inspiration for a beginner with a strong feel for letters in their broadest sense—letters in terms of life, and in relation to life—than was George Meredith in his early prime'. As so often happens with men who are actually creating literature themselves, Meredith was much less 'literary' than the critics— less so than the young Morley:

288

'My interest and love for a book as a book he had no share in: it was to him no more than a respectable superstition, with which for himself he had no more sympathy than Darwin had. Loud and constant was his exhortation. No musical note from a flute, it was the call of the trumpet from live lips. Live with the world. No cloister. No languor. Play your part. Fill the day. Ponder well and loiter not. Let laughter brace you. Exist in everyday communion with Nature.'[1]

Morley continues for a while to praise Meredith for his natural magic, in a passage which seems at first to be 'pure criticism', but which soon turns out to be a 'life'-judgment.

'Nobody in prose, and I almost dare to say nobody in verse, has surpassed Meredith in precision of eye and colour and force of words for landscape, from great masterpieces like the opening pages of *Vittoria*, or the night on the Adriatic in *Beauchamp*, down to the thousand vignettes, miniatures, touches, that in all his work bring the air, clouds, winds, trees, light, storm, with magic truth and fascination for background and illumination to his stage. . . . These divine and changing effects were not only poetry to him, nor scenery; what Wordsworth calls the "business of the elements" was an essence of his life. To love this deep companionship of the large refreshing natural world brought unspeakable fulness of being to him, as it was one of his most priceless lessons to men of disposition more prosaic than his own.'

It is significant that, although Meredith respected Tennyson as a 'fine natural singer', he hated what he called the 'lisping and vowelled purity', 'the mere dandiacal fluting', of the *Idylls*, and described the *Holy Grail* as 'lines in satin lengths'.

Other examples in the *Recollections* are Morley's praise for Arnold as a critic 'in the front line of my generation in serious drift, influence, importance, and social insight'—his aim in all his work was *social*; he had a 'rare feel for life'— and his mild censure of Leslie Stephen (unmerited, one would have thought) for not sufficiently seeking the social bearings or contemporary setting of a book. Morley's own instinct as a critic was always to look first for precisely those things. He was concerned to show writers as 'representative'

[1] *Recollections*, vol. i, p. 36 ff.

men, as men representative, that is, of great historical 'forces' and the 'general march of the human mind'. Speaking of Voltaire, he tells us that in 'mere letters', in 'purely literary qualities', Voltaire was in his day supreme, but that he would have been of little importance if he had not used his literary powers, as he did, for the overthrow of the infamous thing. Literary gifts and graces are 'a fragile and secondary good' unless begotten by 'living forces' and serving to direct them.[1] Again, of Rousseau he says that his eloquence 'struck new chords in minds satiated or untouched by the brilliance of mere literature'.[2] In a passage on Rousseau's *Letter to D'Alembert*, in which Rousseau opposed on puritan-primit-ivist grounds the idea of opening a theatre in Geneva, Morley disposes with truly Johnsonian sturdiness of the whole age-long discussion on the moral effect of the drama. What has all the solemn fuss been about? 'As if', he says (his favourite gesture of scorn), 'as if the effect or object of a stage play in the modern era, where grave sentiment clothes itself in other forms, were substantially anything more serious than an evening's entertainment.' *As if* the public were at the play all day long, and as if they were subject to no other moral influences whatever! This curt relegation of the drama to its 'proper' place in the scheme of things may be taken along with a remark about Voltaire's tragedies, which will seem crude and even offensive to those who have devoted much thought to the theory of tragedy. Voltaire, he has been saying, did not use tragedy as a means of propa-gating heterodoxy; 'With Voltaire tragedy is, as all art ought to be, a manner of disinterested presentation. This is not the noblest energy of the human intelligence, but it is truly art, and Voltaire did not forget it.'[3]

Let us take, as a good example of Morley's literary criticism, his essay on Byron, for here we can not only see his technique in vigorous action but also hear his explicit views on poetry and on critical method. Byron is first, as we should expect, taken as a 'representative' figure; he is the poet of the Revolution. Wonderful that England, 'the most rootedly conservative country in Europe', should have produced him!

[1] *Voltaire*, pp. 6-7.　　[2] *Rousseau*, vol. i, p. 324.　　[3] *Voltaire*, p. 130.

At any rate, having done so, she did her best to repudiate him, for it is only in England that his influence has been slight. He is still read by Englishmen for pleasure and delight, but not, as in continental liberal circles, for inspiration and encouragement. Endeavouring, then, to give Byron his proper place in the 'general march of the human mind', he pronounces that Byron was for the Revolutionary era what Dante was for Catholicism, Shakespeare for Feudalism, Milton for Protestantism, Goethe for—what? 'that new faith which is as yet without any universally recognized label, but whose heaven is an ever-closer harmony between the consciousness of man and all the natural forces of the universe; whose liturgy is culture, and whose deity is a certain high composure of the human heart'.[1] Art, he declares, is 'only the transformation into ideal and imaginative shapes of a predominant system and philosophy of life'; great poets represent 'great historic forces'—'the hope and energies, the dreams and the consummation, of the human intelligence in its most enormous movements'. Why a *predominant* system necessarily? Morley simply takes this for granted, and it is one of his typical gestures of dismissal to say of a writer that he is not in the central stream of tendency, that he is outside the main column of advance, and so forth. It does not seem to have occurred to Morley, as it did to Wordsworth for instance, that a poet may himself have to create the stream of tendency of which he will afterwards be recognized as representative. The fact is that Morley was more interested in tendencies than in poets; or, putting it the other way, he was chiefly interested in poets when they were clearly representative of one of the great moments or phases, produced by extra-literary forces, in the onward march of history. Byron, for him, has this quality, and he recommends 'the noble freedom and genuine modernism of his poetic spirit' to an age like his own, which seems to be 'only forsaking the clerical idyll of one school [Tennyson], for the reactionary mediaevalism or paganism . . . [Rossetti and Swinburne, presumably], of another'. Byron shows 'that subordination . . . of aesthetic to social intention'

[1] *Crit. Misc.*, vol. i, p. 211 (Olympus really civilized at last!).

which is one of the distinctive marks of the 'truly modern
spirit'. He has the virtue of 'poetical worldliness' and familiarity with 'the wide medley of expressly human things'.
Beneath all his posturings there is a firm basis of 'plain
sincerity and rational sobriety'; his admiration for Pope was
no mere eccentricity. He is indeed essentially a *political* poet,
a virtue which Morley claims also for Milton, and even for
Shakespeare (meaning no more than that he was concerned
with ideas of government and the movement of men in
society). Byron had, however, the defect of this virtue; he
was vastly inferior, for example, to Shelley in 'the rarer
qualities of the specially poetic mind'. It is always interesting
to note what qualities are regarded by any critic, or any
period, as 'specially poetic'. For Morley they were 'the
power of transfiguring action, character and thought, in the
serene radiance of the purest imaginative intelligence, and
the gift of expressing these transformed products in the
finest articulate vibrations of emotional speech'. Now Shelley
'transports the spirit to the highest bound and limit of the
intelligible'; he has a 'volatile and unseizable element' lacking in Byron; his thought is more 'rarefied', he has 'rare
gifts of spiritual imagination and winged melodiousness',
'his muse seeks the vague translucent spaces', etc. In all this
Morley is really damning Shelley with loud praise, since for
a man of his stamp the 'purer', the more 'poetic', poetry
becomes, the 'merer' it is. Shelley was 'markedly wanting' in
feeling for real events and people—not, of course, that as a
man he lacked benevolence or indignation against injustice,
but that as a poet, on his 'remote pinnacle', he was barely
conscious of mankind. Morley preferred Byron's 'poetical
worldliness'. True, he lacked Tennyson's *curiosa felicitas* in
landscape-painting, but then Tennyson is apt to be 'narrow
in subject and feeble in moral treatment'. Byron, without any
'wide intellectual comprehension of things', yet had the
copiousness and force which made him the incomparable
'interpreter of the moral tumult of the epoch'. All the passions and fits of the period from 1789 to Vendémiaire,
Fructidor, Floréal and Brumaire are summed up in the
'Byronic epos': 'overthrow, rage, intense material energy,

crime, profound melancholy, half-cynical dejection'. His excess of passion over reflection, his lack of self-knowledge, his unrest and weariness, drove him, in the spirit of Rousseau and Senancour, to Nature, 'the seeming freedom of mountain and forest and ocean'. He made a goddess of Nature, instead of regarding it (as a good positivist should) as a 'stern force to be tamed and mastered', and to this extent he was 'out of the right modern way of thinking'. He had 'no systematic conception of her [Nature's] work and of human relations with her'; he had, that is, no science, no 'positivity'. For 'Byronism', the true remedy, we now know, is Comtism. However, in this age of complacent philistinism, hail to the Samson who shakes down 'the unlovely temple of comfort'! 'As for Great Britain,' says Morley, with a flash of the waspishness which he normally kept so well under control, 'she deserved *Don Juan.*'

Morley's essay on Wordsworth appeared originally as the Introduction to Macmillan's 1888 edition of the poetical works. Like most Victorian essays on Wordsworth (and on most other poets), it could be accused of not being 'real criticism' at all, for its essential theme is what Wordsworth can do for us, and what we can learn from him. The Victorian attitude to Wordsworth was summed up once and for all by Arnold when he invented the phrase 'Wordsworth's healing power'. This may not qualify as a literary *aperçu*, but it says something both true and important about Wordsworth, and if it is not 'criticism' need we greatly care?

Morley's reverence for Wordsworth, as for Burke, is an example of his power to recognize the greatness of men whose later politics he did not share, although with the younger 'revolutionary' Wordsworth, as with the younger 'liberal' Burke, he is in full sympathy. He extols the *Prelude*, Books IX, X and XI (1850), as the finest existing imaginative account of the impact of the Revolution upon a sensitive and ardent mind. Those books, he says, are 'an abiding lesson to brave men how to bear themselves in hours of public stress'. But Wordsworth, for him, is not, as Byron was, a 'representative' poet, or not in the same sense. Wordsworth cannot be accounted for as the poet either of

293

revolution or of reaction. Morley begins, it is true, in his accustomed manner, by sketching in, with a few sweeping strokes, the appropriate historical setting. We hear of the American War of Independence, the French Revolution, the Napoleonic struggle and the Industrial Revolution, but it is only to be told that, throughout the latter part of this era of storm and stress, the birth-pangs of the nineteenth century, Wordsworth 'dwelt sequestered in unbroken composure and steadfastness'.

Wordsworth, he admits, will disappoint those who are looking for 'fire, passion, and ravishing music', or who think that the end of poetry is 'intoxication, fever, or rainbow-dreams'. What Wordsworth has to give (varying Mill's phrase, 'culture of the feelings') is 'education of the heart'; 'composure deep and pure'; 'self-government'. Echoing Matthew Arnold, he declares that 'Wordsworth's claim, his special gift, his lasting contribution, lies in the extraordinary strenuousness, sincerity, and insight with which he first idealizes and glorifies the vast universe around us, and then makes of it, not a theatre on which men play their parts, but an animate presence, intermingling with our works, pouring its companionable spirit about us, and "breathing grandeur upon the very humblest face of human life"'. Further, he saw Nature with his own eyes and gives us, 'not the copying of a literary phrase, but the result of direct observation'. That which he did not see, that from which he averted his ken, was the 'nature red in tooth and claw' with which we have since become painfully familiar. But we must take great men as we find them, and Wordsworth can 'lead us . . . into inner moods of settled peace', giving us 'quietness, strength, steadfastness, and purpose, whether to do or to endure'. In return for all this, in return for all that he has meant to Mill, George Eliot, Arnold, Morley himself and a host of other sufferers from the *Zeitgeist*, we can forgive Wordsworth for having opposed Catholic Emancipation and the Reform Bill. Morley makes short work of the vexed question about Wordsworth's poetic decline: 'Waterloo', he says, 'may be taken for the date at which his social grasp began to fail, and with it his poetic glow.'

In one sense alone Wordsworth admits of the historical classification that Morley habitually sought to impose: he exhibits the revolutionary impulse towards 'simplification', combined with a Burkean respect for 'the symbols, the traditions and the great institutes of social order'. But Wordsworth 'is a teacher, or he is nothing'—though Morley carefully distinguishes (again following Arnold) the genuinely poetic kind of 'teaching' from mere preaching or systematic thought.

The shortcomings of this kind of criticism are obvious enough; they are typified in Morley's neglect of quotation. He seldom takes actual passages of the poetry for analysis, comparison or illustration. He simply tells us, for instance, that Wordsworth's defects are prolixity, prosiness, solemnity, lack of air, fire, colour and music—just as he has similarly enumerated his great merits. But if we do not go to Morley expecting what only a later type of criticism can give, we shall find him a trustworthy mediator of a poet's inmost message, and of its probable value to us as part of 'human nature's daily food'.

I want to conclude by saying something about the essays on Carlyle and Macaulay, of which the latter is probably Morley's best. But there is a frightful skeleton in his critical cupboard, and lest I should seem to be trying to ignore it, let us have it out first and be done with it. It is, of course, his review of Swinburne's *Poems and Ballads*, which appeared in the *Saturday Review* for August 4, 1866. Like all articles in that Review, it was unsigned, but there seems to have been little secret about its authorship. It is a pity that *Poems and Ballads* was given to Morley to review. One must remember that he was still a comparatively inexperienced critic and that this may account for the violently abusive tone of his article, and the comparative lack of the dignity and elevation which we find in all his mature work. Morley was not a prude; he relished Byron, he waded through the obscenities of Voltaire, Rousseau and Diderot without losing his appreciation of them; he thought Tennyson namby-pamby; he knew that hardly any great literature, from the Bible and Shakespeare downwards, could be read aloud to 'young persons' without embarrassment, and that its morality could not be tested by that criterion. But, like Arnold, he was only really at home with what he called the 'loftier masters', whose high seriousness made disagreeables evaporate or gave them their place in a sane and comprehensive reading of life. Beauties of diction, form and treatment were, to him, matters of secondary concern, unless they were accompanied by truth and seriousness of substance. Now this was where Swinburne seemed to him to fail; he had nothing important to say, and said it with incomparable mastery. At a first glance it might seem that Morley was merely a Victorian prude holding up horrified hands at Swinburne's audacities. He writes, for instance:

> '. . . he deserves credit for the audacious courage with which he has revealed to the world a mind all aflame with the feverish carnality of a schoolboy over the dirtiest passages of Lemprière. It is not every poet who would ask us all to go hear him tune his lyre in a stye [*sic*].'

If Swinburne were a genuine rebel against 'the fat-headed Philistines and poor-blooded Puritans', it would be a different matter, but this is 'the spurious passion of a putrescent imagination'. What really shocks Morley is not so much Swinburne's nameless, shameless loves, his roses and raptures of vice, his predilection for sterile kisses and fruitless flowers, for blood and poison and thighs and fangs and the rest of it—not so much all this (though it exasperated him where we are now more likely to yawn), as the worse than barrenness of Swinburne's field of experience. For what are his moods? What impulses impelled him to passionate utterance? 'He is either', Morley replies, 'the vindictive and scornful apostle of a crushing, iron-shod despair, or else he is the libidinous laureate of a pack of satyrs.' The passion seemed to him *spurious*, 'the audacious counterfeiting of strong and noble passion by mad, intoxicated sensuality'. He was not deaf to Swinburne's lyrical power and the superb impetuosity of his rhetoric; he illustrates these merits fully and fairly. But his final judgment is that 'never have such bountifulness of imagination, such mastery of the music of verse, been yoked with such thinness of contemplation and such poverty of genuinely impassioned thought'. If Morley had spiced his article with a little raillery, we might perhaps have been readier to admit that that final judgment is not, after all, so wildly wrong.

Morley's article created such a panic that Payne, of the firm of Moxon the publisher, withdrew *Poems and Ballads* from sale.[1] It says something for the sanity and magnanimity of both Morley and Swinburne that their personal friendship (dating from Oxford days) continued unbroken, and that frequent contributions by Swinburne appeared in the *Fortnightly* under Morley's editorship. Morley praised Swinburne later for his noble ardour on behalf of oppressed persons and nations, and (rather excessively?) for his powers as a critic.

As an offset to the Swinburne review, however, consider another of Morley's un-reprinted essays, the review of Pater's *Renaissance* which lies buried in the files of the *Fortnightly*.[2] If Pater had really been like Mallock's 'Mr Rose', Morley might well have disapproved of him strongly; and in any case the gospel of the 'hard, gemlike flame' is not one for which we should expect him to show much enthusiasm. Interestingly enough, as it happens, he takes Pater as an exemplar of Arnoldian culture and critical disinterestedness. Pater represents the new and hopeful stir of critical energy, which is, we trust, the precursor of a new creative epoch. England needs this critical preparation, for 'the most popular of our two elder living poets [Tennyson] is too narrowly provincial, too blind to the new forces, too content with moral prettinesses, as the other of them [Browning] is too singular in form and too metaphysical in direction, to be in the central current of European ideas'.

Mr Pater not only associates art with the 'actual moods and purposes of men in life', but he has a distinct theory of the good life; it is, to impart 'the highest quality to your

---

[1] Thus leaving the field open for Hotten, founder of Chatto & Windus, who 'took over the poet as a going concern'. See Oliver Warner's Introduction to *A Century of Writers* (Chatto & Windus's Centenary Volume, 1855-1955), pp. 14-15.
[2] April 1873.

moments as they pass, and simply for those moments' sake.'
Now, of course, Pater knows quite well that our daily lives
are woven of 'homespun substance', and presuppose the
humbler virtues of industry, punctuality and the like. But
what interests him is 'what remains for a man seriously to do
or feel, over and above earning his living and respecting the
laws'. Morley sees the Paterian aesthetic religion as 'one
more wave of the great current of reactionary force which
the Oxford movement first released . . . a return upon the
older manifestations of the human spirit'. Since the original
attempt 'to revive a gracious spirituality in the country by
a renovation of sacramentalism, science has come'. Mill and
Grote replaced Newman at Oxford. Men have ceased to find
aesthetic satisfaction in religion, so now they are beginning
to find a religion in aesthetic satisfaction.

> 'Then Mr Ruskin came, and the Prae-Raphaelite painters, and
> Mr Swinburne, and Mr Morris, and now lastly a critic like Mr
> Pater, *all with faces averted from theology*,[1] most of them indeed
> blessed with a simple and happy unconsciousness of the very exist-
> ence of the conventional gods.'

Oblivious, too, mostly, of conventional politics and philan-
thropy; though Mr Ruskin has plunged chivalrously, and
not too successfully, into 'the difficult career of the social
reconstructor'. 'But there is Mr Pater courageously saying
that the love of art for art's sake has most of the true wisdom
that makes life full.' The fact that Pater can do this, can
'raise aesthetic interest to the throne lately filled by religion',
only shows how void the old theologies have become.

In this very Arnoldian essay, then, Pater is praised for
promoting a 'free play of mind' over the whole field of culture. In this country of ours, so preoccupied with material
and political interests, we need never fear that there will not
be plenty of 'energetic social action'. What we do need is to
have 'wedges driven', at many points, into 'the prodigious
block of our philistinism'. Yet Morley ends by hinting
mildly that 'art for art's sake' will only give us, so to speak,
an interim-ethic. Just as Pater's prose style *might* degenerate

[1] My italics.

(though not in his own hands) into 'effeminate and flaccid mannerism', so his gospel might leave us unstrung unless it is merely the precursor of 'that directly effective social action which some of us think calculated to give *a higher quality to the moments as they pass than art and song* [my italics], just because it is not "simply for those moments' sake" '.

The essay on Carlyle[1] (1870), unlike that on Macaulay, is almost devoid of 'literary' criticism. The 'message' of Carlyle was far too exciting to leave space for anything else. The influence of Arnold on Morley appears again when he urges that what England needed was not Carlyle's medicine of 'increased moral earnestness', but 'a more open intelligence' and 'accessibility to new ideas'; and when he decides that Carlyle was outside the 'central march of European thought'. Having called Rousseau the grand type of the 'triumphant and dangerous sophistry of the emotions', Morley designates Carlyle 'the Rousseau of these times for English-speaking nations'. The nemesis of his brand of emotionalism is that, beginning with introspection and the eternities, he ends with blood and iron. It is well enough to worship heroes; such *ersatz* divinities are better than the conventional ones; and in an age of coarse money-worship like our own, a dose of real reverence for virtue is all to the good. But it adds a 'finer holiness to the ethical sense' to care more than Carlyle did for the 'unnumbered millions' who, in his view, deserved nothing better than to be 'thoroughly well drilled by the elect'. Carlyle has restored to our age something of the spiritual vision for the lack of which it was perishing, but the 'extreme inefficiency, or worse, of his solutions' leaves Morley wondering whether, after all, he had done as much good as the Bentham he vilified.

Perhaps because in Macaulay there was no particular 'message' to arouse either approval or disapproval, Morley was left free, in writing of him, to deal more directly than usual with his style. He realized, as he seldom did when mainly interested in a writer's ideas, that Macaulay's style was the man; that what he had to say, and his way of saying it, were but two aspects of the same thing.

[1] *Crit. Misc.*, vol. i, pp. 135 ff.

Macaulay was 'the most universally popular of the serious authors of a generation', and the style of such a man, 'in its relation to ideas and feelings, its commerce with thought, and its reaction on what one may call the temper or conscience of the intellect' must inevitably, not only express the preconceptions of those who so eagerly read him, but set its own stamp upon their minds. Macaulay has influenced the style of modern journalism, and through this, 'the style and temper of its enormous uncounted public'. Public men have caught his manner in their speeches; 'if Mill taught some of them to reason, Macaulay taught more of them to declaim'. His gift of narration, his bustle, colour and sound, his immense range of knowledge, and his resplendent rhetoric, have made his writings 'an incomparable vade-mecum for a busy uneducated man'. To such a man his Essays are 'as good as a library'. He abounded in the 'Commonplace'— not necessarily in a derogatory sense, but in the sense in which Shakespeare too may be said to abound in it: the 'noble Commonplace' of the 'topics eternally old, yet of eternal freshness', the 'perennial truisms' of human experience. But Morley also means, more precisely, that Macaulay was 'one of the middle-class crowd in his heart'; he was 'in exact accord with the common average sentiment of his day on every subject on which he spoke'. He had, for instance, a 'sincere and hearty faith' in two of the cardinal tenets of the popular creed: England's greatness, and the glories of Freedom, and he was thus able, in all sincerity, to 'offer incense' to these and other 'popular prepossessions'. It is in his analysis of the modes in which all this gets translated into rhetoric that Morley shows his best critical insight. To begin with, Macaulay never 'wrote an obscure sentence in his life' —not that Morley holds this against him, but it is none the less connected with the absence, in Macaulay, of any 'deep abstract meditation and surrender to the "fruitful leisures of the spirit" '. The rhythms of his prose are 'emphatically the measures of spoken deliverance'; its chief notes are 'overweeningness and self-confident will'. He has 'no benignity'; he 'marches through the intricacies of things in a blaze of certainty'. 'We are never conscious of inward agitation in him'; he had 'no wonder, no tumult of spirit to repress'. In order to demonstrate these points, Morley does what is rare with him but has since become common critical practice: he takes particular examples of Macaulay's prose and compares them with that of other writers. Clarendon's character of Falkland is shown to be superior to Macaulay's character of Somers, because Clarendon's 'heart is engaged', and he attains a sweetness and harmony beyond Macaulay's reach. Macaulay is shown to be 'flashy and shallow' beside the ground-bass of Burke; and over-emphatic in his 'stamping emphasis' and his 'unlovely staccato' when juxtaposed with Southey. And perhaps most effectively of all, Morley invites us to compare any imaginative passage in Macaulay 'with that sudden and lovely apostrophe in Carlyle, after describing the bloody horrors that followed the fall of the Bastille in 1789:—

> ' "O evening sun of July, how, at this hour, thy beams fall slant on reapers amid peaceful woody fields; on old women spinning in cottages; on ships far out in the silent main. . . ." Who does not feel in this the breath of poetic inspiration, and how different it is from the mere composite of the rhetorician's imagination, assiduously working to order! . . . nor can any beauty of decoration be in the least a substitute for that touching and penetrative music, which is made in prose by the repressed trouble of grave and high souls.'

Macaulay is 'everlastingly playing for us rapid solos on a silver trumpet.'

It will be seen from these samples, I think, not only that Morley was capable of applying a more than superficial analysis to prose style, but also that his own prose, though its usual pace is deliberate, its tone Olympian and its colour sober, can quicken when need be into effective spurts of imagery and vivid phrase.

INDEX

303